C000257336

BUILDING COMPETEN
SCHOOL CONSULTATIᴏɴ

Building Competence in School Consultation, Second Edition, directly addresses the need for practical, comprehensive consultation training, including support materials, for school psychologists, counselors, and other professionals working in schools. School psychologists consistently indicate that consultation is a crucial component of their duties but that they lack sufficient opportunities to develop their corresponding knowledge, skills, and confidence during graduate training. Drawing from evidence-based approaches as well as experienced instructors' real-world toolkits, these essential perspectives and activities approach the standard and less common challenges of the school consultant role.

Written by two leading experts in consultation, this book brings school psychology research directly to graduate students and both novice and experienced practitioners, providing invaluable context, reflection activities, videos from fellow consultation experts, and resources that translate academic findings into skills ready for immediate use. This revised and expanded second edition includes two new chapters – one on collaboration and consultation on teams and another on teleconsultation – along with thoroughly updated content related to socially just and culturally responsive consultation practices; refreshed practice materials including rubrics and videos; references to newly published research and the latest professional standards; and updated activities for readers, all of which are freely downloadable.

Daniel S. Newman is Associate Professor and Program Coordinator of the School Psychology Program at the University of Cincinnati, USA, and Editor of the *Journal of Educational and Psychological Consultation*.

Sylvia A. Rosenfield is Professor Emerita of School Psychology in the Department of Counseling, Higher Education, and Special Education at the University of Maryland, USA.

CONSULTATION, SUPERVISION, AND PROFESSIONAL LEARNING IN SCHOOL PSYCHOLOGY
Series Editor: Daniel S. Newman

Building Competence in School Consultation
A Developmental Approach, 2nd Edition
By Daniel S. Newman and Sylvia A. Rosenfield

Supervision in School Psychology
The Developmental, Ecological, Problem-solving Model
By Dennis J. Simon and Mark E. Swerdlik

The School Psychology Supervisor's Toolkit
By Meaghan C. Guiney

Technology Applications in School Psychology Consultation, Supervision, and Training
Edited by Aaron J. Fischer, Tai A. Collins, Evan H. Dart, and Keith C. Radley

Problem-solving Parent Conferences in Schools
Ecological-Behavioral Perspectives
By Dennis J. Simon

School-Based Consultation and Students with Autism Spectrum Disorder
By Elizabeth L. W. McKenney

Handbook of University and Professional Careers in School Psychology
Edited by Randy G. Floyd and Tanya L. Eckert

Critical Theories for School Psychology and Counseling
A Foundation for Equity and Inclusion in School-Based Practice
Edited by Sherrie L. Proctor and David P. Rivera

CONSULTATION AND INTERVENTION IN SCHOOL PSYCHOLOGY
Series Editor: Sylvia Rosenfield

Becoming a School Consultant
Lessons Learned
Edited by Sylvia Rosenfield

Crisis Counseling, Intervention and Prevention in the Schools, Third Edition
Edited by Jonathan H. Sandoval

An Introduction to Consultee-Centered Consultation in the Schools
By Jonathan H. Sandoval

Handbook of Research in School Consultation, Second Edition
Edited by William P. Erchul and Susan M. Sheridan

Consultee-Centered Consultation
Improving the Quality of Professional Services in Schools and Community Organizations
Edited by Nadine M. Lambert, Ingrid Hylander, and Jonathan H. Sandoval

Consultation Across Cultural Contexts
Consultee-Centered Case Studies
Edited by Antoinette Halsell Miranda

Handbook of Multicultural School Psychology
An Interdisciplinary Perspective, Second Edition
Edited by Emilia C. Lopez, Sara G. Nahari, and Sherrie L. Proctor

International Handbook of Consultation in Educational Settings
Edited by Chryse Hatzichristou and Sylvia Rosenfield

Building Competence in School Consultation
A Developmental Approach
By Daniel S. Newman and Sylvia A. Rosenfield

For more information about this series, please visit: https://www.routledge.com/Consultation-Supervision-and-Professional-Learning-in-School-Psychology-Series/book-series/CSAPLISPS

BUILDING COMPETENCE IN SCHOOL CONSULTATION

A Developmental Approach

Second Edition

Daniel S. Newman and Sylvia A. Rosenfield

Routledge
Taylor & Francis Group

NEW YORK AND LONDON

Designed cover image: © Shutterstock

Second edition published 2024
by Routledge
605 Third Avenue, New York, NY 10158

and by Routledge
4 Park Square, Milton Park, Abingdon, Oxon, OX14 4RN

Routledge is an imprint of the Taylor & Francis Group, an informa business

© 2024 Daniel S. Newman and Sylvia A. Rosenfield

The right of Daniel S. Newman and Sylvia A. Rosenfield to be identified as authors of this work has been asserted in accordance with sections 77 and 78 of the Copyright, Designs and Patents Act 1988.

All rights reserved. No part of this book may be reprinted or reproduced or utilised in any form or by any electronic, mechanical, or other means, now known or hereafter invented, including photocopying and recording, or in any information storage or retrieval system, without permission in writing from the publishers.

Trademark notice: Product or corporate names may be trademarks or registered trademarks, and are used only for identification and explanation without intent to infringe.

First edition published by Routledge 2019

ISBN: 978-1-032-62228-6 (hbk)
ISBN: 978-1-032-62231-6 (pbk)
ISBN: 978-1-032-62233-0 (ebk)

DOI: 10.4324/9781032622330

Typeset in Bembo
by Apex CoVantage, LLC

Access the Support Material: www.routledge.com/9781032622316

CONTENTS

PREFACE

We're not saying it's easy. We're saying it's worth it.

Consultation is a core skill for school psychologists and other professionals working in schools. As with every skill, most especially core skills, consultation requires professional training. In this second edition, we hope once again to provide a basic set of principles and activities for developing your skills as a school consultant based on our combined experience of over five decades of practicing, teaching, and researching consultation. Our goal is to make a difference in the quality of school consultation training provided to school psychologists, as well as school counselors and others who will enact the consultant role in schools, by supporting the development of self-efficacy and competence to provide effective consultation services. We also hope that this text will be a support to university-trainers' and field supervisors' self-efficacy and competence to instruct and supervise consultation. Accordingly, we have updated content and materials across all chapters and added two new chapters – one focused on the growing area of teleconsultation and another on the role of consultation skills in teaming.

In training professionals, some approaches to training are considered more effective than others. Best practice in learning to be a school consultant has been of interest for decades. In 1980, the National Conference on Consultation Training (Alpert & Meyers, 1983), supported by the American Psychological Association (APA) and multiple divisions of APA, was held at McGill University in Canada. Most of the topics discussed at the Conference continue to be relevant to consultation training today, including: (a) understanding the context/system within which consultation will be done, (b) recognizing the importance of consultation processes, and (c) building skills for successfully conducting the processes. However, evidence has existed for decades demonstrating gaps in the quality and quantity of consultation training provided to school psychologists at the pre-service level, including: (a) limited coursework (i.e., too many programs provide only one course), (b) few supervision supports, and (c) limited attention given to complex processes such as building relationships or cross-cultural consultation (see Anton-LaHart & Rosenfield, 2004; Hazel et al., 2010, 2016; Newman et al., 2015).

It is counterintuitive to expect individuals to consult effectively when they do not have sufficient opportunities to develop the knowledge, skills, or confidence to do so at the pre-service level. School psychologist practitioners have historically reported spending limited time engaged in school consultation (e.g., Castillo et al., 2012). Recent data suggest more time may be spent consulting than prior reports (e.g., Bahr et al., 2017; Farmer et al., 2021). However, it is not always clear what comprises consulting or if they are engaging in high-quality consultation practices. For example, Newman et al. (2018) found that early career school psychologists did not necessarily incorporate traditional features of consultation in their work. It is not as if school psychologists do not want to consult; they consistently indicate that consultation is a preferred role (e.g., Bahr et al., 2017; Guiney et al., 2014). Yet, school psychologists continue to spend most of their time devoted to special education-related activities (Farmer et al., 2021).

Lack of skills, including skill in entering the school culture as a consultant, remains a critical reason why school psychologists are not engaging in more consultation practice. If consultation is to be considered a pivotal clinical skill, like other clinical skills (e.g., assessment, counseling), opportunities for practice and feedback through coaching or supervision at the pre-service level, as well as the in-service level, are needed to develop competence, proficiency, and eventually expertise over time (Newell et al., 2020; Rosenfield et al., 2010).

In this book, we hope to bring you methods and activities that have engaged and prepared school consultants to work both at a systems level and an individual consultee level. We include several transcribed examples which reflect the reality of school-based consultation. In the case material presented, names and other identifying information about consultants, consultees, and students have been altered according to characteristics common in the case literature and are presented in an unidentifiable manner.

This is a relatively short book, but don't be misled – it is filled with activities for you to develop your thinking and skills. If you simply read through without doing the activities, you will miss the opportunity to make the most of this book. To make it easier to complete the book's activities, printable online versions of all activities can be found on the book's webpage at the following URL: https://www.routledge.com/Building-Competence-in-School-Consultation-A-Developmental-Approach/Newman-Rosenfield/p/book/9781032622316. Some of the activities are to be completed individually, and some with a partner or small group. The variety of activities will enable individual readers (including those instructing and supervising as well as those learning consultation) to pinpoint content to best match their needs at a given point in time. No matter your role, we hope that you will consider keeping this book and revisiting the content and the activities in the future to continue your consultation learning process.

Practice with feedback and supervision is the road to competence in every professional domain. As you learn and practice the skills and concepts provided in this book, they will come alive if you also are spending time in a school where you can observe how the school works as an organization (i.e., its culture, structure, and staff) and have the opportunity to engage with a teacher in a consultation experience. We don't expect that every experience in which you participate will be successful, and we do know that many will challenge you.

The activities in this book will also involve a great deal of reflection and deliberate practice on your part. We anticipate that you will need to record your interactions to be more aware of your verbal and non-verbal behavior – we have found many times that novice consultants are not aware of the words and content of their interactions with teachers. A response in supervision that we have heard often is, "*Did I really say that?*" Also, there is a need for coaching and supervision of your work to provide you with invaluable feedback. When we don't know what we don't know, it is easy to make unknowing errors in content and process, and worse yet, to have those errors become comfortable and repeated over time. We strongly believe in constant personal reflection as well as feedback from more experienced consultants.

Our hope is that through this work, you come to see consultation as a crucial component of your school practice. And that in learning the skills here, you will become so much more comfortable and confident with the process that you will use consultation in your practice in the schools.

Daniel S. Newman
Sylvia A. Rosenfield

ACKNOWLEDGMENTS

We wish to acknowledge all the students we have taught at Fordham University, Temple University, the University of Maryland, National Louis University, and the University of Cincinnati. Without their feedback and participation, this book could not have been written, or perhaps not written in the way we have constructed it.

Thank you to Hallie Fetterman for her feedback and logistical support on the first edition of the text when she was a doctoral student at the University of Cincinnati, Megan Leamon for researching content to support chapter development, and Kandace Mossing for indexing the text. Thanks as well to Jud Phay (JP) Leong, Multimedia Coordinator, for consulting on the book's video resources and to school psychology graduate students Nimah Araf and Alison Smith for coordinating the videos. Our thanks also to many colleagues who, over time, have participated with us in research and extended conversations about training. Daniel would like to thank his current and former colleagues at the University of Cincinnati: Tai Collins, Janet Graden, Renee Hawkins, Julie Morrison, and Lori Vincent for being wonderful collaborators and models of school psychology training. Sylvia would like to extend appreciation and thanks to Todd Gravois for his incredible influence on this book through his work in co-constructing the IC Team model, developing the highest implementation standards for the work, and partnering in our joint research together over so many years. So many others in the schools and in the Lab for IC Teams have also contributed to my thinking and the way in which this book has been written – thank you.

We are grateful for the support of Daniel Schwartz, Editor at Routledge, for believing in this project and supporting its development. Thanks as well to our past editors with whom we have worked toward this point: Lane Akers and Rebecca Novack.

Finally, we would like to thank the consultation experts who contributed a video or other materials to this book: Courtenay Barrett (Michigan State University), Mary Kate Gerrard (University of Cincinnati), Janet Graden (University of Cincinnati), Kamontá Heidelburg (Ohio State University), Lauren Kaiser (Millersville University), Danielle Levine (The Seven Hills School), Hannah McIntire (University of Cincinnati), Antoinette Miranda (Ohio State University), Colette Ingraham (San Diego State University), Julie Smith (University of Cincinnati), Elise Pas (Johns Hopkins University), Arlene Silva (Wayland Public Schools), Markeda Newell (Loyola University Chicago), Sujay Sabnis (Miami University of Ohio), David Shriberg (Indiana University), Julia Villarreal (University of Cincinnati), and Stacy Williams (University at Albany). We are grateful that you have been willing to share your wisdom with the readers.

1

CONSULTATION TRAINING

Making It Work

Everything starts somewhere.

(*Terry Pratchett,* Hogfather)

One of the critical domains of school psychology practice is consultation. Our purpose here is to provide you with the beginning knowledge, attitudes, and skills to enter the profession able to engage in consultation. But consultation is a term with many meanings. So how is school consultation defined?

A good place to begin is to examine what your current perception of school consultation is as a part of your role. First, consider your own personal image of a consultant in the schools.

ACTIVITY 1.1 (INDIVIDUAL)

Warm-Up Questions: Introduction

Write down your own assumptions regarding what you consider to be the purpose of the consultant in the school setting. You can write sentences or just key words.

1   What do you think a consultant does?
2   How does the role of consultant fit into your own image of the role of a school psychologist or school counselor?

DOI: 10.4324/9781032622330-1

(To make it easier to complete the book's activities, printable online versions of all activities can be found on the book's webpage at the following URL: https://www.routledge.com/Building-Competence-in-School-Consultation-A-Developmental-Approach/Newman-Rosenfield/p/book/9781032622316).

Now that you have thought about your own assumptions, we will share ours. We begin this text with two key assumptions:

> **Assumption 1:** Consultation is a *pivotal clinical skill* for school psychologists. There is no other skill more foundational than consultation (Ysseldyke et al., 2006). Indeed, consultation is considered by the American Psychological Association (APA) to be one of six foundational competencies required for all psychologists (Fouad et al., 2009) and by the National Association of School Psychologists as a core domain in training and practice (NASP, 2020b). Further, it is rare for any assessments or interventions to occur without consultation, as the interactions leading to those decisions happen within a social context: "Someone must decide that an intervention is needed. Someone must select an intervention . . . Finally, someone must determine whether the intervention has been successful and make adjustments . . . and determine follow-up . . . adding a consultant layer . . . is a straightforward notion" (VanDerHeyden, 2014, p. 140).

> **Assumption 2:** As with other clinical skills, developing *competency* in consultation requires adequate content knowledge as well as sufficient opportunities for distributed practice over time, supported by developmentally appropriate supervision. The assumption that psychologists prepared for direct service are also prepared for indirect service has been rightfully challenged (Gutkin & Conoley, 1990). We support the caution that without appropriate training, consultants risk causing harm to consultees and clients based on action or lack of action in a case (O'Roark, 2002).

Being a school consultant is an enormous responsibility. Consultants have the potential to impact individuals directly (e.g., teachers, administrators, parents) and indirectly (e.g., students) as well as to influence systems (e.g., classrooms, teams, schools, and even school districts). However, we can't expect consultants-in-training (CITs) to consult effectively in *real life* if they do not have sufficient opportunities to practice these skills with a safety net, if they do not receive meaningful feedback via supervision, or if they do not know what they do not know. This assumption raises the question that is at the heart and purpose of this text: How can we build competence in consultation?

Why Assumptions Are Important

These assumptions may not seem particularly controversial to you. However, we do not believe that the majority of trainees, practitioners, or graduate educators consistently share these assumptions or that they are regularly reflected in actual consultation training or practice. In short, there is tension between the purported value of consultation in school psychology and how consultation training and practice ensues in graduate training programs and in the field. As a result of reading this book, we hope you come to view consultation as: (a) a distinct competency area that is complex yet well-defined, (b) teachable and learnable with the proper tools and support, and (c) worth the effort to teach, supervise, learn, and practice given the potential benefits that result for consultants, consultees (e.g., teachers, parents), clients (e.g., students), and systems (e.g., schools, districts).

To begin, let us consider in more detail what school consultation is and how it is implemented in contemporary school settings. Imagine you are approached by a teacher in the hallway who shares a concern and then asks, "What should I do?" On first thought, it might seem simpler or more efficient to tell the teacher what to do rather than to schedule a time to explore problems and solutions in greater depth. Yet when the teacher does not do what you suggested, when the problem persists, when the student gets an inappropriate referral for a special education evaluation, or when the implemented intervention clearly does not match the problem, you may wind up asking yourself, "Was this really a more efficient way to consult?" To answer this question, it is helpful for us to define school consultation more specifically.

School Consultation Defined

We know that consultation means different things to different people. It may even be devoid of meaning altogether for some, given the wide variety of contexts, relationships, and actions that consultation may describe. Here we present definitions of school consultation that we will tie in later in the chapter to our core model of School Consultation.

To a layperson, consultation is "meeting with someone to talk about a problem," a definition that is accurate but oversimplified. How each component of the layperson's definition (i.e., meeting; someone; to talk; problem) is elaborated likely diverges based on one's view of consultation training and practice. Such a broad definition also fails to differentiate between consultation and related areas such as counseling or therapy, coaching, supervision, mentoring, and teaching.

Consultation is *not* supervision, nor is it coaching, counseling/therapy, mentoring, or teaching. Although each of these services shares several commonalities, and all are interpersonal processes to provide support, they are in several ways unique (see Table 1.1). In the sections that follow, we highlight distinct features of consultation, beginning with a definition.

Zins and Erchul (2002) provide a well-articulated definition of school consultation that links with practices considered hallmarks of competent practice:

> School consultation is defined as a method of providing preventively oriented psychological and educational services in which consultants and consultees form cooperative partnerships and engage in a reciprocal, systematic problem-solving process guided by ecobehavioral principles. The goal is to

TABLE 1.1 Comparison of Features of Consultation and Related Services

Definitional Feature	Consultation	Related Service				
		Counseling/Therapy	Coaching	Supervision	Mentoring	Teaching
Hierarchical	N	Y	Y	Y	S	Y
Evaluative	N	N	S	Y	N	Y
Ongoing	S	Y	Y	Y	Y	Y
Confidential	S	Y	S	Y	S	N
Voluntary participation	Y	Y	S	N	Y	N
Choice of partner	Y	Y	S	N	Y	N
Guided by a priori content/curricula	N	N	N	N	N	Y
Gatekeeping function	N	N	N	Y	N	Y
Addresses professional problems	Y	S	Y	Y	Y	N
Addresses personal problems	N	Y	N	N	S	N
Involves professional learning	Y	N	Y	Y	Y	Y

Note: Y = Yes; N = No; S = Sometimes.

enhance and empower consultee systems, thereby promoting students' well-being and performance.

(p. 626)

First, this definition articulates a clear purpose of consultation: to support the staff and/or caregivers that are responsible for students and to enhance their knowledge and skills. Further, the definition refers to consultation as a *preventative orientation* or framework. Consultation is inherently linked to primary prevention, risk reduction, early intervention, and treatment efforts (see Meyers & Nastasi, 1999; Meyers et al., 2004). In addition, consultation can support a salutogenic approach, which focuses on promoting health and well-being, rather than only preventing or addressing problems (Hylander, 2017). School consultants aim to empower teachers, administrators, and other consultees with the knowledge and skills not only to tackle the problem at hand but also to learn from the process and apply new skills to prevent problems from occurring in the future, as well as to sustain healthy and thriving students (Hylander, 2017; Rosenfield, 2014; Sandoval, 2014).

Consultation is typically considered a method of *indirect service delivery* in which the consultee ultimately maintains problem ownership. Although consultants may have some role in intervention delivery, the primary responsibility for intervention implementation usually lies with the consultee. This speaks to the need for consultees to maintain as much as possible a sense of ownership over the problem and solution during the consultation process. Both consultants and consultees keep an eye on promoting positive academic, behavioral, and social-emotional outcomes for students; however, consultants also maintain a focus on promoting positive consultee outcomes at the forefront of their efforts.

Within the *cooperative partnership*, "consultants structure and guide the overall process, while consultees supply much of the content of the discussion" (Zins & Erchul, 2002, p. 627) since it is the consultee who brings the problem to the process. The relationship is one of equals, with the parties bringing divergent knowledge to the table and taking on different mutually agreed-upon responsibilities during a systematic problem-solving process with clearly defined stages. The relationship includes reciprocal interactions, where consultants and consultees both may change their conceptions of the problem along the way. Consultees have a story to tell, and change is the evolution of a new story (Clare, 2022). For example, a teacher may experience a *turning* (see Hylander, 2012, 2017) where they begin to view a student as lacking sufficient prior knowledge to be successful in the curriculum in contrast to their initial perception of the student as *disabled* or *lazy*. This new frame may be considered *ecological* or *ecobehavioral* in that the dyad moves away from defining the problem in language that focuses on student deficits in isolation but rather on the student's strengths and needs within a larger context (e.g., in schools, an instructional environment including task demands and instructional supports).

Novice, Routine, and Competent Consultation

For school-based practitioners to embrace this model in their work, it is essential that they have the skills required. There are different levels of competence in the development of consultation skill and practice. In what we subsequently define as novice consultation, routine consultation, and competent consultation, the components of a layperson's definition of consultation are elaborated differently (see Table 1.2).

Novice Consultation

Novice consultation is practiced by those such as graduate students prior to receiving consultation training or early in the training process, or practitioners with limited to no consultation training. Novice consultation may be reflected by a consultant's lack of awareness of particular communication skills or their purposes or feeling robotic in their application (see Chapter 4). In novice consultation, a consultant may also be focused on being liked by the consultee (i.e., a personal relationship) rather than prioritizing the enhancement of the consultee's professional functioning (i.e., a professional working relationship), which we address in Chapter 3. There may not be a systematic problem-solving process, but a quick attempt to resolve a problem with advice.

Routine Consultation

Routine consultation refers to performing consultation without engaging in ongoing self-evaluation, goal-setting, and deliberate practice, the last of which refers to continuously practicing a skill with ongoing assessment and ongoing corrective feedback from a coach or supervisor (Rousmaniere et al., 2017). Veteran practitioners engaged in routine consultation may have a more nuanced understanding of school practice than novices (e.g., knowledge of systems and recognition of complexities in problem-solving) and may have engaged in more consultation over the years. However, time spent consulting without deliberate practice of skills is unlikely to link with the development of competence or eventual expertise (Rousmaniere et al., 2017). Consequently, routine consultation tends to look more like what we define as novice consultation than what we define as competent consultation.

In routine consultation, a consultant may argue that there's not time to do formal, structured, or systematic consultation (or not be aware of or competent in the process) or that one cannot stop and think about what communication skills they should use at a given moment. In a routine context, consultation is viewed as asking questions, getting answers, and providing research-based solutions. In contrast, competent consultation includes a clear, systematic framework including where, when, how often, and with whom consultation occurs, how communication ensues, and how problems are addressed.

TABLE 1.2 Differences in Understanding and Application of Consultation: Novice, Routine, and Competent Consultation

Component of Layperson Definition	Novice Consultation	Routine Consultation	Competent Consultation
Meeting	• Brief • Mostly one-time • Mostly "On-the-fly" • Any location (e.g., in the hallway)	• Brief • Mostly one-time • Mostly "On-the-fly" • Any location (e.g., in the hallway)	• Sufficient time for problem-solving • Mostly ongoing • Mostly pre-scheduled • Contract to establish meeting times, structure, and process for consultation • Quiet location free from interruptions
Someone	• One teacher • Caregiver • Focus on personal relationship with consultee	• One teacher • Caregiver • Administrator • Teams (grade-level; multidisciplinary) • Focus on professional relationship with consultee(s)	• One teacher • Caregiver • Administrator • Teams (grade-level; multidisciplinary) • Focus on professional relationship with consultee(s)
To Talk	• Lack of communication skill awareness/viewed as "common sense" or awareness of skills but rigid application • Ask leading questions directing conversation toward own problem conceptualization • Offer information/advice/solutions before active listening	• Lack of communication skill awareness/viewed as "common sense" • Ask leading questions directing conversation toward own problem conceptualization • Offer information/advice/solutions before active listening	• Purposeful, flexible application of communication skills • Ask clarifying questions to understand the problem in observable/measurable terms • Use a variety of communication skills (e.g., paraphrasing, summarizing, reflecting feelings) in addition to asking questions • Active listening before offering information/advice/solutions • Communication skills used to build the consultation relationship
About a Problem	• Student-deficit focus • High inference problem definitions • Constructed *for* consultee • Jump prematurely into intervention stage • Overwhelmed by so many problems	• Student-deficit focus or ecological focus • Low inference (i.e., observable/measurable) or high inference problem definitions • Constructed *for* consultee • Jump prematurely into intervention stage • Work quickly on several problems	• Ecological focus • Low inference (i.e., observable/measurable) problem definitions • Constructed *with* consultee • Work systematically through problem-solving stages • Work with consultee to prioritize problems

Given gaps in the availability of supervision for school-based professionals (Silva et al., 2016), it is likely that many professionals are engaged in routine consultation. Further, routine consultation might be explained by a lack of extensive pre-service training in consultation or a lack of deep training in any particular consultation model; a school culture that is non-receptive to collaborative consultation often combined with a lack of skill in supporting or developing a culture in which consultation can occur; or an attempt to work as efficiently as possible, perhaps with limited training, in the time-crunched realities of schools (Newman et al., 2018).

Whatever the explanation, *quick and dirty* or unsystematic modes of consultation are likely what many students observe in the field and engage in themselves during practicum and internship experiences. Or they may not see supervisors or practitioners consulting at all. Tarquin and Truscott (2006) found practicum students and interns tend to observe supervisors engaged primarily in a special education assessment-driven role with a limited focus on consultation. Given that school psychologists' consultation practices may be variable (Newman et al., 2018), trainees may go on to become early career practitioners engaging in unsystematic consultation practices with the justification of "this is what consultation looks like in the real world." Such practices become routine over time, creating a cyclic problem.

Competence in Consultation

The development of competence in professional psychology, and in school psychology as a specialty, has received increased attention over the past several years (e.g., Belar, 2009; Daly et al., 2011; Fenning et al., 2015; Fouad et al., 2009). Competence is "an individual's capability and demonstrated ability to understand and do certain tasks in an appropriate and effective manner consistent with the expectations for a person qualified by education and training in a particular profession or specialty" (Kaslow, 2004, p. 775). Competence includes engaging in critical thinking and analysis, applying professional judgment in decision-making, and adapting decisions based on situational context (Newman, 2020).

Professional organizations have developed sets of competencies in the domains of practice, including consultation. For example, the APA's Society of Consulting Psychology (Division 13) has specified 11 overarching competencies and ten level-specific competencies for all consulting psychologists. The competencies are embedded in the overarching principles of adhering to a scientist-practitioner approach. The competencies are organized into personal, knowledge-based, and procedural domains, with ethics and professional standards providing a foundational anchor (see APA, 2017b, for further details).

Several of these competencies (e.g., relationship development; diversity competence; assessment and intervention; process consultation) are particularly relevant for school consultants, as these competencies also link well to the NASP (2020b) *Standards for the Graduate Training and Preparation of School Psychologists*. The NASP consultation competencies are presented in Table 1.3. The importance

TABLE 1.3 National Association of School Psychologists (NASP, 2020b) Practice Model, Domain 2: Consultation and Collaboration

Summary	Examples of Professional Practices
School psychologists understand varied models and strategies of consultation and collaboration applicable to individuals, families, groups, and systems, as well as methods to promote effective implementation of services. As part of a systematic and comprehensive process of effective decision-making and problem-solving that permeates all aspects of service delivery, school psychologists demonstrate skills to consult, collaborate, and communicate effectively with others.	• Using a consultative problem-solving process as a vehicle for planning, implementing, and evaluating academic and mental and behavioral health services. • Effectively communicating information verbally and in writing for diverse audiences (e.g., parents, teachers, school personnel, policy-makers, community leaders). • Consulting and collaborating with education professionals at the individual, family, group, and systems levels. • Facilitating communication and collaboration among all stakeholders by demonstrating effective and appropriate interpersonal communication techniques. • Participating on a variety of school- and district-based leadership teams to promote positive outcomes for students, school staff, and school systems. • Consulting and collaborating within and across disciplines to share resources and improve practices. • Advocating for needed change at the individual student, classroom, building, district, state, or national levels. • Applying psychological and education principles to enhance collaboration and achieve effective service delivery.

of organizational competence is highlighted within and integrated across several APA Division 13 consultation competency areas. Organizational or systems-level understanding and intervention (Borgelt & Conoley, 1999; Curtis et al., 2008; Newell & Coffee, 2015), including consulting on grade-, building-, and district-level teams, is also a pivotal competency area for school consultation. However, neither the NASP nor APA Division 13 competencies provide sufficient specificity for the development of consultation skills.

A Developmental Approach to Consultation Competency Development

Although delineating competencies provides a helpful starting point to consider your development as a consultant, the framework is broad, leaving it challenging for the evaluation of growth (Newell et al., 2020). Furthermore, focusing too narrowly on competencies may result in mechanically listing competencies without recognizing how they are interrelated, interactive, and dynamic (Belar, 2009). Therefore, it may be helpful to view consultation competencies within a developmental framework, including matching appropriate training and supervision approaches with commensurate levels of CIT knowledge and skill levels (Rosenfield, 2012; Rosenfield et al., 2010; Stoltenberg, 1993).

As is illustrated in Figure 1.1, as you learn to consult, it is theorized that you will move through the stages of developing awareness, conceptual understanding, skill acquisition, and skill application (Rosenfield et al., 2010). At the *awareness* level, you will have a cursory knowledge of theories, practices, and content, which develops into a deeper *conceptual understanding* of content, as well as more awareness of consultant-consultee relational dynamics. Eventually, you will engage in *skill acquisition*, applying new skills in action for the first time in structured situations, followed by the *application of skills* in context with increased automaticity and flexibility. To move along this continuum, particular training and supervision strategies may fit best at each level.

We hope that the content of the text allows you to enhance your awareness and conceptual understanding of consultation. We include initial presentation of consultation content and videos of experts speaking about consultation.

The stage of skill acquisition includes any number of scaffolds, such as physical, verbal, or visual prompts. For example, as you are acquiring new skills, you may practice consulting in a simulated problem-solving session while using a checklist

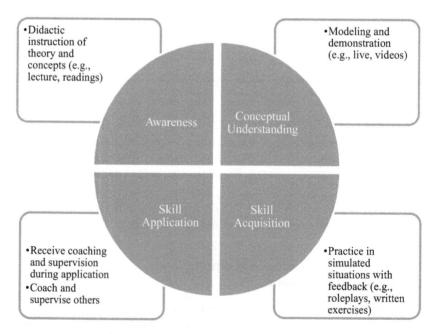

FIGURE 1.1   A Developmental Approach to Teaching and Learning Consultation

from this book as a visual prompt about what to do during that problem-solving stage. This text contains numerous activities, including simulated case examples, which can be supported by course instructors or supervisors.

Finally, skill application is when you can perform a skill without any physical, verbal, or visual prompts. During this stage, performance monitoring and feedback continue to be essential. You can receive feedback through coaching or supervision, including audio- or video-recording and reviewing consultation sessions, transcribing, and engaging in written reflection, all linked to action-oriented planning for the future (Newman, 2012). In Chapter 12, we highlight several actions for CITs as well as instructors and supervisors to use to support the increasingly independent application of school consultation in action.

One reason monitoring and feedback are critical even at later stages of skill development is because you may inadvertently be practicing errors (e.g., consistently asking questions in rapid sequence without listening actively or carefully to consultee responses). While *perfect* practice makes perfect, *imperfect* practice makes imperfect performance. For example, I (D. N.) recently borrowed my 9-year-old son's ukulele and started to learn some tunes with instructional videos on YouTube. In a matter of hours, I felt as accomplished as Israel Kamakawiwo'ole (if you haven't viewed his version of *Somewhere Over the Rainbow*, go check it out after you finish reading this chapter)! When I began lessons with an instructor a few weeks later, it was clear that I had learned several detrimental habits through online videos. My rhythm was irregular, my fingers were twisted and awkward on chords, and if I continued to hold the ukulele that way, carpel tunnel syndrome was in my future. My ongoing lessons include instructor modeling, observation of my playing, physical prompting, verbal feedback, and a whole lot of independent practice in between. I even video-record myself playing melody and "duet" with myself, strumming the rhythm to get the timing right. It has taken continued deliberate practice, with an instructor's observation and feedback, to learn the fundamentals and to unlearn the poor habits I had practiced so diligently. In other words, errors can be very difficult to undo once rehearsed a number of times (Archer & Hughes, 2011). Further, my instructor warned me that without frequent, repeated practice of the "right" habits, when the pressure is on (e.g., a performance), I will likely fall back on poor habits. The same is true of learning new consultation behaviors, unlearning ineffective habits of practice, and applying skills the right way during actual consultation. When the pressure is on in professional practice (e.g., consulting with a real teacher), without having had sufficient practice, it is easy to fall back on poor habits or not use the more effective skills that you've been learning.

Another aspect of training that we will focus on is that of reflection. Doing is not enough – reflecting upon your actions facilitates learning. According to Di Stefano et al. (2014), learning is augmented "when individuals can not only 'do' but also 'think' about what they have been doing" (p. 4). They argue that "learning from direct experience can be more effective if coupled with reflection – that is, the intentional attempt to synthesize, abstract, and articulate the key lessons taught by experience" (p. 4). Their research shows that self-efficacy can be generated by reflection, as you make explicit your thinking about what you have learned. Their work confirms Schon's (1983) model of reflective practice as a critical adjunct to practitioner learning. Thus, we will provide some structures to enable you to reflect upon your experiences as a school consultant.

Finally, it is essential to recognize that learning to be a skilled consultant is not always easy, natural, or comfortable. As in so many other areas, opportunities for learning often arise out of error and failure as much as success. Although focused on leadership training, Hackman and Wageman's (2007) wisdom resonates in our experience for CITs as well:

> failures generate data that can be mined for insight into how one's assumptions and models of action might be improved. Overcoming the impulse to reason defensively, however, can be a significant personal challenge. It . . . involves asking anxiety-arousing questions (e.g., about the validity of deeply held assumptions or about personal flaws in diagnosis or execution). . . such activities are neither natural nor comfortable.
>
> *(p. 46)*

Hackman and Wageman go on to stress that emotional maturity is required "to move toward anxiety-arousing states of affairs in the interest of learning about them, rather than moving away from them to get anxieties reduced as quickly as possible" (p. 47).

The Need for Competent Consultants in Contemporary Schools

The educational landscape has changed a great deal over the past two decades, potentially impacting how novice and experienced consultants enact consultation in contemporary school settings (Newman et al., 2018; Rosenfield, 2013). In fact, since the publication of the previous edition of this text in 2019, major ripples in the nested systems in which schools are embedded have further shifted the context for consultation. In the first edition of this text, we identified four educational issues begging for increased attention to consultation training and practice: (1) the implementation of Multi-tiered Systems of Support (MTSS) or Response to Intervention (RtI), (2) increased national attention to issues of teacher training and practice, (3) burgeoning knowledge about the positive effects of collaboration, and (4) the increasing diversity of students. In conjunction with each of these issues, which are even more pertinent than before, needs emerging from the COVID-19 pandemic, including the shifting role of technology as a tool for consultation training and practice, have arguably impacted the context for consultation service delivery.

MTSS/RtI

The implementation of the Individuals with Disabilities in Education Improvement Act (2004) brought with it the implementation of RtI in schools. RtI can be defined generally as "the practice of (1) providing high-quality instruction/intervention matched to student needs and (2) using learning rate over time and level of performance to (3) make important educational decisions" (Batsche et al., 2005, p. 5). The term MTSS has become more common in educational vernacular because, unlike RtI, which developed from special education law, MTSS "focuses on providing instruction and intervention, rather than using data to identify disabilities" and "has a more explicit focus on general education" (Burns et al., 2016, p. 720). Therefore, we use the term MTSS throughout this text when discussing it in relation to school consultation, with RtI subsumed within MTSS. The precise convergence of school consultation and MTSS is not yet clear, although there seems to be some consensus that skilled consultation services are relevant, if not pivotal, to effective MTSS implementation (Gutkin & Curtis, 2009; Newman et al., 2014; Reschly & Reschly, 2014; Sabnis et al., 2020). Team-based consultation services are usually integrated into MTSS processes, and much of the content of this text is useful for working with teams. We have added a chapter, Chapter 10, which focuses on applying consultation skills in team settings.

An essential component of MTSS is the concept of three tiers of service, each addressing concerns at a more intensive level. We view consultation as relevant at *all tiers* of MTSS. For example, at Tier 1 (universal supports), school consultants might consult at a systems level with administrators regarding school-wide academic or behavioral data and observe and consult with teachers about either individual or class-wide issues. Notably, such consultations are prevention or well-being focused, with the goal of *giving psychology away* (Miller, 1969), working to improve systems and support large groups of students and staff. In some schools, consultation around individual students about whom teachers have questions is also in play. At Tier 2 (targeted intervention), school consultants are often active members of problem-solving teams and help select or design interventions and continue to be involved in data collection and analysis in collaboration with teachers and other consultees.

Consultation continues to be relevant at more intensive tiers, even at Tier 3 (intensive, individualized intervention), where a consultant can support a teacher consultee in working on an individual student's concern. Sometimes, a concern can be indicative of problems at an earlier level (Tier 1 or 2), and the consultation provides an opportunity to affect more than the student who is initially of concern to the teacher. For example, a fourth-grade student with a severe problem in writing was one of several fourth-grade students referred to a school-based problem-solving team for writing concerns. Further examination revealed that the school did not have a consistent and explicit writing curriculum in the previous grades; as a result, students could not meet the expectations of the fourth-grade teachers. One of the outcomes was to move back to a Tier 1 intervention, the development of a school-wide writing program with specific competencies at each grade level.

Tiers as static entities or just another way to label students (e.g., "He's a Tier 3 kid.") is a danger in the present system, reflecting a failure to address the deficit model in current practice. In a recent qualitative study, Sabnis et al. (2020) found that the MTSS process for six teachers emphasized compliance to procedures in a manner that depersonalized students and defined/explained problems in deficit-oriented ways (e.g., using tiers as typologies and focusing on what a student "can't do" or "won't do") rather than considering broader problem ecologies. In sum, consultants must hold a flexible, prevention and systems-level orientation focusing on the nested systems in which problem-solving is situated rather than reifying the medical model of practice.

Consultation does not end at Tier 3. Even if a student qualifies for special education services, teachers supporting the student might need additional supports themselves. For example, general education teachers still might require consultative support regarding instruction in the general education setting since most students spend a good deal of instructional time in regular classrooms as part of their IEPs. Moreover, special education teachers can also benefit from consultation in their work with students (see, e.g., Pas, 2012; Tsakiris, 2012, for how consultation can support special education teachers), such as conceptualizing differentiated instructional and intervention supports for students with a variety of needs. Much of the content in this text around knowledge, skills, objectivity, and self-confidence applies to members of teams. For example, communication, relationships, and problem-solving are inherent in team-based services, just as in dyadic consultation.

Teacher Professional Learning

A spotlight on teacher training, effectiveness, and evaluation burns brighter and hotter than ever before. In their book, *Professional Capital: Transforming Teaching in Every School*, Hargreaves and Fullan (2012) argue that "overload, isolation, increasing expectations, contradictory demands, and no real forum for ordinary teachers to make themselves heard" (p. 36) have been norms in teaching for decades and continue to persist and intensify in contemporary settings despite evidence that collaboration is increasingly viewed as a powerful mechanism for productive outcomes. Teacher stressors and risk for burnout are exacerbated by the COVID-19 pandemic (Baker et al., 2021; Pressley, 2021). Teachers are expected to deliver high-quality instruction via new modalities (e.g., combining online, hybrid, and in-person instruction) while simultaneously playing whack-a-mole with student absenteeism, engagement, and responsiveness (Leech et al., 2022) for a variety of reasons such as illnesses, quarantines, limited access to technology, and limited caregiver supervision. Moreover, students' academic and social-emotional needs have likely worsened and will continue to expand, given inconsistent educational experiences and opportunities. Burnout and stress may also intersect with problematic professional practices. For example, there is some evidence that the odds of disproportional exclusionary discipline (e.g., office disciplinary referrals, suspensions) are at an approximately three times greater rate for Black students compared to White students when teachers are emotionally exhausted (Eddy et al., 2020).

Despite the clear need for teacher supports during this stressful time (Darling-Hammond et al., 2020), prior evidence suggests teachers lack sufficient opportunities for professional development and professional collaboration at the in-service level (Farbman, 2015; Organization for Economic Cooperation and Development [OECD], 2019). It is not clear that new supports are presently emerging, and teachers are leaving the profession in startling numbers (National Education Association, 2022). School consultation models focused on consultee empowerment may be viewed as forms of ongoing, embedded professional development for teachers and other educators. Such supports for teachers may be particularly relevant in relation to the COVID-19 pandemic (Newman, 2021).

The Value of Collaboration

Sarason (2003) concludes that: "If the conditions for productive learning do not exist for teachers, they cannot create and sustain those conditions for students" (p. 44). Consistent with this belief, evidence is emerging to suggest that collaborative approaches to professional learning result in positive outcomes for teachers (e.g., building strong working relationships) *and* students (e.g., enhancing academic achievement) (Darling-Hammond et al., 2020). An international survey by the Organization for Economic Cooperation and Development (OECD, 2019) suggested that teacher collaboration is associated with increased levels of job satisfaction, self-efficacy, and innovative instruction. Collaboration may also be viewed as serving a social support function in schools, acting as a protective factor for teachers or others against stress, burnout, professional isolation, or professional stagnation (Conoley & Conoley, 2010; Hargreaves, 2019). Collaboration is also conceptually aligned with the establishment of collective self-efficacy, namely, a group of educators' shared beliefs that they can make a difference for students, which has emerged as a significant factor influencing student achievement (Donohoo, 2017). Competent school consultants are well-positioned to collaborate effectively with teachers and to encourage collaboration in the school setting at large, ideally resulting in positive outcomes for teachers and students alike.

Student Diversity

An additional challenge is how educators can be culturally responsive, given the growing diversity of students in schools in terms of culture, race, ethnicity, and language. The number of racially and ethnically minoritized students enrolled in public schools in the United States is larger than non-Hispanic white students and continues to increase (de Brey et al., 2019). However, the racial and ethnic diversity of educators lags significantly behind (e.g., Meckler & Rabinowitz, 2019). So too, does the recognition of the socially and racially unjust practices that continue to permeate educational institutions, resulting in educational inequities for many minoritized students (U.S. Commission on Civil Rights, 2018). Such inequities appear to have been exacerbated by COVID-19 (Sullivan et al., 2021). Meeting the needs of students and staff in this increasingly complex world requires consultants to have an appreciation of culture at the individual, interpersonal, and organizational levels and the skills to integrate this awareness into practice.

Evans (2021) provides a format for us as psychologists to approach the challenge of racism and equity. He asks us to focus on the system level of analysis, in our case, the community and school, rather than just the interpersonal level, to address the structural and institutional factors that impact our practice. He encourages us to use an equity, diversity, and inclusion (EDI) lens in all our work rather than see it as separate and apart from the main work we do: "If we can more routinely apply an EDI lens to our thinking and consider the EDI implications across all issues – even those seemingly unrelated to race and racism – we will have a much better shot at developing effective solutions" (p. 10). Rodriguez and Walls (2000) remind us that "multicultural rhetoric does not necessarily translate into quantifiably better services for culturally diverse clients" (p. 89). We will further explore these variables across all the chapters and the skills within them.

Technology

The use of technology in education has exploded since the onset of COVID-19, and its proliferation is likely to continue in the coming years. Indeed, it is extremely likely that you will engage in technology-mediated consultation during your training and practice. Yet research on teleconsultation, or the practice of providing consultation via videoconferencing or other technology, is in its early stages (King et al., 2022). Extant studies, which primarily stem from behavioral models, suggest the acceptability of teleconsultation by consultees (Bice-Urbach & Kratochwill, 2016; Fischer et al., 2017; Witte et al., 2022) and the potential to impact positively students' academics and behavior (King et al., 2022). However, issues related to interpersonal communication, relationship initiation and maintenance, and collaboration in teleconsultation have received less attention in the literature. We devote Chapter 11 to considering how technology may be most effectively incorporated across the consultative problem-solving stages in a manner that is consistent with the model presented in this text.

The Need for Ethical Consultants in Contemporary Schools

Before moving on to discuss the framework of this book, there is an additional topic to consider. The changing educational landscape and the organizational nature of work in schools generate several ethical issues relevant to school consultation practice, yet ethics in school consultation is an area that has received less attention than would be expected. School-based practitioners, whether internal or external to a particular building or district, work at three different levels: with individuals, groups such as teams, and the school or district as an organization. Of course, some issues are relevant to all the activities of practitioners. Lowman and Cooper (2017) acknowledge the following concerns that are likely to raise ethical issues in practice with particular relevance to consultants: (a) competence, (b) contracting and informed consent, (c) confidentiality, (d) multiple relationships, (e) conflicts of interest, (f) failure to use research science and evidence-based practices, and (g) conflicts between organizational demands and ethics.

Competence

Working within your competency areas is an ethical expectation, which is why becoming a competent school consultant is an ethical issue. Developing multicultural competence for working with diverse students, parents, and school staff is also a generic ethical issue that has a significant relationship to consultation. The NASP (2020b) *Principles for Professional Ethics* Guiding Principle I.3 (Fairness, Equity, and Justice) under the Broad Theme of *Respecting the Dignity and Rights of All Persons* specifies that, in providing services, school psychologists

> use their expertise to cultivate school climates that are safe, welcoming, and equitable to all persons regardless of actual or perceived characteristics, including race, ethnicity, color, religion, ancestry, national origin, immigration status, socioeconomic status, primary language, gender, sexual orientation, gender expression, disability, or any distinguishing characteristics.

Additional consideration will be given to these issues of diversity in Chapter 2.

Contracting, Informed Consent, and Confidentiality

Lowman and Cooper (2017) found that even the most recent edition of the APA Code of Ethics does not pay sufficient attention to the practice of psychology in organizations, although the 2002 revision did include Standard 3.11, Psychological Services Delivered to or Through Organizations. This standard addresses contracting and the informed consent process; in Chapter 6, some of these specific ethical issues will be elaborated upon, along with the limits of privacy and confidentiality.

Multiple Relationships and Conflicts of Interest

Ethics codes also discuss concerns related to multiple relationships. In the complex culture of schools, multiple relationships are common. For example, teachers and other staff develop personal friendships, which sometimes become a concern when they impair the objectivity or effectiveness of professionals in conducting their professional functions, including consultation. In one case, the teacher backed out of the process for personal reasons; because the CIT and the teacher had developed a personal relationship, the CIT was so sympathetic to the teacher that she did not suggest some alternatives that might have allowed the consultation to continue, depriving the student client of further intervention support. In many situations, multiple individuals are involved, and their needs and interest can be in conflict. For example, a bilingual teacher scheduled a group of students at a convenient time for the bilingual teacher's schedule, but the students were not well matched for their needs. A CIT working with the classroom teacher and the bilingual teacher saw that the student they were concerned about was not making progress and losing class time as well, but she found it difficult to address the conflict of interest between the bilingual teacher's scheduling issues and the teacher's concern about the student's progress.

Failure to Use Research Science and Evidence-Based Practices

There is a priority for consultants to consider practices that are likely to work as a starting point in their work. However, there are not always evidence-based practices and research to support all assessment and intervention activities. Further, just because there is an evidence base does not mean the practices align with the context in which they may be implemented (Truscott et al., 2022). For example, an intervention that has proven effective in elementary grades may not be as effective in middle school, or a study conducted with an affluent population may not be applicable in a setting with fewer available resources. Because consultants work indirectly, and the consultee is usually responsible for the implementation, consultants have additional considerations in suggesting interventions, even those which are evidence-based. These issues are addressed in multiple chapters of this book, especially Chapter 8.

Conflicts Between Organizational Demands and Ethics

All school practitioners are sometimes faced with this type of issue, but it can be especially difficult for consultants. Most consultants lack power within the organization, although their consultation and advocacy skills are the tools they have to try to work through these issues when they arise. Consultants often see processes in schools that are mandated but not in the best interests of some of the students and staff with whom they work. There are no easy answers to these kinds of questions. For example, grade retention is often a recognized intervention in a school by administrators at the school and district level but not an empirically supported strategy. When it is recommended by the teacher but perceived as not in the best interest of a particular child about whom the teacher has requested consultation, it is difficult to challenge (see Pickering, 2012, for a case in which retention was an issue that impacted the consultation process).

Issues also arise in which minoritized communities are negatively impacted by local or national policies, and social justice issues are therefore likely to be present during consultation (Kaiser & Newman, 2023). Although individual consultants may be able to address social justice issues through consultation (see Chapter 3), change is also supported through larger institutions. For example, state and national organizations have a responsibility to advocate for the best interests of students and families. The NASP (2022a) Advocacy Toolkit provides useful guidance and references for school psychologists to engage with and advocate for policies that support students and families.

A Framework for School Consultation

The School Consultation (SC) framework presented in this text reflects our own assumptions and beliefs about consultation, which are built upon both scientific evidence and practice experience. Several consultation models are reflected in SC, including Consultee-Centered Consultation (Caplan, 1970; Lambert et al., 2004; Newman & Ingraham, 2017; Sandoval, 2014); Instructional Consultation (Kaiser & Newman, 2023; Rosenfield, 1987; Rosenfield et al., 2014; Rosenfield et al., in press); Process Consultation (Schein, 1999, 2009, 2013, 2016); Multicultural School Consultation (Ingraham, 2000, 2014); Behavioral/Problem-Solving Consultation (Bergan & Kratochwill, 1990; Kratochwill et al., 2014); and Organizational Consultation (Illback, 2014).

In Chapter 2, we introduce the concept of school culture and the process of entry into the school as a consultant. We examine the rationale for assessing the culture of a school in which you plan to provide services as a consultant, beginning with a historical overview of staff collaboration in American schools; introduce the concepts of norms and regularities in organizational life and provide some activities to support your understanding of these concepts; examine some multicultural parameters related to consultation; and provide strategies for assessing school culture and for increasing your opportunity for effective entry into the school.

In Chapter 3, relationships are the focus. We describe the differences between working relationships and personal relationships; discuss the expert-collaborative continuum in consultation; examine the perils of being the helper versus the helpee; the importance of self-knowledge as a consultant; and how to conduct difficult conversations that arise in your relationships.

In Chapter 4, the communication skills that will support and enhance your work are presented. We agree with Kegan and Lahey (2001) "that work settings are language communities" (p. 8), and your awareness of, and skill in, how you communicate with your consultee is essential to becoming a competent consultant. The impact of language on creating the problem to be addressed will be described, and nuances that distinguish between communication skills in consultation and counseling considered. The specific strategies include: (a) listening and the challenges that listening involves, (b) obtaining information through clarification and questioning, (c) paraphrasing to ensure that the consultee's communication is clear, and (d) reflecting feelings to acknowledge that feelings and emotions are also heard. Activities to practice your skills are included in the chapter as well.

Chapter 5 provides a brief history of how problem-solving emerged from research into clinical work. The stages of problem-solving that will be elaborated on in the following chapters are introduced here.

It is critical that the purpose and processes of consultation are transparent to the consultee, especially if the consultation model is collaborative. Obtaining informed consent from the consultee to engage in the process is key. In Chapter 6, the rationale for *Contracting* is explored, along with providing the nuts and bolts of the contracting process. Activities to practice contracting are provided.

It is not intervention but *Problem Identification and Analysis (PID/PA)* that is the critical first step in problem-solving – any intervention must address the right problem. Chapter 7 introduces the four different types of consultee problems that you will encounter (lack of knowledge, skill, objectivity, and confidence) and provides the nuts and bolts of the *PID/PA* process. The chapter also presents six Big Ideas that undergird the *PID/PA* process, along with activities to support building your problem identification and analysis skills.

Designing and implementing intervention skills are the focus of Chapter 8, which covers two related stages: (1) *Intervention Planning* and (2) *Intervention Implementation, Monitoring, and Performance Feedback*. Once again, the details of the process are explored. The importance of the consultant supporting the implementation and documenting that the intervention has actually taken place are critical aspects of these stages.

Consultation is a relationship, so it is important to say hello (contracting) and goodbye (closure), whether or not the problem has been resolved. Chapter 9 addresses the nuts and bolts of *Post-Intervention Planning and Closure (PIPC)*. Sometimes the closure stage leads to a new issue for consultation, or it simply leaves the door open for a future opportunity.

Although we often focus on the traditional consultation triad in this text (consultant, consultee, and client), consultation and collaboration in schools also frequently take place in the context of teams. In Chapter 10, new to this edition, we provide a brief history of teams in schools. Further, we consider how the skills covered throughout the text can be applied to optimize participation in teams and support successful facilitation.

Next, Chapter 11 provides an overview of teleconsultation, a rapidly developing area of consultation research and practice. Consistent with the text as a whole, the chapter is framed with a relationally oriented perspective, including how the online context may influence relational dynamics and problem-solving across all stages.

The final chapter, Chapter 12, explores the concept that this is just the beginning of your consultation training and experience. We provide a roadmap for continuing learning to be a consultant. Assessing your consultation skills and the outcomes of your consultation work are ongoing processes requiring feedback, supervision, and deliberate practice. We hope that the final chapter will encourage you to expand your thinking about consultation training and how to move toward becoming an ever more competent consultation professional.

Making the Most of This Text

You will benefit most from this text if you are taking a course in consultation and are placed in a school site to engage in studying the culture and conducting entry as a consultant, as well as engaging in problem-solving consultation activities. Involvement in the school, whether with students or adults, can be an anxiety-producing activity but a necessary one in order to develop your skills – consider reframing your anxiety to excitement as you begin the path to competence. Becoming a competent school consultant is not just about learning academics/ knowledge but about working as a novice professional in a school building under quality supervision. Scan QR code 1.1, which links to an introduction to the text by the authors, Daniel S. Newman and Sylvia A. Rosenfield.

QR CODE 1.1 Daniel S. Newman and Sylvia A. Rosenfield Video

If you do not have the advantage of having classmates to discuss your responses to activities, you might consider asking a colleague or fellow student to join you, or you might participate in a study group in your professional setting. It is important in any case that you be comfortable with how much you want to share about your responses as well as to be respectful in how you respond to your partner(s) as you work your way through this text, using the opportunity to build trust and open communication.

As you read the book, you will find several recurring features in each chapter. Each chapter begins with a quick write reflection activity to help you identify your thinking and assumptions about the topic of the chapter. Within the chapters, there will be opportunities for you to engage in individual and group activities, and the text will alert you and your class instructor, if you are in a consultation course, to activities that we have found useful in the class context. We also offer several models of how consultants might strategically use language during consultation. We hope these examples serve as building blocks to aid you in finding your own consultation voice. Finally, experts on school consultation and problem-solving discuss aspects of the consultation process in videos linked to pertinent content throughout the book. To access these videos, scan the QR code with your phone or tablet, and you will be linked to a relevant video. We hope these videos act as resources to further support your understanding of school consultation provided by voices in addition to our own.

Back to Assumptions and Goals About School Consultation

How does school consultation, as we have defined and contextualized it here, fit with what you previously thought? Based on our collective experiences educating CITs, we imagine that many of you are thinking school consultation is more complex than you expected. Indeed, complicating your thinking about consultation is an outcome of learning to consult (Worrell et al., 2017). In the chapters that follow, we further explore key facets of school consultation overviewed in this introduction and pair this content with interactive training activities. As you work through the text, we encourage you to continue to question your assumptions about consultation and to set goals for your knowledge and skill development. Activities throughout this text will help you do just that for this initial stage of learning.

ACTIVITY 1.2 (INDIVIDUAL)

Developing Your Own Map of Consultation

At the beginning of this chapter, you wrote down your initial thoughts about consultation. Now take your initial sentences/thoughts and your new knowledge from this chapter and design a map to diagram your current understanding of school consultation. Underneath the map, write a brief written summary of your map. We will revisit this map at the end of the book to see how your understanding of school consultation evolves over time.

2

UNDERSTANDING SCHOOL CULTURE

What is essential is invisible to the eye.
(Antoine de Saint-Exupery, The Little Prince)

The most damaging phrase in the language is: "We've always done it this way."
(Grace Hopper)

Consultation does not take place in a vacuum. Every school has a culture that serves as an important context for consultation services. When we make the commitment to support the residents in that culture to make change, it is essential that we bring an understanding of that culture into our awareness and our actual work. The culture view is critical since, as participants in the culture, we too often fail to see that it is the culture, rather than the individual, that has an impact on the behavior of those within the culture. Because we cannot *"see the structure in the same way that one sees an individual . . . we have trouble grasping and acting in terms of its existence"* (italics in the original; Sarason, 1982, p. 27). In this chapter, we will focus on helping you to develop that awareness as well as learn the importance of the entry process into that culture. Learning how to enter a school with consultation as an important aspect of your service delivery is a critical skill.

To begin, consider these warm-up questions regarding school culture.

DOI: 10.4324/9781032622330-2

ACTIVITY 2.1 (INDIVIDUAL)

Warm-Up Questions: School Culture

Write down your own responses to the following questions. You can write sentences or just key words.

1   What is your definition of culture?
2   How do you define collaboration? What do you see as the benefits of collaboration?
3   How would you go about entering a new school setting with the goal of providing services as a consultant?
4   How do the assumptions teachers, administrators, and other professionals in the school have about the school consultant role at your practicum or internship site impact the entry process? What are the implications for engaging in consultation?

What Do We Mean by Culture?

Too often, culture is viewed as a variable or category of variables, not as "a paradigm or worldview that permeates one's thoughts and actions" (Ingraham, 2014, p. 343). As one consultant in training (CIT) stated:

> Initially, I had great difficulties understanding school culture probably because I did not relate the concept of culture to school. My understanding of culture has always related to ethnicity and race. Thus, culture as an environmental component was difficult for me to grasp. The environmental component of culture seemed so abstract.

Organizational Culture of Schools

Perhaps no one has better articulated the concept of school culture and its profound effect on the work of those in schools than Sarason, especially in his classic book, *The Culture of the School and the Problem of Change* (1971; see also Sarason, 1982, 1996). Much of our work as school consultants involves change, and sometimes these changes conflict with cultural regularities of those with whom we work. For example, a programmatic regularity in many schools, as we will detail in what follows, is a belief in teachers working independently, even though current research supports teacher collaboration (e.g., Donohoo, 2017; Organization for Economic Cooperation and Development [OECD], 2019). Lowman (2015) reminds us "consultants are always crossing cultural boundaries, even within their own cultures, because every organization they work with has a unique culture of its own, as do the groups and individuals within those organizations" (p. x).

So, what do we need to know as consultants about the culture of schools? First, schools are organizational settings with unique cultures. Secondly, collaboration and consultation have not always been the way the work is done. While collaborative structures have become more commonplace in American schools, serving multiple functions, such structures are relatively new (e.g., Hargreaves & Fullan, 2012). Hargreaves (2019) describes 30 years of research on collaboration in schools, including the perils of individualism (e.g., teachers working in isolated silos), the promise of teacher collaboration, and the complexity of establishing effective professional learning communities to promulgate collaborative schools. For example, rather than establishing the intended practice of deep collaboration and professional learning through joint work (Little, 1990, as cited by Hargreaves, 2019), an emphasis on collaboration may result in surface-level collaboration reflected in polite communities filled with storytelling, celebrations, or unilaterally sharing materials. Or, on the other end of the pendulum, an administrative push or pull toward collaboration may produce teacher resentment for contrived or micromanaged collaboration requirements while inadvertently stifling collaboration (for example, teachers sitting in required meetings grading papers or swiping on their smartphones).

Why Collaboration and Teaming

Roots in independence and isolation continue to impact school culture, even as school staff members have sought to move to more collaborative structures. For example, student test scores from individual teachers have been used as part of teacher accountability for several years. Even with the implementation of the Every Student Succeeds Act, which deemphasizes standardized testing, many states continue to require or allow testing to be part of teacher evaluation (34 as of 2019). Accordingly, it is not surprising that teachers may still see themselves as independent professionals within the context of their own classroom (Visone et al., 2022). In fact, across systems and organizations in the United States, a primary goal is often to optimize and reward individual performance, as true in schools as in our society at large (Quintero, 2017).

The push for collaboration and teaming in schools emerged from research and policy that identified collaboration and teaming as structures enabling schools to educate an increasingly diverse population of students more effectively. Student diversity, including culture, race, ethnicity, and language, has generated concern about how best to address all students' educational and mental health needs. Along with the increased diversity of the student population, and in part, a response to that diversity, there has been a proliferation of specialists, such as reading teachers; teachers who support students whose first language is not English; and mental health providers, such as school counselors and school psychologists, leading to the fragmentation of services. This development has accelerated the need for collaborative and interdisciplinary structures, including co-teaching, consultation, and teams. It has also increased the need for comprehensive professional service delivery approaches requiring collaboration at the district, school, and classroom levels (Gravois, 2013). Even as schools have developed overarching policies such as Multi-tiered Systems of Support (MTSS), consultation and collaboration within those systems remain important skills for the effective implementation of services to students.

Because of the concerns around the special education process and the least restrictive environment policies, researchers and practitioners have turned to teams with different names and structures, generically termed problem-solving teams. These teams are intended to reduce the number of inappropriate referrals for special education evaluation and provide support to teachers who are increasingly being assigned students who present additional challenges to teach and manage in the classroom. Policy options such as mainstreaming and the least restrictive environment in special education law have increased the amount of time that students experiencing academic and behavioral issues spend in regular education settings rather than in special education settings. These policies have enhanced the need for collaboration among regular educators and specialists, a collaboration that is still being negotiated (Blanton et al., 2018). Although these teams do not have a strong research base (Rosenfield et al., 2018), they have proliferated in schools since their emergence in the 1970s and 1980s (Truscott et al., 2005).

Along with the development of problem-solving team structures, schools also incorporated more collaborative structures in other areas, including teacher professional development and school reform. Examples of structures include professional learning communities, collaborative planning time, collaborative inquiry, peer observations and review, self-evaluation, and data teams (Hargreaves, 2019). A growing literature has emerged about teachers' workplaces, detailing how school culture affects teachers' knowledge, skills, and morale. For example, Hargreaves (2019) recently discussed the notion of *collaborative professionalism*, an enriching process of collaborative inquiry and action and collective responsibility that includes dialogues that are "neither too comfortable nor too contrived. Nor . . . simply a balanced mid-point in between these things" but rather "deep and demanding, yet trusting and respectful at the same time" (p. 15). Although a professional community can empower "teachers' effectiveness and strengthen the overall capacity of a school to pursue improvements" (Little, 2007, p. 54) and collective self-efficacy is associated with student achievement (Donohoo, 2017), a challenging balance remains between collaboration and individualism (Hargreaves, 2019; Visone et al., 2022). This is especially problematic given current accountability measures that focus on the academic performance of an individual teacher's students (Visone et al., 2022).

The school reform movement also embraced collaboration and teaming, with the need for staff to collaborate on decisions and implementation of change (e.g., Hall & Hord, 2020). The concept of a school that learns involves team learning as key to improvement, with collaboration to "be fostered inside classrooms, between parents and teachers, among members of the community, and in the 'pilot groups' that pursue successful school change" (Senge et al., 2012, p. 8). Just as in other organizational settings, Senge's work spoke to educators as a way to foster improvement and change.

One of the purposes of this book is to alert you, as a new consultant, to the cultural issues that have the capacity to impede or enhance your collaboration with other school staff as you seek to embed consultation services into your work with individuals and with teams. This is a concern because insufficient attention has been paid to training and implementation issues as educators seek to change and sustain a more collaborative school culture. We will come back to some of these issues in Chapter 10 on teams.

ACTIVITY 2.2 (INDIVIDUAL, GROUP)

Time for Collaboration

One of the major issues around collaboration has been that of time. Given the demands on teachers and staff, how do they find time to work together when collaboration is not always viewed as essential? Reflect on the following questions individually or with a small group:

1 How do teachers in your school find time to collaborate?
2 What do teachers perceive as the major barriers in finding time to collaborate with each other and with consultants?
3 What do the issues around time in your school alert you to in terms of school culture and collaboration?
4 Working together, can you generate three ways in which time for collaboration might be found in a school?

Organizational Boundaries

Schools have permeable boundaries with the community, and the nested systems within which schools are embedded undoubtedly affect the school consultation role in some ways (American Psychological Association [APA], 2017c). In this text, we have not focused on family or community, both of which are relevant to the work of school consultants. Our focus has been on the school. However, family caregivers are also key participants in the workings of the school. The Conjoint Behavioral Consultation (CBC) model, also referred to as Teachers and Parents as Partners (TAPP), is a unique consultation approach in that it includes caregivers as part of the behavioral consultation problem-solving process (Sheridan & Kratochwill, 2008; TAPP, 2022). By including caregivers, family-school partnerships can be strengthened in support of students (Sheridan et al., 2014; Sheridan & Garbacz, 2021). A full review of CBC/TAPP is beyond the scope of this book, but research (including randomized controlled studies) by Sheridan and colleagues on CBC/TAPP has consistently demonstrated enhanced academic, social-emotional, and behavioral outcomes for students (see Sheridan et al., 2014, and the TAPP website for comprehensive summaries). The consultation skills presented in this book are equally important in the work of consultants with caregivers.

Learning About Norms and Regularities That Impact Helping

As true today as when he wrote those words, Sarason acknowledges that the "helping role inevitably involves changing someone or something" and that people, not just school staff, "do not take kindly to departures from their accustomed ways of thinking and acting even when they proclaim they are motivated to do so" (Sarason, 1995, p. 66). To help that change, he believed it was critical to learn "how their structure, practices, regularities, goals, and rationales combine as justification for what is and rejection of alternatives about what could or should be" (Sarason, 1995, p. 66).

ACTIVITY 2.3 (INDIVIDUAL, GROUP)

Man From Mars

Read the following excerpt from Sarason's (1996) classic book The Culture of the School and the Problem of Change and answer the subsequent questions individually. If possible, compare responses with a partner or in a small group.

Let us approach the general problem of outcomes by indulging in a fantasy. Imagine a being from outer space who finds himself and his invisible space platform directly above an elementary school. Being superior to earthly beings, he is able to see everything that goes on in the school. But he does operate under certain restrictions: he does not comprehend the meaning of written or spoken language, and it can never occur to him that things go on inside of what we call heads. He can see and hear everything and, being an *avant-garde* outer-spacer, he, of course, possesses a kind of computer that records and categorizes events on any number of dimensions, allowing him to discern what we shall call the existing regularities. (Let me anticipate the discussion of the latter part of this chapter by advancing the hypothesis that *any attempt to introduce change into the school setting requires, among other things, changing the existing regularities in some way.*

The intended outcomes involve changing an existing regularity, eliminating one or more of them, or producing new ones.)

Let us start with one of the more obvious regularities. Our outer-spacer will discern (but not understand) that for five consecutive days, the school is densely populated, while for two consecutive days, it is devoid of humans. That puzzles him. Why this 5-2 pattern? Why not a 4-3 or some other kind of pattern like 2-1-2-1-1?

What if the outer-spacer could talk to us and demanded an explanation for this existing regularity? Many of us earthlings would quickly become aware that we have a tendency to assume that the way things are is the way things should be. But our outer-spacer persists. Is this the way it has always been? Is this the way it is in other countries? Is it demonstrably the best pattern for achieving the purposes of schooling? Does the existing regularity reflect noneducational considerations like religion, work patterns, and leisure time? Is it possible that the existing regularity has no intrinsic relationship to learning and education?

From Sarason, S.B. (1996). *Revisiting "The culture of school and the problem of change."* (p. 96). New York: Teachers College Press.

Questions for Reflection:

1   According to this passage, how do you define an existing regularity?
2   Name a few school-based regularities that you are aware of/have noticed from your own experiences as a student or working in the schools.
3   Why do you think each of these regularities was in place?
4   What are some alternatives to the existing regularities you identified?

When we take an ecological perspective on problems brought to us within any school, we are, in part, acknowledging that it is the roles and relationships within a school that determine how goals and problems will be defined and approached. In many cases, this will present a conflict with the norms and regularities that structure the way the school culture has viewed problem behavior in students from a deficit approach.

To develop a clearer sense of the concept of norms, you might begin by examining those within your own university class or professional development unit.

ACTIVITY 2.4 (INDIVIDUAL, GROUP)

Assessing Norms and Regularities in Your Class Culture

Individually, complete the survey. Next, answer the subsequent questions individually and, if possible, compare responses with your classmates.

In any class, there are informal "dos" and "don'ts." They are rarely written down, but they serve as a kind of code, making it clear what people in the system should and should not do if they are to be accepted by others. Following is a list of specific things that a student or instructor might do or say. Estimate what most people in your consultation class would feel about each item (not what you feel, but what you think others would feel). That is, <u>what do you feel the predominant feeling of most of the students in this class</u> is concerning whether one should or should not do or say the thing in question? You can indicate your answer by placing a checkmark in the appropriate column beside each item.

Questions for Reflection:

1   What are the items you think the majority of students would feel someone "Should" do? What are the implications?
2   What are the items you think the majority of students would feel someone "Should Not" do? What are the implications?
3   If you do this with your class, what are the items in which the opinion of the class is split? What are the implications?
4   Would you like to see some changes in the norms? Why? What would be the implications of those changes?

The majority of students feel that someone	Should	Should Not
1. Ask others who seem upset to express their feelings directly		
2. Tell colleagues what you really think of their work		
3. Look for ulterior motives in other students' behavior		
4. Avoid disagreement and conflict whenever possible		
5. Question ways of doing things		
6. Disagree with the instructor if you happen to know more about the issue than s/he does		
7. Withhold personal feelings and stick to the merits of the case		
8. Push for new ideas, even if they are vague or unusual		
9. Ask others to tell you what they really think of your work		
10. Keep your real thoughts and reactions to yourself, by and large		
11. Trust others not to take advantage of you		
12. Be skeptical about things		
13. Point out other people's mistakes to improve working effectiveness		
14. Listen to others' ideas, but reserve the decision to yourself		
15. Try out new ways of doing things even if it is uncertain how they will work out		
16. Stay cool – keep your distance from others		

Sarason (1996) reminds us that the existing culture is one of many possible alternatives, even though that may not be obvious to those living within the current culture. Sarason helps us to see the arbitrariness of some of our norms – like why schools operate from September to June in most places and are empty during the summer months. Is that really the only calendar for schools to operate on? Generating an alternative is tough because it requires us to change our actions, our thinking, and how the setting will operate. When some schools in the United States tried to move to an all-year schedule, with breaks scattered throughout the year, it was difficult for many communities to adjust to that model. Or, more recently, in some school districts, arguments have been made in favor of changing school start times to allow high school students a later start than elementary students, given the myriad positive effects that have been demonstrated from a change that considers adolescent sleep patterns. This effort encountered opposition because of logistical issues (e.g., related to buses), but also in large part because it is different from how things have been done before.

Recognizing how difficult it is to change a norm or regularity in schools, Sarason (1996) asks us to acknowledge "there are no better ways to comprehend the culture of the school than either by looking at how it responds to pressures for change or how it responds to someone who is trying to be helpful to people within it" (p. vii). A good place to begin to understand how change will be perceived in a school in which you are working is by answering questions about the norms, regularities, and unwritten rules about help-seeking and working with a consultant.

ACTIVITY 2.5 (INDIVIDUAL, GROUP)

Norms and Regularities, Outcomes, and Alternative Regularities

1　Individually or as a class, read through the norms/regularities table.
2　Individually complete the first alternative regularities for: "Teachers do not ask for help."
3　Individually think of additional norms/regularities, intended outcomes, and alternatives for the final row. Although there is only one blank row, it might be helpful to think of more than one series of norms, outcomes, and alternatives.
4　In a small group or individually, discuss/reflect on your responses guided by these questions:
　　a.　Do the intended outcomes and actual outcomes of the norms you investigated converge or diverge?
　　b.　If the intended outcomes diverge from the actual outcomes, what are some alternative possibilities to achieve the intended outcomes?

c. How do you think a school consultant might support the consideration of alternative regularities in a school when intended outcomes are divergent from actual outcomes?

Norms/ Regularities/ Unwritten Rules in Your School	Intended Outcomes (What are the regularities supposed to accomplish?)	Actual Outcomes (What do the regularities actually accomplish?)	Alternative Regularities (What are some different ways to do things?)
School psychologists primarily function as "testers" and special education gatekeepers	• Get at the root of the problem • Put a label on it for parents • Provide "comprehensive" recommendations • Meet the school's legal obligations • Get kids in special education, which is more effective • "Professional preciousness" • Fits with professional training • Shifting roles would be hard	• Focus on student, miss alternative roles for school psychologist • Ecological perspectives in problem-solving • Cross-disciplinary collaboration • Clear assessment questions • Recommendations linked to instruction	• Alternative roles for school psychologist • Ecological perspectives in problem-solving • Cross-disciplinary collaboration • Clear assessment questions • Recommendations linked to instruction
Teachers do not ask for help	• Avoid negative evaluation, criticism/save face • Avoid lengthy processes that may be ineffective • Maintain professional autonomy	• Professional isolation • Students may not get what they need • Focus on student (fundamental attribution error)	?
?	?	?	?

Assumptions That Impact Consultation

Embedded in this activity around norms is a set of assumptions that impact school consultation work. Here are some very important assumptions that are critical to the success of the school consultant.

Broken Child Versus Broken Match

In a school, is the problem referred to the consultant or the problem-solving team viewed as situated: (a) within the child, or (b) within the relationship between the student's skills, the teacher's skills, and other issues within the context? If there is a substantial difference between the school culture, the individual consultee, and the consultant, awareness of that discrepancy is essential. In one situation (Pickering, 2012), the school culture and teacher consultee valued retention of students not reaching standards in kindergarten, while the CIT was focused on research that recommended promotion and was focused on an intervention to support the student building his early reading skills. The teacher was less focused on the student making progress, as she had already decided he should be retained in kindergarten for another year. In another example, the school psychologist was so wedded to the broken child assumption that he could not refrain from assessing the student's cognitive and achievement profile when he was developing his consultation skills in case he "missed a learning disability."

Maital (2017) makes the case even more complex, as she reminds us that our consultees, as well as consultants, often have hidden competing commitments and competing priorities based not only on school culture but their own individual beliefs about students. Citing the work of Kegan and Lahey (2001) on competing commitments, Maital (2017) finds that even after developing skills in consultation, energy may continue to be devoted to goals or beliefs counter to using those skills: "psychologists, trained to seek intrapsychic factors in individual difficulties, may assume that reliance on . . . consultation may not really resolve psychological difficulties" (p. 246). It is not unusual in our experience for school psychologists to express the concern that they might miss the real problem if they consult with the teacher rather than do a complete traditional psychoeducational assessment.

Value of Collaboration and Consultation

We have earlier provided you an introduction to the history of collaboration in schools. Within each school, collaboration can be valued along a continuum, and it is important that you assess the school, your consultee, and yourself. Sometimes school psychologists so value their role as experts that they are less willing to develop collaborative relationships with teachers. We have heard school psychologists state that they are unwilling to give up their expert role. Of course, psychologists maintain their expertise as psychologists and as experts in the process of consultation, confusing their role in assessment or treatment with their expertise in general.

In some schools, the culture is one of self-reliance, and teachers are expected to resolve their own problems or send any student exhibiting problems for special education assessment. Other schools have been described as balkanized cultures (Hargreaves & Fullan, 2012), pockets, or cliques (Visone et al., 2022), where only some teachers work together. Hargreaves and Fullan (2012) describe collaboration at the school level along a continuum. There can be *comfortable collaboration*, where teachers get along but do not work on problems together. This can be puzzling to a novice consultant. In one school, teachers ate together and planned parties together but did not work together on school, classroom, or curriculum concerns. While it seemed collegial, the collaboration was not about the work. Sometimes an administrator can attempt to encourage collaboration, setting up time to meet and organizing teams for different purposes. This *contrived collegiality* can be seen in schools where time is allocated for meetings, but teachers are observed grading papers and on their smartphones rather than focused on working together. Of course, some teams may function better than others, but it is important to be aware of the lack of a culture of collaboration among a group with which you as a consultant want to work. A more promising setting for consultation is schools that have an interactive and functional professional culture in which consultation and collaboration thrive. While most schools have a mixture of these types of collaboration, the consultant needs to be alert to the impact these varying levels of collaboration may have on consultation.

Value of Diversity and Culturally Responsive School Consultation

In contemporary schools, it is necessary to consider the numerous intersectional identities and cultures of the students, families, and educators that comprise the school community as part of school culture. Much of the professional psychology literature on culture focuses on multicultural and cross-cultural issues, often on the race, gender, or ethnicity of those involved in treating and treatment. The lens of intersectionality is helpful in understanding relational interactions between consultants, consultees, and clients. Intersectionality refers to "the merging or intersection of multiple marginalized identities" such as race, culture, sexual orientation, language proficiency, gender identity, disability status, economic status, and numerous other variables (National Association of School Psychologists, 2017). It also highlights that within a particular minoritized group, there are numerous individual identities, each with multiple axes. The APA (2017c) recognizes intersectionality as an essential lens for psychology practice, including consulting at the individual and systems levels.

> Consultants can . . . inform educational institutions that intersectional identities comprise both a personal agentic process of self-definition (e.g., this is how I choose to identify myself) and structural institutional dynamics and labels (e.g., this is how others, including the institution, identify me). Psychologists can point to intersectional oppression when explaining the complexities of identity and self-definition.
>
> (APA, 2017c)

Guiney and Proctor (2022) explore the case of a high-achieving 16-year-old high school student who suddenly began struggling academically. The student immigrated to the United States with her family from Honduras when she was six, and the family was undocumented. Recent local and national policies related to immigration resulted in the student feeling overwhelmed with the possibility of being "outed" and deported. She also identified as gay but has not yet come out to her traditional Catholic family. She confided in a trusted classmate, who subsequently shared this information, resulting in harassment from peers.

Imagine a teacher consultee asked for your support on such a case. What information would be important for you to have as a consultant? What questions might you ask of the teacher? What identities (your own, the consultee, the student) are pertinent to think about? Which ecological layers of individuals and systems are relevant? Of course, there are no easy answers here. That is the point. Being a humble consultant, including consulting with cultural humility, requires complex thinking and ongoing learning. We return to these issues later in the chapter and throughout the book.

Although it is critical that school consultants have the requisite consultation skills, the application of those skills in culturally diverse settings requires additional training (Ingraham, 2017, 2022). Ingraham's (2000) Multicultural School Consultation (MSC) framework consists of five components designed to bring a multicultural lens to the practice of consultation. MSC integrates cultural responsiveness and awareness into the consultation process at all levels, from entry to intervention implementation.

- The first component, Consultant Learning and Development, summarizes knowledge and skill areas expected of culturally competent consultants, including understanding one's own culture, the cultures of others, and the impact of culture in supporting consultees and clients.
- Consultee Learning and Development, the second component, focuses on the knowledge, skill, objectivity, and confidence areas for consultees that might be supported during the consultation process.
- Component three, Cultural Variations in the Consultation Constellation (Figure 2.1), highlights cultural similarities and differences between consultants, consultees, and clients and how these might be relevant to the consultation process.
- The fourth component is Contextual and Power Influences, which explores power differentials between individuals engaging in the consultation and also considers the nested systems in which the consultation takes place.
- The final component is Hypothesized Methods for Supporting Consultee and Client Success, which includes the consultant's careful construction of a problem frame in collaboration with the consultee, incorporating culturally responsive consultation strategies, and continuing, always, to engage in professional learning and self-reflection about culture.

Recent articles demonstrate the continued applicability of Ingraham's (2000) classic framework to contemporary consultation practice (Brown et al., 2022;

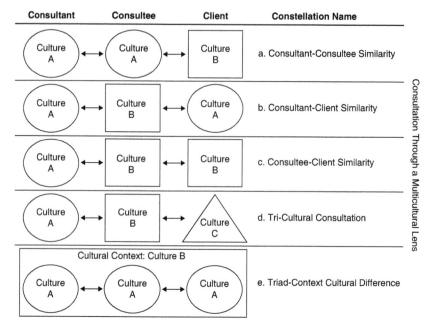

FIGURE 2.1 Constellations of Consultation Relationships (Ingraham, 2000)

Parker et al., 2020). Parker et al. (2020) interviewed 15 school psychologists about their application of culturally responsive consultation. Four qualitative themes from this study reflect how consultants attempted to support consultee and client success (Component Five from Ingraham's, 2000, framework):

1. Involve others in problem-solving (e.g., teachers, parents, administrators, and other professionals), although facilitating parental engagement was sometimes viewed as a challenge.
2. Teach consultees about culturally diverse students through strategies such as offering information, asking questions, dialoguing, and modeling how to think about diversity, although some teachers were viewed by consultants as having limited interest in culturally responsive practice.
3. Demonstrate support for teachers, parents, and students through emotional support mechanisms, including affirming and praising teachers' culturally responsive interventions, valuing professional relationships with parents, including learning about their backgrounds and finding effective means of communication, and continuously advocating for the best interests of students.
4. Engage in systems-level consultation to help groups of culturally diverse students, including providing schoolwide professional learning opportunities and interventions. However, a systems-level role was not always supported by school administrators.

Brown et al. (2022) adapted the Ingraham (2000) framework for specific consideration in working with Gender and Sexually Diverse students, including those from ethnically and racially minoritized backgrounds, by incorporating a minority stress model (i.e., recognizing that individuals holding minoritized identities experience increased mental health difficulties resulting from structural prejudice and discrimination) and intersectionality frameworks. The authors argue that "at every stage of the consultation process, the consultant must consider how sexual orientation, gender identity, race, and ethnicity shape the consultant-consultee-client triad [and broader social context]" (Brown et al., 2022, p. 19).

The complexity of consultation in diverse schools goes beyond the knowledge base. Miranda (2016) provides a series of cases that support a more culturally responsive school consultation practice. We will come back to these issues in later chapters. Establishing multicultural and cross-cultural school consultation competency is an ongoing process for all of us. Once you have developed increased self-awareness around these issues, you can seek out additional resources and consult with more knowledgeable others (e.g., supervisors) regarding your areas of need; developing a plan for further learning can include applied experiences during your professional training.

Scan the first QR code to view Dr. Antoinette Miranda present some aspects of the urban multicultural context.

QR CODE 2.1   Antoinette Miranda Video

Using the second QR code, you may listen to Dr. Miranda speak about this content as a guest on the *Conversations About Consultation Podcast.*

QR CODE 2.2   Antoinette Miranda Consultation Podcast

In a consultation case, it is important to examine the cultural constellation to determine the relevance of cultural issues to the process, consistent with the third component of Ingraham's (2000) Multicultural School Consultation framework (Figure 2.1). Pickering (2012) provides a good example of a cultural consultation constellation issue in a case in which the CIT identified with the student who shared his ethnic background. In another case, one CIT was concerned about a dysfunctional grade-level team with which she was working on a curriculum assessment issue. Three of the teachers were White, and one was African American; the three White teachers had bonded into a group, and the African-American teacher was not participating in the team meetings. The CIT had not considered this as part of the constellation until it was pointed out in supervision.

ACTIVITY 2.6 (INDIVIDUAL, GROUP)

Cultural Constellation

If you are currently consulting with a consultee or consultees, complete and answer the following questions.

1 Identify the constellation, including any intrapersonal intersectional identities, of your consultation triad in Figure 2.1.
2 What are the implications of this constellation for your work, if any?
3 How do you determine which, if any, cultural issues are *salient* in your case?
4 Discuss your responses with a partner.

Globalization of School Psychology Consultation

Before leaving the topic of multicultural consultation, it is relevant to introduce the growth of a global perspective in psychology. There is increasing interest in globalization across school psychology as well as a history of school psychologists with an interest in consultation theory, training, practice, and research connecting with one another around the world. For example, psychologists from Australia, Canada, England, Greece, Hong Kong, Israel, Sweden, and the United States contributed chapters to the *International Handbook of Consultation in Educational Settings* (Hatzichristou & Rosenfield, 2017), which provides a resource to learn more about this aspect of school consultation.

Strategies for Uncovering School Culture

We are hopeful that you are now considering how important it is to focus on school culture rather than just on the problems of individual children or teachers. Rhona Weinstein, a clinical psychology faculty member at the UC-Berkeley, attending the APA/Carnegie Conference on Urban Schools (1997), commented most eloquently on looking in at schools:

> I think we need to teach psychologists about schooling – getting to know classrooms and schools and the children, teachers, and principals inside of

schools. Those of us with interest in schooling share a fascination with the personality of classrooms and schools and districts, much like others' fascination with the personality of individuals. We need to instill this excitement and raise awareness of the importance of schooling environments in children's development.

Where are some places you can learn about a school culture? For sure, one place is the school faculty meeting. To prepare for such a visit, here is an activity you can do by yourself or with your consultation class:

ACTIVITY 2.7 (INDIVIDUAL, GROUP)

School Culture Case Example

Read the following case example and then answer the subsequent questions individually and, if possible, compare responses with a partner or in a small group.

Case Example:

You are asked at a faculty meeting to introduce yourself as the new school psychologist and to talk about consultation. The principal introduces you to the staff and announces that the superintendent has indicated an interest in the school's participation in building more collaborative working relationships among staff, including the school psychologist. However, he states that the program is voluntary. The principal runs into your time by making several announcements regarding school procedures.

As you finally get up to talk, some teachers listen attentively while others chat with each other. When you ask for questions, there is a pause. Then one teacher asks how this collaboration thing differs from other new programs that have come and gone in the past. Others ask what proof there is that consultation makes a difference for students and how much extra work is involved for teachers.

Questions for Reflection:

1   What information did you pick up from the meeting about the norms and regularities of this school culture?
2   What information did you pick up about the roles of the principal and the teachers?
3   What else is important for you to confirm/learn about this school culture?
4   Taking an ecological point of view, how might you have responded to these questions?

Other ways you can learn about school culture include:

- Talking with individual teachers about their experiences with consulting and collaborating with colleagues,
- Spending time in the teacher lounge and listening to conversations,
- Sitting in on team meetings at the grade and school level,
- Interviewing the principal about consultation and collaboration as a school norm.

Additional information can be gleaned from students' caregivers, of course, and from students, who may have little or no opportunity to collaborate with each other. In fact, students are often the most perceptive purveyors of the school culture. One high school student mentioned that she knew how the teachers felt about her school because they couldn't get out of the building fast enough when the afternoon bell rang.

Developing a map of the relationships among the staff is helpful for new consultants. Knowing the names of all the staff members, their roles, and how they interact with each other can be very informative and useful for understanding the school culture and, thus, helpful in establishing a consultant role. Learning the pattern of relationships (e.g., who eats with whom) is also useful information, as is examining where staff and classes are placed in relationship to each other. For example, the placement of special education classrooms, bilingual classrooms, and specialists, including counselors and school psychologists, often represents how they are perceived in the school. Wyner (1991) reminds us that, given space is often at a premium, especially in urban schools, space allocations "reflect implicit, unvoiced priorities" (p. 99). Her description of the suboptimal placements of English as a Second Language (ESL) teachers clearly indicated their status in a school. School psychologists sometimes post social media pictures of their offices at the beginning of each school year. Much can be gleaned about the place of the school psychologist based on shared images of small, windowless spaces that were made in closets as an afterthought and misspellings of "psychologist" versus ample space, new office supplies, and prime locations by the front office.

An important aspect of school culture relevant for consultation is the degree of collaboration engaged in by staff. Activity 2.8 references a school collaboration scale (Appendix A) that you can use in the setting where you are consulting. This scale was part of a larger study, and data on the scale and its relationship to consultation outcomes can be found in Vu et al. (2013).

ACTIVITY 2.8 (INDIVIDUAL, GROUP)

Assessing School Climate for Consultation

Using the survey provided in Appendix A, do the following at your practicum site, internship site, or school where you are employed:

1 Complete the survey yourself.

2   Administer the survey to two other individuals at your school. Try to survey staff members with distinct roles (e.g., general education teacher, special education teacher, school psychologist, nurse).

3   Reflect in writing and/or discussion on what the data suggest about your school's climate:

    a.   What results were *surprising* or *unsurprising* to you? Why?

    b.   What are the implications of the data for your enacting a consultant role at this site?

What Do We Mean by Entry?

We now move on to the concept of entry, the process of the consultant entering and being accepted into the culture of a system or organization, in this case, a school. Effective consultants, whether internal or external to the system, must do two things: (1) learn about the norms and regularities of the school that comprise its culture, which we have discussed previously, and (2) make entry into the school as a professional who seeks to include consultation in his or her scope of practice. Simply walking in the door and greeting the staff is not sufficient as an entry process.

Entering the School as a Consultant: The Entry Process

One of us (S. R.) was asked the following question (only slightly modified for clarity):

> We are curious to hear from you on what advice you have for us going out into our internship year. During class time lecture and instruction, we are taught best practice by using the Multi-tiered Systems of Support (MTSS) framework. But many of our internship sites are struggling to implement it. Would you be willing to share your thoughts on how best we, as soon-to-be interns, can implement and successfully use instructional consultation? Thank you for taking the time to read this email; we hope to hear back from you soon!

Basically, these two interns were asking how to enter a school to be able to provide consultation services, given that most schools do not expect the school psychologist to include much consultation within their scope of practice or perhaps even have clear ideas of what consultation services might look like. They were also acknowledging that what they were taught as best practice in their training might not be in place in the schools. In a focus group interview, an experienced intern supervisor noted that his interns came with many new ideas but were frustrated because they did not have the skill to introduce them to the school setting in which they were placed.

For consultation to become a norm within a particular school, the teachers and other staff members need to understand what engaging in consultation, no matter the model, requires of them and to accept the role of consultee. This introduction needs to happen at two levels: (1) entry into the school as a practitioner expecting to do consultation as part of regular service delivery, and (2) contracting with a specific staff member who is seeking support either for a student or for themself in their professional role. We will come back to the second, contracting, in Chapter 6.

Sarason and his colleagues (1966) recognize the need for a Port of Entry presentation when an external consultant entered a school to provide consultation services. However, an internal consultant (i.e., an individual such as a school counselor or school psychologist who works in the setting) also needs to assess how and where to enter a school as a consultant, presenting a service delivery model that may or may not be new to the staff. Engaging with the principal, who is the legitimate leader of the school (big rule: never blindside a principal), to ensure that they know about the intended consultation service delivery to determine the level of support, or to build support, is an important first step. It is also possible, for consultants who feel less experienced and wish to begin small, to find a responsive teacher with whom to practice together the roles of consultant and consultee around a concern. Sometimes a brief introduction at the first faculty meeting, followed later by a more extensive presentation, will work best, especially when there are some teachers in the room who have experienced success with the consultant.

In beginning her career as a school psychologist, Carner (1982), recognizing the potential to move to a broader role, described her process to restructure a school psychology position in which consultation would be foundational rather than peripheral. She concluded that "there can be a great deal of latitude in creating a consultative role in school psychology – and, moreover, that it is up to the psychologist to demonstrate what is possible" (p. 9). She made her case in her hiring interview, developed an understanding of the school cultures in her assigned schools, worked with the principals, and spoke at faculty meetings – all part of her entry into the schools as a consultant. In schools, as in other organizational settings, effective consultants assess the needs of the system, communicate with clarity about what they have to offer to support those needs, and subsequently develop, implement, and evaluate a mechanism of support (e.g., a structure for consultation) that matches the organization's needs (London & Diamante, 2018). We will discuss these issues further in Chapter 6 in an overview of contracting for consultation.

Dr. Lauren Kaiser, currently a faculty member in the school psychology program at Millersville University, discussed her experiences introducing consultation to her school-based sites as an intern. Scan QR code 2.3 to learn about how she was able to do so.

QR CODE 2.3 Lauren Kaiser Video

Entry Strategies

In his book about the school psychology internship, Newman (2020) highlights several key actions interns can take in entering their internship sites, which are summarized and applied to school consultation in Table 2.1. These strategies are relevant for graduate students entering schools as practicum students or interns but also might be useful for early career and experienced practitioners who are entering a new building and wish to incorporate a consultation framework in their practice.

TABLE 2.1 Actions to Support the Consultation Entry Process in a New Setting

Action	Examples of Actions
Be proactive	• Learn about the school's existing regularities and potential entry points for consultation services. • Get out of your office whenever possible and spend time in classrooms; provide direct support to teachers. • Engage in self-assessment and set goals related to consultation knowledge development and skill application. • Work with supervisors to make sure opportunities for consultation are available.
Walk around the school and meet people	• Introduce yourself to teachers and other staff members during orientation, before kids begin; let teachers know that you are available to consult about student concerns. • Send an email, or place a letter in staff mailboxes, introducing yourself and the services you provide, including consultation. • Print out a staff list and write down notes about the new people you are meeting (e.g., personal information learned in establishing rapport; professional needs for support articulated).
Ask questions	• Ask clarifying questions if you are unsure of a school policy, procedure, or terminology. • Asking clarifying questions to students, teachers, and other staff members may unveil hidden regularities in the school culture that might impact your ability to provide consultative services.
Move beyond comfort zones	• Engage in school consultation even if it is new to you and outside of your comfort zone. • Seek out supports such as mentoring and supervision, including observation and feedback, especially if you have had limited school consultation training.

However, no matter how the process is introduced at the school level, a teacher receiving consultation services needs to be provided the opportunity for informed consent to engage in the process. Although the consultant role may be introduced at a universal level, such as a school faculty meeting, in our experience, such presentations do not always result in teachers' clear understanding of consultation. Our discussion of contracting in Chapter 6 will provide information on the content and process of contracting to enable consultees to make an informed decision to commit to consultation.

From Culture and Context to Consultation

Having explored the concept of school culture and entry into that culture, we move on to two of the most basic domains of consultation: building relationships with consultees (Chapter 3) and developing effective communication skills (Chapter 4). When working with a consultee, content is only one aspect of an effective consultant's toolbox. The following two chapters are designed to help you build the skills you will need in those critical domains.

3

CONSULTATION RELATIONSHIPS

Building Working Relationships

Human relationships are not rocket science — they are far, far more complicated.
(*James Pennebaker*)

We can easily acknowledge that consultation is a helping relationship but helping is not a simple concept. Perhaps Silverstein (1974, p. 101) put it most succinctly in his poem:

And some kind of help
Is the kind of help
That helping's all about
And some kind of help
Is the kind of help
We all can do without.

Before we explore the complexities of relationships in consultation, consider these questions:

ACTIVITY 3.1 (INDIVIDUAL)

Warm-Up Questions: Relationships

Write down responses to the following questions. You can write sentences or just key words.

1   What does it mean to have a working relationship with a consultee?
2   How does a consultation relationship differ from a therapy relationship? A personal relationship?

DOI: 10.4324/9781032622330-3

3   What assumptions do you have about teachers seeking help from con-
    sultants in schools?
4   What is the relationship of trust to building a working relationship?
5   What have you noticed so far about the help-seeking efforts of teach-
    ers at your practicum or internship site? What are the implications for
    engaging in consultation?

The relationship is core to the success of any helping process, such as consultation, although Schein suggests that there is still a lot to be learned about the nature of that relationship (see Schein et al., 2021). Much of the literature about consultation focuses on the problem-solving process, but we believe that the essence of consultation begins with the establishment of a solid working relationship, one that is perceived by the consultee as helpful. In providing help, there must be understanding and trust:

> Understanding is needed for the helper to know when to offer help and what would be helpful if asked for help. Trust is needed for the client to reveal what is the real problem, to be able to accept what is offered, and to implement whatever resolution might come out of the conversation with the helper.
>
> *(Schein, 2009, p. x)*

Let's begin by differentiating the working relationship from a personal or friendly relationship. Although there can be personal and friendly aspects to a working relationship, sometimes friendly relationships get in the way of working relationships. As one consultant commented, she needed to focus less on being liked and more on getting down to what needed to be done. Sometimes novice consultants work to build a personal relationship, but when a problem in the process occurs, or there is a difference in perspective, they discover they do not have a working relationship with the consultee and are unable to productively move the problem-solving process forward. In one such case, the consultant-in-training (CIT) did not even attempt to move forward in the problem-solving process with a teacher because the CIT had become so sympathetic to personal issues impacting the teacher, resulting in the referred student not receiving the support he needed. Although one consultation relationship between a CIT and a teacher eventually led to their marriage (well after the consultation case was over), in another case, a female CIT needed to receive supervisory support on coping with a male teacher who was obviously interested in a personal relationship that she did not want to encourage. With support, she was able to build a working relationship in this situation and provide a successful outcome for the teacher and his students.

Nor is consultation a therapeutic relationship (Sandoval, 2014). The personal issues of the consultee are not the focus – the *work* of the consultee is. When personal issues arise in the process, it is best to acknowledge them and move on or help the consultee receive an appropriate referral. The key point is that a relationship between two or more individuals can take many directions.

Schein (2009) provides a different kind of distinction about relationships, suggesting that there are three ways that a consultant can offer help, although we can shift back and forth among them: we can be an expert resource to provide information or services; we can diagnose problems and prescribe solutions; or we can be a process consultant who builds a non-hierarchical relationship that begins by clarifying the kind of help that is needed. At times, all these forms of help can be relevant, but we argue that it is this third kind of helping relationship that school consultants should embrace most often for maximum effectiveness.

Expert Versus Collaborative Relationship

Over many years, there have been discussions about the distinction between expert and collaborative relationships in the consultation literature (see, e.g., Erchul et al., 2014 for a discussion of this literature). Consultation relationships were seen as either collaborative, that is, two or more professionals, each with their own areas of expertise, working in a non-hierarchical relationship to resolve a problem – more like Schein's (2009) process consultant, or as expert in which the consultant's expertise is the source of the consultee's acceptance of what the consultant has to offer – similar to Schein's first two roles.

Of course, one should view the expert-collaborative dimension as a continuum, but it is helpful to be aware of where one is on the continuum and if that is the right place. Collaboration has been seen as a way for school consultants to produce change by partnering with the consultee in a way to minimize resistance (Erchul et al., 2014) and enhance acceptance and implementation fidelity of interventions, since in most instances, school personnel, aside from administrators, do not have formal or legitimate power over one another. For the expert consultant engaged in a relationship with another school professional, too often, the expectation is that the consultant's unique knowledge base will provide solutions that will resolve problems – the expert providing resources. Our confidence or belief in interventions, particularly those that are "evidence-based" according to our literature, seems self-evident to many consultants – but often not to our consultees.

Richard Thaler and Daniel Kahneman both won Nobel Prizes for their work on people's propensity for acting in irrational ways, challenging the belief that people always behave rationally even when it might be in their own interest. Therefore, even if you think you have the correct solution to a consultee's problem, they might not accept the solution you have to offer. Or, maybe the consultee's perspective (e.g., about why a solution is not acceptable) is rational in ways that we need to explore more deeply through our communication skills. When interventions do not get implemented or do not work as expected, the reputation of consultants as experts suffers, and their impact on future problem-solving efforts is at risk. So, it is imperative to focus our thinking on how to influence our consultees other than simply telling them what we know to be best, moving away from the expert and diagnostic-prescriptive roles as often as possible. Rather than call the teacher resistant, the consultant needs to explore these relationship alternatives instead.

Social Influence/Interpersonal Influence

Relationships also serve as conduits for change. Given that consultation is an indirect service delivery model, the consultant's ability to influence the behavior of consultees through an interpersonal influence process is crucial (Erchul et al., 2014). Acknowledging that "power and influence are integral to all human relationships" (p. 350), Erchul et al. (2014) recognize that our role is to influence our consultees, a truth that is sometimes uncomfortable for new consultants. In fact, novice consultants often feel a lack of power in their interactions, worrying about whether they are imposters in trying to provide services to consultees, often experienced teachers and administrators. Women and minoritized CITs, in particular, often suffer from imposter syndrome. Thinking through issues of power is helpful to the new consultant.

There is a research base in the consultation literature around the kind of social power bases that consultants bring to the process; that is, how consultants can influence their consultees to change in some way, whether it is their beliefs about a problem or student, their attitude toward a situation, or their behavior. Erchul and colleagues (2019) summarize the French and Raven (1959) concept of social power in the school consultation literature as a well-known framework for examining social influence, one that has changed over time. According to Erchul et al. (2019), survey research of school psychologists has demonstrated that consultants seem to perceive soft bases (e.g., direct informational, positive expert, and positive referent power) as more effective (i.e., influential) than harsh bases. Erchul et al. (2001) stated that "soft (weak) bases tend to be more subtle, positive, and noncoercive; hard (harsh) bases tend to be more overt, punitive, and 'heavy-handed.'" (p. 487). In a study of teacher perceptions of social influence strategies, Owens et al. (2017) found some evidence that teachers may have different preferences for expertise and power dynamics in the relationship, which may impact changes in their classroom management practices. The authors contend that knowing what sources of power influence specific teachers would be helpful in knowing how to approach individual teachers.

Research on social power and actual change in teacher behavior remains limited, although Erchul et al. (2019) conclude that for behavioral consultants, soft power bases may be most effective. We would also like to acknowledge that social influence may be viewed differently in different consultation models. For example, a consultee-centered consultation framework would consider bidirectional influence a meaningful aspect of the consultation process; consultant perceptions may shift alongside consultee perceptions, not just the other way around. In that way, consultants are more than influencers, and consultees are partners rather than just targets of influence.

One way in which social power is bidirectional involves what consultants term resistance. Aguilar and Cohen (2022) describe multiple ways that teachers and administrators negotiate power or give up power in situations but remind us that there is always power to be negotiated in social situations. One way to conceptualize resistance is as a power struggle, reflecting an unmet need resulting in anger, fear, or sadness (Aguilar & Cohen, 2022). Aguilar and Cohen suggest that power struggles emerge "when people are not aligned in purpose or in process, or sometimes both" (p. 112). One of the important functions of the contracting phase, which we will consider later in the book, is to develop a shared understanding of purpose and process. Building a relationship of trust is also directed at reducing the need for using resistance to maintain a level playing field of power. Additional strategies for developing working relationships will be provided throughout the chapter.

The Perils of One-Down Status Position in the Relationship

Developing a collaborative relationship in a helping situation is not simple. In all relationships, there are issues of status positioning, that is, our desire to have the status and position we feel we deserve (Schein, 2009). There is agreement that in most helping relationships, there is a power differential where the helper is perceived as one-up over the helpee. After all, who has the problem, and who has been called in to help resolve it? In essence, there are professional costs to asking for help.

There are multiple examples of specific costs to the consultee who is being helped (Rosenfield, 1987). First, school staff members are busy, and it is difficult to ask for help from a busy professional. An unintended message sent by the busy staff members is that they are too overloaded to take the time to help, and the consultee may feel like they are burdening their colleague, which does not encourage asking for help. Key to being approached for help is that the school consultant develops relationships that convey the message of availability for consultation rather than having no time to listen or provide support.

It is also important to provide information to school staff, both in faculty meetings, memos, and personally, that using the consultant's services is appropriate and within the scope of services provided by the consultant. This is most crucial when beginning work in a school where collaboration and helping are not part of the school culture. For example, one early career school psychologist struggled to incorporate a consultation-oriented role because staff members were used to the psychologist role being focused on special education decision-making, the emphasis of her recently retired predecessor. Beyond role expectations, in American schools, there is a long-standing tradition of praising teacher self-reliance, as we noted in an earlier chapter. Recent changes in school norms to more collaborative relationships need to be encouraged and not necessarily assumed (Rosenfield et al., 2018). Examining your school culture to assess if norms of collaboration and helping are valued will help you to address issues of teacher autonomy as they arise.

Third, help seekers may be perceived and may perceive themselves as less competent. Both helpers and those asking for help enter a relationship with a belief about their own value, and how the relationship evolves depends in part on how much the consultee "grants value to the helper and the degree to which the helper grants value to the [consultee]" (Schein, 2009, p. 14). Consultants who are trying to form collaborative relationships need to be authentic in their respect for classroom teachers requesting consultation. Teaching is a very difficult job, and consultants need to be humble in developing an appreciation for the complexities of managing a classroom of diverse students with mixed entry-level skills, motivation, and academic histories, in a context in which there is a considerable lack of respect for the teaching profession, often limited support, and high accountability. Appreciating the very human need of the consultee to save face is critical to the success of the relationship.

Diversity in the Consultation Relationship

In addition, perceptions of competency may be affected by diversity, including microaggressions against minoritized educators. Before the helping relationship even materializes, some minoritized consultants and consultees may find themselves one-down due to local and systemic factors, including prejudice or racism. The one-down position may reflect a lack of respect or confidence in their school setting, both perceived and actual (Brown, 2019; Kohli, 2021). Brown (2019) cites a number of studies documenting the concerns of African-American teachers, usually few in number, in a traditionally white female workplace. She describes racial microaggressions experienced by African-American teachers in their schools, including being treated as second-class citizens, a one-down position before the consultation relationship even begins. Recognition of these issues for both consultants and consultees requires self-reflection on our own biases, a topic we will return to later as we consider the importance of self-reflection for consultants.

Trust

Given the critical need to save face in many helping relationships, both by the consultant and the consultee, there must be a sense of trust between them. In a

New Yorker article about why some healthcare innovations spread swiftly and others sluggishly, surgeon and author Atul Gawande (2013) asserts that change is *not* best accomplished via friendly requests, coercive demands for action, providing the most up-to-date technology, or even offering lucrative incentives.

> To create new norms, you have to understand people's existing norms and barriers to change. You have to understand what's getting in their way . . . people follow the lead of other people they know and trust when they decide whether to take it up. Every change requires effort, and the decision to make that effort is a social process.

In a consultation context, trust also means "that no matter what we choose to reveal about our thoughts, feelings, or intentions, the other person will not belittle us, make us look bad, or take advantage of what we have said" (Schein, 2009, p. 18). The consultee will often not reveal what is really going on until trust is established. Here is where our relationship factors come into play, including our communication skills, our ability to convey a sense of interest in the other person (described as *personizing* by Schein et al., 2021), our nonverbal behavior, and our capacity to listen, as described in Chapter 4. Allowing a teacher to be vulnerable about their professional skills, rather than placing the burden for the problem on the student, requires trust. At the most basic level, "trust means safety for our self-esteem" (Schein, 2009, p. 19).

Being trustworthy also requires keeping time and other commitments. One simple but critical behavior to build and establish trust is being on time for appointments or having a way to communicate with the consultee when a problem arises. Fulfilling task commitments is also essential, such as doing what you said you would do before the next consultation meeting. Even if the teacher does not follow through on their commitments, the consultant is still obliged to do so.

However, the consultant also can expect the teacher to be there for appointments and to follow through on tasks. When that is not happening, it is important to discuss the reasons and perhaps re-contract on expectations for both parties to the relationship (see Chapter 6 for a discussion of contracting). Consistently missing appointments and failing to follow through on tasks are signs that the relationship is not mutually satisfying or there are issues unknown to the consultant which are impacting the relationship (such as an illness in the consultee's family). An open discussion is essential. Sometimes that means that the teacher does not want to continue the relationship, the tasks are either not meaningful or practical from the teacher's perspective, or there are teacher concerns unrelated to the consultation relationship distracting the consultee. These are important signs not to be dismissed as resistance but as relationship issues that require openness and communication.

Scan QR code 3.1 to listen to Dr. Courtenay Barrett, a faculty member in the school psychology program at Michigan State University, who discusses the importance of trust in the consultation relationship. She also comments on cultural humility in the relationship, a construct we revisit later in this chapter.

QR CODE 3.1 Courtenay Barrett Video

The Peril of One-Up Status in the Relationship

There are also perils to the one-up status position of the helper, including multiple traps that the one-up relationship can generate for the consultant (Rosenfield, 1987; Schein, 2009). First, until trust is built, the consultee may not be comfortable sharing the real problem. As a result, to protect the teacher's sense of efficacy, the initial focus of the first concern the teacher brings to the table is often a student deficit or problem rather than one related to instruction or management in the classroom. If the consultant moves too quickly to an intervention on the first problem presented by the consultee, it is not likely to be successful if the intervention does not address the real problem. This issue is often exacerbated on problem-solving teams, where the teacher's self-efficacy is at risk in front of multiple colleagues. In addition, many problem-solving teams allow only a brief period for identifying the problem and move quickly to intervention without sufficient analysis of the problem itself. Even an evidence-based intervention is ineffective if it is used for the wrong problem.

Second, once the consultee has shared a problem, there is often a sense that it is now the consultant's job to resolve it. Consultees often feel as if they have handed over the problem to the consultant for action once the concern has been shared. The pull to solve the problem is strong, and many CITs have been surprised, when listening retrospectively to recordings of consultation sessions, to hear themselves suggesting solutions well before there is a clear delineation of the problem. Consistent with research on soft power bases such as exerting positive expert power (Owens et al., 2017), consultants should possess content expertise (for novice consultants, this can be achieved in conjunction with support from supervisors), as they sometimes need to offer essential information to consultees. Doing so in a way that balances collaboration in synchrony with directiveness may best achieve the intentions of indirect service delivery (Gutkin, 1999).

Further, the process of giving intervention suggestions must be done carefully, as telling someone what to do maintains a one-up status position for the consultant and a one-down status position for the consultee. In medicine, for example, as much as 30% of medication prescriptions go unfilled, and approximately 50% of medications for chronic diseases are not taken as prescribed (Viswanathan et al., 2012). Glaucoma patients have been found to go blind because they do not use the prescribed eye drops. Upon his retirement from the National Institute of Health in December 2021, former Director Francis Collins reflected,

> To have now 60 million people still holding off of taking advantage of life-saving [COVID-19] vaccines is pretty unexpected . . . We used to think that if knowledge was made available from credible sources, it would win the day. That's not happening now.

Of course, there are several explanations regarding this final example, but the point is that, even in matters of life or death, just because something is evidence-based or seems to you to be logical, it does not mean it will be accepted by someone else. We will return to the issue of intervention implementation in Chapter 8.

In school consultation, the intervention suggestion might be something the consultee has already tried, and the consultee may find it condescending (e.g., "Of course I've tried moving her seat!"). If the initial intervention is not useful or practical, the consultant also risks being seen as irrelevant or not a credible source of support. Relatedly, sometimes the consultee does not want help but validation for their perspective, reassurance that they are doing everything that needs to be done, or just an opportunity to vent about the issues. For example, Guva (2004) makes the case for the importance of understanding why the consultee has come to the consultant rather than assuming they are asking for help. Sometimes, she says, they are handing over a question (what do we need to do to get this student assessed for special education?), or a task (a request for direct services, such as counseling), or communicating "the *feeling* that something has to be done" (italics in original; p. 256). We will return to these issues in Chapter 8, which is focused on interventions.

Knowing Oneself

Novice consultants may not be comfortable seeing themselves as involved in an interpersonal influence process, but the consultant's role is to help bring about change. We need to develop the skills to support change, and our relationship with the consultee is part of that helping process. Engaging in a relationship that supports change requires us to be clear about who we are.

One key issue that concerns CITs, especially those who do not have much professional experience or lack school experience, is their own competence, or specifically, their competence in their new professional role. Stone et al. (1999) reflect on the core identity issues that often underlie our difficulty in professional conversations and list the issue of competence as critical. As one CIT said, "I know that the more confident and professional I act, the more successful I can be." In our experience, CITs often back off from authentic conversations with consultees because they feel incompetent in the face of teacher expertise, believing they have no power or expertise to create change. Their non-verbal behavior and communication reflect this assumption, a disservice to the consultee who likely perceives this feeling. The same CIT, reflecting on a case that had gone well, made it clear that acting professionally "really had a positive impact." Although she was a novice, she "acted as if" she were a professional, and "it worked."

Learning to trust the power of the consultation process is one way to address this issue. It is helpful for the novice consultant to reflect on and understand the usefulness of the consultation process when it is conducted with integrity. We often recommend that at the beginning, CITs *act as if* they trust the process.

Some novice consultants have also used their lack of expertise in the content of the concern to ask authentic and open questions about curriculum, instruction, or behavior management; these "naïve questions" (Garmston & Wellman, 2016) enable the teacher to exhibit their own sense of competence rather than having it called into question because of the request for assistance, and often have led to a more open discussion of the problem. Naïve questions act to lower consultee defenses as well as help to make sure that the consultant and consultee have the same information to move forward in problem-solving.

Having clarity about your own sense of identity is also essential to your work as a consultant. As discussed in Chapter 2, an intersectionality lens can help consider the numerous aspects of your own identity, interactions with the identities of consultees and clients within the consultation constellation, and how these interactions are nested within a school's culture. Maintaining a systems-level view as a consultant is particularly important for another critical issue, namely implicit bias.

Implicit biases are "the attitudes or stereotypes that affect our understanding, actions, and decisions in an unconscious manner" (Staats, 2016). All individuals are vulnerable to implicit biases, including educators. For example, among numerous unfortunate examples, research suggests that teachers hold lower expectations for minoritized students as compared with white students (Van Den Bergh et al., 2010); Black students are over-referred for subjective disciplinary concerns (Bradshaw et al., 2010); and perceptions of collaboration in the consultation relationship vary based on the race of the consultant, consultee, and client (Clinkscales et al., 2022).

Notably, individuals can become aware of their implicit biases and adjust (Staats, 2016). However, doing so is obviously challenging, given that such biases are initially unconscious. While consultants are as vulnerable to holding implicit biases as anyone else, developing self-awareness of such biases, as well as of the systemic biases rampant in educational settings, is a starting point for shifting these dynamics (La Salle et al., 2020). The skills and problem-solving process described throughout this text are intended to help consultants engage in a type of humble inquiry (Schein, 2016), including cultural humility, which supports professional collaboration and opportunities for "safely challenge[ing] a consultee's inferences or biases without being so nondirective or nice that they unintentionally become complicit in oppression" (Kaiser & Newman, 2023). Specific skills to achieve these goals (e.g., clarifying) are expanded upon in the subsequent chapter focused on communication. For more information on implicit biases, interested readers may wish to link to the following podcast interview with Dr. Mahzarin Banaji, a pioneering scholar in this area, using QR code 3.2.

QR CODE 3.2   Mahzarin Banaji Podcast

Scan the QR code 3.3 to view a video of Dr. Stacy Williams, who expands upon the challenges of relationship building in school consultation, including understanding your own identity and navigating the systems in which you are consulting.

QR CODE 3.3   Stacy Williams Video

To help you reflect on your own identities, their intersectionality, and how they may matter within a larger consultation constellation, we provide the following exercise. It can be done individually, with some of your classmates, or within a class.

ACTIVITY 3.2 (INDIVIDUAL, GROUP)

Circles of Identity (Adapted from Laidley et al., 2001)

Think about your "circles of identity" and create one for yourself (see the following example). These are (a) descriptors or words that shape who you are and interact with the world and (b) descriptors or words that other people use to identify you.

Questions for Reflection:

1   With which descriptors do you identify most strongly? Why?
2   With which descriptors do others identify you most strongly? How do you feel about that?

3   Describe a time when your perceptions of a child/student's identity caused you to do something that moved her/him forward.
4   Describe a time when your perceptions of a child/student's identity caused you to do something that held her/him back.
5   How does *your* identity, either descriptors you chose or others choose for you, impact who you are as a consultant?

Possible Group Activity

Get into groups of three (classmates you do not always work with). Look at one question at a time. Take one minute to think. Each partner has one full minute to speak while others listen. If the person finishes speaking before one minute is up, the group should sit in silence. Switch persons at the end of each minute.

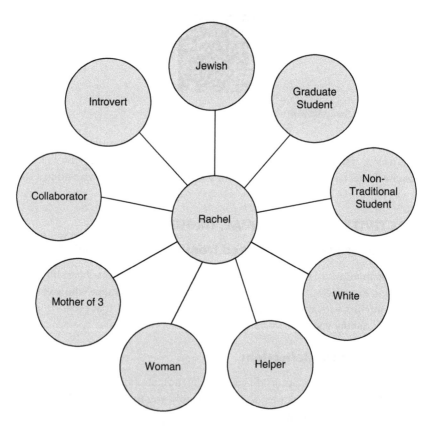

FIGURE 3.1   Example of a Circle of Identity

Difficult Conversations Within the Context of a Consultation Relationship

We have introduced one source of tension that can lead to a difficult conversation, that is, whether the consultee is meeting agreed-upon commitments. Other sources of tension can arise from different perspectives about issues and practices, such as whether rewarding students is a good practice. Teachers often resist rewarding student behavior, which the empirical literature supports, because they believe it should not be necessary to do so. The discrepancy between the teacher's perspective and the literature can provide a barrier to a consultant's objectivity with a teacher who pushes against a practice that is supported in the research. There is a tendency in such situations to simply repeat what the research says over and over in different ways, but that will not necessarily change the perspective of the teacher who has her own response to reward.

Stone et al. (1999) stress that all difficult conversations have an underlying structure, which includes:

- What is the situation that calls for the conversation?
- What are the underlying feelings about the situation?
- And, least likely to be acknowledged, what the situation means to our sense of who we are.

ACTIVITY 3.3 (INDIVIDUAL, GROUP)

Unpacking a Difficult Situation

Read the following case example, and then answer the subsequent questions individually. If possible, compare responses with a partner or in a small group.

Case Example:

In one case, a teacher was missing appointments on a regular basis but kept promising she would do better; the CIT was reluctant to have a conversation about this situation, and the lack of progress and meeting dragged on.

Questions for Reflection:

Using Stone et al.'s (1999) structure, how would you assess the issues in the situation for the consultant?

1 What is the nature of the situation that requires a conversation?
2 What are the underlying feelings that the teacher and the CIT had?
3 What did the situation mean for the consultant?

Stone et al. (1999) invite us to think about intentions that we attribute to our colleagues — what assumptions are we making about the teacher's intentions? Did we assume they wanted to end the relationship? In one case, a teacher's daughter was getting married, and the teacher was frantically trying to attend to all the details while working full-time — there was just not enough time to incorporate the consultation meetings into her day. However, the CIT assumed a different intention, that she was not interested in the consultation process. Although it is not always possible or appropriate to talk about feelings, sometimes it can be helpful to do so. The teacher, in this case, had some feelings that needed to be addressed and the feelings of the CIT needed to be addressed as well. The communication skill of reflecting feelings, presented in Chapter 4, can be helpful in discussing feelings that are present but might otherwise go unacknowledged. In many situations, there is a quick tendency to assess blame, especially to label the teacher as "resistant." We need to move from blame to assessing what caused the problem and how we might move forward. In the next chapter, we will introduce the Ladder of Inference to help understand and unpack the inference-making process.

The third aspect of the Stone et al. (1999) structure has to do with what the issue has to say about oneself. For a CIT, holding a difficult conversation can be especially troubling if the self-message is: "I am not doing this consultation thing very well," instead of: "How can I get better at this and learn from this experience while I have good supervision, and maybe I am not seeing this accurately anyway." One CIT expressed it this way:

> Because I was concerned about offending or frustrating Mrs. Smith, I often felt myself attempting to avoid areas that I thought might be sensitive or apologizing to her . . . Specifically, I have learned the importance of checking in gently with a teacher regarding her perceptions instead of making assumptions about them . . . Additionally, I have learned to make my communications more direct and pointed and then to move on, rather than lingering over sensitive topics in an attempt to soothe or apologize. By being direct and stating my concerns briefly before moving on, I allow the teacher to hear me without creating a prolonged and perhaps difficult conversation about subjects that have already been discussed.

We all have internal doubts when learning a new set of skills, and having the confidence and persistence to move forward can be intimidating, especially in the face of a difficult situation. Perhaps the best advice comes from Stone et al. (1999):

> Instead of wanting to persuade and get your way, you want to understand what has happened from the other person's point of view, explain your point of view, share and understand feeling, and work together to figure out a way to manage the problem going forward . . . Changing our stance means

inviting the other person into the conversation with us, to help us figure things out . . . We need to have a learning conversation.

(p. 16–17)

As one CIT expressed it,

> I am learning the importance of developing a sense of confidence in my own competence so that an upset teacher does not in turn upset me. By becoming upset myself, I make it more difficult to communicate in a clear and effective manner that truly addresses what the teacher is saying.

The Helping Relationship

A helping relationship needs to be built – it can't be assumed. It begins with the very first contact between the consultant and potential consultee – perhaps even before, if we consider how the consultant enters the culture of the school. Recognizing that the relationship is unbalanced at the beginning (the one-down status position of the consultee), that trust must be built, that communication matters, and that an open discussion of the process is essential to avoid misunderstanding (likely to occur anyway) will help the consultant to negotiate a productive working relationship. Understanding the many facets of your own culture and how who you are may intersect with the consultees, clients, and systems you work with is also critical. In Chapter 6, we will discuss the importance of the initial contracting session to the process of building the relationship. First, let us explore the communication skills that act as the building blocks of the consultation relationship.

4

COMMUNICATION SKILLS

The single biggest problem in communication is the illusion that it has taken place.

(George Bernard Shaw)

Most of the consultation process takes place through verbal and non-verbal communication between the consultant and consultee. However, the role of these consultation conversations is far more complex than they seem on the surface. Not just simple information sharing, these conversations are

> dynamic, interactive, and inclusive. They evolve and impact the way we connect, engage, interact, and influence others, enabling us to shape reality, mind-sets, events, and outcomes in a collaborative way . . . giving us the exquisite ability to get on the same page with our fellow humans.
>
> *(Glaser, 2014, p. xiii)*

The words we choose and the tone we use, as well as our non-verbal communication, make a difference in the message we intend to convey. Through our interpersonal communication, we obtain and provide content but also sustain the collaborative relationship and build trust.

Communication skills are at the heart of effective consultation, and they are learnable. The goal of this chapter is to begin the process of developing communication skills that will support and enhance your consultation experiences. Consultants-in-training (CITs) who listen to their recorded consultation sessions are often surprised at what they actually said and how they said it versus what they intended to communicate. In this chapter, we will discuss several techniques and how they are useful to you as a CIT, as well as give you the opportunity to

DOI: 10.4324/9781032622330-4

practice and reflect on your emerging communication skills. To begin, reflect on the role of communication in school consultation in Activity 4.1.

ACTIVITY 4.1 (INDIVIDUAL)

Warm-Up Questions: Communication Skills

Write down responses to the following questions. You can write sentences or just key words.

1   How do you use communication skills to build relationships in your day-to-day life?
2   How do you suppose communication skills in school consultation would be similar to and/or different from day-to-day communication?

The Power of Words

Consultation is fundamentally a conversation between the consultant and the consultee. It is often difficult for us to understand that "language does not so much reflect reality as create it" (Watzlawick, 1978, p. 16), a phenomenon that has a long history in psychology and the other helping professions, even though it may be new to many consultants. For example, family therapists (e.g., Anderson & Goolishian, 1988) have long recognized that we generate meaning as we interact with each other through language.

Social psychologists have also provided research that supports the importance of language and communication in consultation. Higgins (1999) researched the way verbal interactions shape reality for the communicators:

1   Audience Tuning: We modify our message to take into account our perceptions about what our listener wants to hear. When speaking to a school psychologist about a potential referral, our consultees may think school psychologists or counselors want to hear about the possibility of, and evidence that suggests, a disability.
2   Shared Reality: Talking about a topic with another person generates beliefs about the objectivity of the message. So, if our consultee teachers talk about a potential learning disability, they may become even more convinced about the certainty of that diagnosis. In one school, grade-level teacher teams that had discussed student issues and decided the specific students had disabilities were less open to the school-based prereferral team's suggestions for classroom interventions (Benn, 2004).
3   Correspondence Bias: There is a tendency to see the person rather than the situation as the source of behavior. School consultants often struggle to help

teachers understand the importance of their own instruction and management strategies in student problem behavior rather than continue to embrace the assumption that the students have a deficit unrelated to the classroom context.

You will see these and other communication issues arise as you work in the schools as a consultant.

Communication Strategies

There are specific communication strategies that will support your work as a consultant. We often hear graduate educators and CITs comment that the communication skills they learned in counseling are the same ones we use in consultation. Indeed, several of the skills we will discuss in this chapter overlap significantly with the well-established basic listening skills that are described in counseling research, practice, and training (e.g., Ivey et al., 2018). However, there are subtle differences in how these skills are used in consultation. In this chapter, the following communication skills will be discussed: listening and its challenges; obtaining information, including the art of questioning and clarifying; paraphrasing to ensure you understand the speaker; reflecting feelings[1]. When affect is involved; and the bond and move strategy when applying more than one skill will be more effective.

It is critical for you to record your consultation sessions since reflecting on the communication skills you use is essential for the development of your own competence in consultation. We will provide some exercises for you to practice these skills, but deliberate practice requires you to reflect on your actual communication behavior in the context of a consultation session, preferably with feedback from a supervisor.

Listening

Michael Francis, conductor of The Florida Orchestra, claims that when we listen together, we come together. While he was talking about the power of music, we will consider how this also applies to the power of listening to each other. He also contrasts listening with hearing. Just hearing is not enough. Hearing is so automatic that we often do not realize how difficult it is to listen accurately and effectively in a consultation session, nor how much what we hear is shaped by our own thoughts as we listen. CITs practicing listening skills often comment that it is hard work, as it is an active, not a passive, process. Although you often find the term *active listening* to label such responses as eye contact, facial expressions, nodding, "yes," and "uh-huh," they are just a subcategory of listening skills, although certainly, they support the perception of the consultant as attentive and involved during the session.

---

[1] In the previous edition of the text, we used the term perception checking, but now we refer to this skill as reflecting feelings.

As organizational psychologist and author Adam Grant (2021) reflects in his popular book *Think Again*, good listening "is more than a matter of talking less. It's a set of skills in asking and responding. It starts with showing more interest in other people's interests rather than trying to judge their status or prove our own" (p. 156). Grant cautions, "we can easily slip into the mode of a preacher perched on a pulpit, a prosecutor making a closing argument or a politician giving a stump speech" (p. 156) if we're not careful in how we communicate, particularly when we're interested in catalyzing change (e.g., of a consultee's perspectives or actions).

Strategies to Address Typical Listening Challenges

The following are several common challenges that you will need to be prepared to address as a competent listener.

Develop Awareness of How Often we Jump to Conclusions/Make False Inferences

From research on memory, we know that we don't register communication by others as if we were audio-recording the words. We hear the message filtered through our own biases and perspective (see, e.g., Roediger III et al., 2001). We remember something as having been said when it was only inferred since we continue to make multiple inferences during our conversations with others (Roediger III et al., 2001). Even a single word (e.g., "anxious") may have a significantly different meaning to the speaker and listener, carry with it a connotation beyond what the speaker intended (e.g., level of severity), and shift the direction of the conversation.

A useful concept to keep in mind is the power of the Ladder of Inference (Argyris et al., 1985; Senge et al., 1994), that is, our propensity to reach conclusions without really thinking through how we got there. This reflexive loop moves us from observable data and experiences, such as a video recorder might capture, from which we select data, add our own meaning (cultural and personal), make assumptions based on the added meaning, draw conclusions, adopt beliefs, and take actions based on those beliefs. At the bottom of the ladder is *sturdy ground* – observable and measurable behaviors for problem-solving, and at the top of the ladder is *shaky ground* – inferential conclusions transformed from the initial observation. An example of the Ladder of Inference idea is provided in Figure 4.1.

So, when a teacher comes to you with an initial description of a student's problem, you often need to work together with the consultee to move this down the Ladder of Inference to the actual behavior of the student. Activity 4.2 presents an opportunity to consider the Ladder of Inference in action. The figure should be viewed from bottom to top.

Shaky ground: Actions are taken based on assumptions and beliefs rather than data.	Irene is referred for a special education evaluation.
Assumptions and beliefs about the world are adopted.	"Some students are just beyond my reach, and that's okay. She'll be better off in another setting."
Conclusions are drawn based on personal and cultural meaning added to the data.	"She is a student in need of specialized instruction, and belongs in special education."
Assumptions and beliefs are made based on meaning that is added to the data.	"There's nothing I can do to help Irene in my classroom. She's too far behind and needs something more than I can give."
Personal and cultural meaning is added to the data.	"Mom has some issues, too; the apple does not fall far from the tree."
Data is selected based on observation.	"Irene is currently on pace to fail the third grade."
Sturdy ground: Observable and measurable data.	Third-grader Irene is significantly behind peers in reading achievement, despite an evidence-based reading curriculum and Tier 2 intervention. She frequently does not complete classwork or homework. She has inconsistent attendance, and has attended multiple schools since Kindergarten.

FIGURE 4.1   Example of the Ladder of Inference Applied to School Consultation

ACTIVITY 4.2 (INDIVIDUAL, GROUP)

Ladder of Inference

If you were listening to this statement, draw a possible ladder of inference (see Figure 4.1 for an example of what this might look like). If possible, compare with a partner or in a small group.

> **Teacher Consultee:** I guess I expect some support in the area of suggestions of how to make some changes in his daily behavior. He challenges me, and he is so impulsive consistently that I need some suggestions. It doesn't seem like the things I've been able to use over the years that were quick fixes seem to work with him. And perhaps additional testing needs to be done with him for behavioral or academic reasons.

Develop the Confidence to Listen to the Speaker Rather Than Plan Your Next Response

Particularly neophytes in consultation often are planning what they are going to say next rather than focusing on what the consultee is saying. Staying with the consultee's own words is often the key to moving the dialogue forward rather than moving on to our own next question. We will come back to that as we discuss the power of clarification responses. Using the same transcribed excerpt that you reflected on in the context of the Ladder of Inference activity, consider what aspects of the teacher's statement would be helpful to clarify further.

ACTIVITY 4.3 (INDIVIDUAL, GROUP)

Identifying Points of Clarification

Review this excerpt from a real teacher consultee. Underline those aspects of what the consultee stated that you think require further clarification. Then answer the subsequent question individually and, if possible, compare responses with a partner or in a small group.

> **Teacher Consultee:** I guess I expect some support in the area of suggestions of how to make some changes in his daily behavior. He challenges me, and he is so impulsive consistently that I need some suggestions. It doesn't seem like the things I've been able to use over the years that were quick fixes seem to work with him. And perhaps additional testing needs to be done with him for behavioral or academic reasons.

Question:

1 Why did you underline what you did as requiring further clarification?

Focus on Non-Verbal Cues in the Consultee and Yourself

Words are only part of what needs your attention as a listener. So much is communicated non-verbally; if you don't attend to that, you will miss the opportunity to really *listen to* what your consultee is saying. In one case, a CIT was busy taking notes and missed the point when the teacher moved back in her seat in response to a question, indicating her concern about what the CIT was asking. As the CIT viewed the video recording, she recognized this non-verbal movement as an indication that the topic was sensitive to the teacher, which helped the CIT in the next session to check in with the teacher consultee about it.

Additionally, your own body language provides messages to the consultee, sometimes unintended. For example, frequent head nodding demonstrates active listening but may also inadvertently suggest agreement even when you do not agree with what the consultee stated. Or looking down at your notes may suggest a lack of listening to the consultee when, in reality, you are just trying to keep an accurate record of what the consultee has said.

Avoid Glossing Over Emotional Tone

If anger or frustration is part of a consultee's message, avoiding it in your responses will suggest to the consultee that you have not really listened to the message being conveyed. For CITs, this is a common challenge because they are eager to move forward in solving the problem, want to avoid getting involved in emotional interactions, or are not sure of the boundaries between appropriate consultee venting and problem admiration (see Chapter 7). However, clarifying that you have heard the feelings being expressed confirms the depth of your listening; often, you are able to respectfully acknowledge the consultee's emotions and, in the same response, move on by seeking additional clarification about the problem at hand. We explore potential consultant responses to emotional tone later in a section on reflecting feelings.

Become Adept at Courteous Interrupting

Consultees often have a lot to share, and sometimes you may feel awkward or rude speaking up when the consultee is speaking. However, being a good listener sometimes requires interjecting to ensure you understand the consultee's experience of the problem. As described by Caplan (1970):

> I sit beside the consultee, actually or metaphorically, and I involve him in questioning the material he presents about the case. I do not allow the consultee to talk for more than a few minutes without interrupting him with questions. I avoid, under all circumstances, a situation in which I listen in relative silence while the consultee tells a long story about the client and turns to me at the end and says, "What do you think about it and what should I do?" First, I probably will not know what he should do. Second, since I may not yet know what the elements in the story really mean to the consultee, I will not wish to say something the inner meaning of which to the consultee I will not know.
>
> *(pp. 85–86)*

Here is an activity for you to consider when and how to interrupt.

ACTIVITY 4.4 (INDIVIDUAL, GROUP)

Interrupting the Consultee

Answer the subsequent questions individually and, if possible, compare responses with a partner or in a small group.

1   How comfortable would you be interrupting a consultee? Why?
2   Given the following transcript dialogue, at what point would you interrupt?

Teacher Consultee: He's doing everything. Messing around in his seat, dropping his pencil, getting up to get Kleenex, moving around, and turning on the fan. Everything but his work. I can get a need to walk around. A lot of kids with ADHD need their outlets, or kids with hyperactivity just need to do something physical. I get that. But a lot of the things he does aren't channeled, whether it's yelling out across the classroom, insulting other students, or falling over in his seat. Sometimes he does do the class clown behavior. A lot of students around him find it annoying because they are trying to do their work. And they'll say, "Scotty, stop it!" That's when he retorts and says, "Shut up, you're an idiot." He'll take any type of comments from his classmates as negative, even if they are trying to do something that's positive. Luckily I have a pretty good class first and second period, so really, they see him as not being a good role model, whereas other classes will see that as clowning and follow along with it. Not the class I currently have. They will say, "Stop it," and that sets him off. It's an anger issue. Often times if you try and correct him without explicitly reasoning with him, and it's something he can't entirely understand, he gets angry about it. For example, if I want him to move to the back of the class because he is disrupting other students, he will object to it. Whether it's throwing little fits, saying, "I don't want to do it," or flat-out refusing to do it. If you don't word it exactly right to him and be like, "Scotty, you are having a little trouble right now, and I don't want you to get in trouble for these things you are doing. Do you think sitting in the back will help?" If you don't word it exactly right with him, he takes it negatively, just like he takes the attention from his classmates negatively.

Obtaining Information

Every consultee brings a concern framed in a story that they tell the consultant. Working with the consultee to develop a narrative that leads to a change in perspective or to a potential solution is the goal of communication. Listening is only one part of the work. Now let us turn to the other side of the listening/speaking communication cycle – how we gain the information needed to support the change from problem to solution. We will begin with the skills required for the art and science of obtaining information for problem-solving, including, but not exclusively, question-asking.

The Art of Questioning

Making sure the *right* problem is found is not as simple as asking direct questions. Berger (2014) found that successful problem-solvers "were exceptionally good at asking questions" (p. 1). In fact, he views good questions as ones that often lead to unexpected and productive answers. His concept of a beautiful question is one "that can begin to shift the way we perceive or think about something – and that might serve as a catalyst to bring about change" (p. 8). That is very similar to Hylander's (2004, 2012) concept of a *turning* in consultation, a conceptual change in the consultee brought about by the consultation process. She and her colleagues developed a set of questions for preschool staff to help them explore the meaning of student behavior from the consultee's perspective in such a way as to shift their perspective.

For example, in exploring issues around anger in preschool settings, Michelsen (2004) discusses the impact of introducing a surprising question. She asks the consultee a comparative gender question: *if he had been a girl? Or, if she had been a boy?* This question helped to widen the frame of reference and "to increase further reflections, consciousness, and emotional and cognitive understanding of anger in girls and boys and the consultee's interactions with angry children" (p. 296). Exploring how questions can be used to shift how a problem is seen as a critical skill to learn.

Schein (2013) views good questions as ones that also help to build positive relationships. In a diverse world, we need to ask questions based on mutual respect, recognizing that our consultees know things that need to be known in order to solve problems. He finds that too often, consultees know things that are critical to resolving a problem but are not expressed because consultants do not listen, do not take the consultee's knowledge seriously, or simply do not ask the right questions. He recommends "humble inquiry," specifically, "the fine art of drawing someone out, of asking questions to which you do not already know the answer, of building a relationship based on curiosity and interest in the other person" (p. 2). Our goal in this section of the chapter is to provide you with some support in learning to ask the right questions.

Who Asks the Questions?

If the consultant comes to the *Problem Identification and Problem Analysis (PID/ PA)* interview with the belief that they should be asking the questions and the consultee providing answers, they risk creating an identified problem that is theirs, one to which they believe they can provide answers. For example, if the consultant, who is a school psychologist, moves the problem toward the possibility of a disability, then they have the instruments to conduct a diagnostic examination. If the consultant knows little about academic content and instruction, then their questions can avoid exploring that area, even if the teacher mentions such an issue. In reviewing transcripts of consultation sessions, teachers often suggest the presence of academic issues as well as behavioral ones; but CITs with more comfort in the behavioral area and without knowledge in the academic domain often fail to follow up on these concerns. Instead, they focus on the behavioral ones, maintaining the expertise of the consultant to identify and address the problem. Activity 4.5 presents such a choice point.

ACTIVITY 4.5 (INDIVIDUAL, GROUP)

Consultant Question Focus

In the following quote from an actual consultation meeting, what would your next question be? Write down a response and, if possible, compare it with a partner.

> **Teacher Consultee**: Well, in phonics, for example, some days he would put all three sounds together; other days he knows the sounds and he can't put them together. He doesn't try.

> **Consultant Response:**

Using the Consultee's Own Words to Explore the Problem: The Clarifying Question

Consultees provide us with information about the concern they want us to address, but it is often an error to assume that we have fully understood the problem without seeking clarification of their presentation. Remember the concept of the Ladder of Inference (Argyris et al., 1985; Senge et al., 1994). Much of our *understanding* comes from what we fill in from the conversation because large sections of what is said by consultees in referral interviews are either unclear or open to multiple interpretations. Some typical examples of problem statements include words such as *immature, poor attention span, doesn't complete work,* or *no discipline.* See Table 4.1 for more examples of high-inference language commonly heard in schools. By bringing your attention to these words, we hope that you will help

TABLE 4.1 Examples of Red Flag Words

ADHD	Lost
All day long	Low achiever/performer
All the kids	Naughty
All the time	Never
Always	None of the kids
Anxious	No number sense
Asocial	On the spectrum
Asperger-y	Parents don't care
Disorganized	Rough home life
Disrespectful	Rude
Doesn't stop	Sassy
He just struggles	Simple
Her parents don't care	Slow processer
Hyperactive	Sluggish pace
Lacks attention	Space cadet
Lazy	Unmotivated

consultees move down the Ladder of Inferences through clarification and consider the clarity of your own language in problem-solving.

There are multiple ways to request clarification, not all of them even questions. Here are some starter sentences to help you request clarification:

- Can you give me an example?
- I am not sure I understand what you just said.
- Tell me more about that.
- What behavior do you see that leads you to consider him immature?
- What is the work he is not completing?

Leading and Irrelevant Questions

It is important to differentiate clarification from other types of questions. In fact, asking *leading questions* (formerly called "relevant questions" in the first edition of this text) when seeking to understand what brought a teacher to the consultation process is the most common strategy. Too many consultants work from a script of questions, while we see the value of building from the consultee's own words as they describe the problem.

Expert-oriented consultants see their goal as obtaining information about "the problem" from the consultee. So, after sometimes allowing the consultee to vent about the situation, consultants will pose a series of questions in which they obtain the information that they want to know. Such a process places the consultant squarely in the expert mode, and according to Dillon (1979), there are some negative consequences of this questioning process:

> Far from encouraging client expressiveness, questions are held to produce blocking, to reduce input, to cut off conversation, and to inhibit response . . . In answering the questions, the client will reveal the information requested, but expressions of problems, feelings, relevant facts, and other data pertinent to understanding the . . . situation will not be forthcoming . . . Questions . . . generally, cause him/her to settle into a passive acquiescent role, or at worst, they provoke a sense of threat, resistance, and defensiveness.
>
> *(p. 76)*

As we have been suggesting, it is essential for consultants to recognize that they are often selective about what they choose to address, which then influences the direction and focus of the *PID/PA* process. Recall Activity 4.5. You had some choices here, which is often true in actual consultation sessions. You could focus on the child's behavior (In what kinds of situations do you see him not trying?), or you could clarify (What do you mean by not try?), which would take you in one direction, or you could focus on his phonics skills (Let's talk about his phonics skills. What sounds does he know and what does he not know?). In this actual case, not trying was the key issue for the teacher, but the lack of vowel knowledge turned out to be the core problem. If the consultant is not comfortable with an academic concern, as discussed previously, it is not unexpected for both the teacher and consultant to focus on the behavior, whether or not that would be the right focus.

Of course, some questions are not relevant to resolving a concern. Sometimes consultants ask questions about the student's family that are not helpful in resolving the classroom problem. Knotek (2003) examined several such instances in problem-solving teams, such as when team members discussed family living arrangements rather than the student issues in the classroom, to the detriment of problem-solving efforts. Such discussions may reflect some educators' implicit biases about students and their families, and even more problematic, may be reflected in their subsequent decision-making.

To focus on the difference between types of questions, Activity 4.6 will provide you with some practice exercises.

ACTIVITY 4.6 (INDIVIDUAL, GROUP)

Clarifying, Leading, and Irrelevant Questions

1   Individually, write down a response for each of these three excerpts.
2   If possible, compare your responses with a partner. Determine if your question is clarifying, leading, or irrelevant. How do you know?
3   If possible, as a whole class, share examples of each with your classmates.

Excerpt 1:

Consultant-in-Training (CIT): Have you ever been involved in any type of problem-solving approaches before?

Teacher Consultee (TC): Probably, but not with that designated name.

CIT:

Excerpt 2:

TC: The particular student that I have some concerns about, his daily work is not up to speed, and I feel like he can be doing a better job on his daily work, and I need to know what I can do to help him improve his daily work score.

CIT:

Excerpt 3:

TC: He's very distractible and tries to change to subjects that are completely off-topic from what is going on in the classroom.

CIT:

Making Sure You Understood: The Art of Paraphrasing

It is often an incorrect assumption that you understood the consultee until you confirm that. By paraphrasing, you are essentially testing your own understanding of the message. For example, if the teacher consultee says *James does not comprehend what he reads*, what does the teacher actually mean here? Is it a comprehension problem? Or is there an underlying decoding skill or language issue? Rather than assuming it is a comprehension problem, it is important to first assure the teacher that you heard what she said. This is the skill of paraphrasing.

A paraphrase does not merely repeat what was said but checks your own understanding by trying to restate the teacher's words with your own words. It is your best attempt to comprehend what the consultee said and to then restate the meaning in your own words. Returning to the teacher consultee quote we previously considered, now think about the use of paraphrasing in that example.

ACTIVITY 4.7 (INDIVIDUAL, GROUP)

Paraphrasing Practice

Review this excerpt from a real teacher consultee. Consider how you might respond to this teacher's statement with a paraphrase, and write your response below. If possible, compare your responses with a partner.

> **Teacher Consultee:** I guess I expect some support in the area of suggestions of how to make some changes in his daily behavior. He challenges me, and he is so impulsive consistently that I need some suggestions. It doesn't seem like the things I've been able to use over the years that were quick fixes seem to work with him. And perhaps additional testing needs to be done with him for behavioral or academic reasons.

Consultant-in-Training (CIT)

Paraphrasing may not be enough of a response, and we will return to this later in the chapter.

Responding to Affect: Reflecting Feelings

Maintaining a collaborative relationship requires also understanding not only the consultee's content, for which you might use a paraphrase or ask for a clarification, but also being open to understanding the consultee's feelings that may be expressed, sometimes by words and sometimes by non-verbal means. You may perceive that there is an emotion but need to consider two issues: (1) how to acknowledge the emotion, and (2) whether your perception is accurate.

Just as in paraphrasing, where you need to confirm that your perception of the content is accurate, in reflecting feelings, you validate that your perception of the feelings is accurate. Reflecting feelings means restating the feelings you think are present in your own words. You may not be correct, but you then give the consultee the opportunity to correct your understanding. Your reflection of feelings should be done in a non-judgmental way and in an even tone.

> **Teacher Consultee**: Today, Drew was really bad. Like, he wouldn't do anything . . . it took him 45 minutes to come to the rug because he was playing with a piece of string. He keeps picking things off the ground, and I can't be monitoring him all the time and making sure there isn't a piece of paper on the ground.
>
> **Consultant-in-Training (CIT)**: Oh wow, that seems frustrating. It sounds like you have your hands full. Was there anything that he did well today?

In this example, the CIT perception checked and used the bond and move strategy, to be discussed next, after reflecting feelings, to reorient the teacher to working on the problem.

CITs sometimes express their concern that it is inappropriate to discuss consultee feelings in a task-oriented problem-solving process. They sometimes fear that they will open a Pandora's box of feelings. But here, the goal is clear communication, not therapy. Consultation is, by its very nature, interpersonal, and attitudes, emotions, and expectations are part of the data gathering. Consultees have very human emotions, which the student's behavior or the teacher's feelings of helplessness can engender.

Also, we are not always rational about our experiences and our reactions. As Bersoff and Grieger (1971) so eloquently stated, "At times. . . teacher concerns about a child's behavior may be based on irrational attitudes and ideas that lead to irrational expectations, demands, and feelings, and inappropriate actions toward the child" who exhibits problem behavior (p. 484). Misunderstanding the feelings that you perceive the consultee is expressing may lead to inferences that are inaccurate and short-circuit an interaction, so it is important to reflect on the feelings being expressed. Moreover, assessing if there are hidden agendas related to feelings can provide information about where the problem is and what interventions will be accepted. There is a difference, for example, between frustration and anger, which would lead a competent consultant to move ahead in different directions. Moreover, a good reflection of feelings, at the very least, can tell the consultee that you want to understand the emotion.

Bond and Move

As we have been suggesting, often, it is not enough to paraphrase or reflect feelings, especially if the consultee's statement is ambiguous to begin with, as it was in the activity dialogue mentioned previously. Combining communication strategies can be even more powerful in moving the problem-solving process along. In the bond and move strategy (Rosenfield, 2012), it is recommended that after paraphrasing or reflecting feelings as a way to demonstrate that the consultee is being heard, the consultant can then move on to obtain additional information, perhaps through clarification. So, for example, after letting the teacher know that you heard she is concerned about the student's comprehension skills, you can clarify just what she means by asking for an example or a request for further information about the student's comprehension.

Developing Awareness of Cultural Communication Styles

Ingraham (2014) provides a window into "how one's communication style can impact their consultation effectiveness" (p. 302). She cites Hall's (1976) concept of *context communication,* specifically differentiating cultures with "high context (where extensive knowledge of the culture is needed to interpret meaning of communications) and low context (where the message is straightforward and does not necessitate knowledge of the culture to infer meaning)" (p. 302). While her concern is particularly important for consultants working in the global arena, it also has relevance for those within a particular culture. She encourages consultants to learn about their own communication style preferences and their intersection with consultees using different communication styles.

Scan QR code 4.1 to view Dr. Colette Ingraham integrating her perspective on multicultural consultation with the communication skills we have been presenting earlier in this chapter, such as questioning.

QR CODE 4.1   Colette Ingraham Video

One of the communication styles that Ingraham (2017) addresses in her training is understanding the difference between direct and indirect communication styles. For example, direct communicators tend to be more forthcoming and quick to provide suggestions, whereas indirect communicators tend to choose their words carefully and may imply rather than say something directly. She has found that "affective reactions of people when they encounter a style divergent from their own can be intense and can jeopardize relationships and consultation" (Ingraham, 2017, p. 302). Sometimes it is also true that a consultant and consultee using the same communication style can be unaware of how that interferes with making progress in problem-solving. In one case, both members of the consultation dyad used indirect communication styles and made little progress in their sessions (Newman, 2012).

A similar cultural communication issue has been described in the work of Tannen (2007, 2017) on traditional gender differences in communication styles. She describes both the unique communication pattern of women as well as the differences between men and women in communication style, describing the often-invisible influence of gender conversational style. Although it is important to point out that not all of us conform to traditional communication patterns, it is useful to be aware of the potential for misunderstanding if differences are not considered. For example, she has found evidence that women will talk about a problem or concern to gain understanding or support, whereas men will be prompt to provide advice when a problem is described. Recall Guva's (2004) paradox presented in the last chapter, namely that teacher consultees do not always ask for help when they ask for consultation; sometimes they are handing "over the *feeling* that 'something has to be done'" (italics in original; p. 256). This can lead to an example of admiring *the problem* rather than focusing on problem-solving. We will see this issue raised again in Chapter 7 within the *PID/PA* process.

Additional Activities for Practice

Practicing communicating as a consultant in both simulated and real-life scenarios is essential to your development of these skills. A combination of self-reflection, assessment, and feedback from a supervisor leads to both increased communication self-efficacy and skill application (Newman, Gerrard et al., 2022; Newman, Villarreal et al., 2022).

We have included an abridged transcript in Activity 4.8 for you to reflect on a CIT's communication skills in action. We have also included a Process Log format (Appendix B) to assist you in reflecting on transcriptions of your own actual consultation recordings. Activity 4.9 provides an opportunity to reflect on your own use of communication skills in action. The tool provided in Activity 4.9 could also be used for observing someone else consulting, whether in person (i.e., real or simulated), on video, or while reading a transcript. Activity 4.10 includes four practice videos with a teacher consultee requesting assistance. You can watch these videos and practice responding. Rubrics for assessing your own performance or for a peer, instructor, or supervisor to assess your work are provided in Appendix C. These activities do not substitute for examining your communication skills in context, but they will provide you with some experience in reflecting on how you communicate.

ACTIVITY 4.8 (INDIVIDUAL, GROUP)

Transcript Reflection

The following is an actual excerpt from the second *Problem Identification/Problem Analysis* session of a CIT's consultation session with a first-year, second-grade teacher. Read the transcript and answer the subsequent questions individually, and, if possible, compare responses with a partner or in a small group.

Teacher Consultee (TC): Spelling he's okay . . . it's more structural . . . getting an actual complete sentence out. I mean, you have that writing sample . . . I mean, he's not horrible; he's definitely lacking some skill sets . . .

Consultant-in-Training (CIT): But would you say that your priority would be to actually get him to start writing, or . . .?

TC: Definitely. Because honestly, I don't care if his words are spelled wrong as long as he's writing, I think that will help him.

CIT: Alright, well, that's good to know. One of the things today, when I was talking to him (following a classroom observation), he wasn't so clear with the directions. Was that something that you have found with him – that it takes more than one time to explain the directions?

TC: Definitely. I think, though, even when you do take the time to explain it, and also, the people . . . I purposely put him with Jesse and Alisha because they're very strong in reading and writing, and they'll try to help him.

CIT: They gave him an A-plus on his paper (referring to a mark they wrote on his paper that morning) (laughs).

TC: (laughs) Yeah, they'll try to help him, and sometimes he doesn't want the help, so. I don't know how much it is another way to get out of it. Maybe he doesn't understand it, and some things, if he really doesn't understand, I don't know . . .

CIT: So you're saying when he doesn't want the help, he's trying to avoid it still?

TC: Like, he'll go, "I don't understand," and they'll try to explain it to him, and he just will totally ignore them and not listen.

CIT: Mm-hm, I see. So when I wrote, "difficulty with writing," I think we can be more specific and say, "with actually producing words." What do you think?

TC: Yeah, definitely. Forming complete thoughts and sentences.

CIT: So, writing complete thoughts and sentences. What do you mean when you say "complete thoughts and sentences"?

TC: Sometimes in his writing, he'll just . . . I can just remember what we were writing about . . . we were writing about: "What's special about you?" and he has this bling-bling necklace . . . and instead of writing, "My necklace makes me special," he'll just write, "Necklace." It's not like a complete thought or something like that.

CIT: So, if we were to look at his production, it's more important that it would be a complete sentence, not necessarily like, "He wrote 30 words . . ."

TC: Yep.

CIT: But you're not worried about spelling or grammar.

TC: Nope.

CIT: Okay. Now, today would you prefer to focus on reading or writing stuff? Where is your gut telling you?

TC: I think writing. He's doing better in reading. I think writing.

CIT: Just one thought that I had with reading – which is an off-the-cuff thing – when he had this spare time to pick a book from the library, the book that he was reading, he brought over to read with me, which I thought was adorable, but, it was something that was really hard for him, I felt like, the book that he was reading. Maybe something that would be helpful for him at that time to keep him on task is if he had a book selection that was a J or below – of books that were at his benchmark level.

TC: Maybe it was because up there in the back, there are books that are benchmarked. But they usually like reading hard books (laughs).

CIT: Yeah, and then sometimes he's reading the hard one and gets up and moves around and stuff because he can't really read it.

TC: Yeah.

CIT: So in terms of his, like right now, his writing, can we look at his journal again and maybe get an idea . . . we can either use that as a baseline for how much he's actually producing, or we could do it another way . . .

TC: That's fine. Because journal I do every single day, so that would be a good way to see . . . (looks in student's desk for his journal) you can see his library books . . . He took out Harry Potter. I mean (laughs) . . . that's not really his level.

CIT: Yeah, one of the things that I talk about in my class a lot is the idea of practicing, of relevant practice, and you know, as he's learning new words, if he's reading something with those words in it where it's easy for him to read, that would be helpful.

TC: So, Harry Potter might not be that helpful (laughs).

CIT: (laughs) He's awfully ambitious!

Questions for Reflection:

1 Identify what communication skills the CIT used during this session (when applicable, write the skills in the left margin of the transcript).
2 What did the CIT do well?
3 What could the CIT have done differently? If you would have responded differently, write what you would have said next to the teacher's response.

ACTIVITY 4.9 (INDIVIDUAL, GROUP)

Communication Skills Reflection Tool (Adapted from Gravois et al., 2011)

Transcribe part or all of a recording of a consultation session with a teacher. Reflect on the consultant's use of communication skills by using the format provided and responding to the subsequent questions. Note that this tool could also be used for self-assessment of your own communication skills or for observing another consultant's communication skills. It is also a helpful way to provide critical feedback to a peer or a supervisee. Remember, this and other activities are available as Word documents at the Publisher's website (https://www.routledge.com/Building-Competence-in-School-Consultation-A-Developmental-Approach/Newman-Rosenfield/p/book/9781032622316#:~:text=Description,other%20professionals%20working%20in%20schools). for you to download and type your responses in a document.

Communication Skill	Tally of Occurrence	Examples	
		Consultant Statement	Consultee Response
Active Listening			
Clarifying Question			
Request for Clarification not in the form of a question			
Paraphrase			
Reflecting Feelings			
Bond and Move (Paraphrase or reflecting feelings combined with another communication skill)			
Offering Information			

Questions for Reflection:

1   What communication skills did the consultant apply well? How do you know? (Hint: The consultee's response often provides important information.)
2   What communication skills need improvement? How do you know? (Hint: The consultee's response often provides important information.)
3   Identify alternative responses for any interactions you believe need improvement.

ACTIVITY 4.10 (INDIVIDUAL, GROUP)

Scan the QR codes to view videos of a teacher consultee requesting assistance with a concern. Practice using one or more of the communication skills presented in this chapter in response to the teacher. Hint: It would be difficult to have a solution with such limited information as is presented in each example. Note: a more extensive outline for practicing communication skills with supervision is outlined in Chapter 12 (Appendix J).

QR CODE 4.10.1   Consultee Request for Assistance #1

QR CODE 4.10.2   Consultee Request for Assistance #2

QR CODE 4.10.3   Consultee Request for Assistance #3

QR CODE 4.10.4   Consultee Request for Assistance #4

Summary

In the past two chapters, we delineated the basic relationship and communication skills required for effective problem-solving. In the next section of the book (Chapters 5 to 9), we describe the stages and work of consultative problem-solving.

5

THE CONSULTATIVE PROBLEM-
SOLVING PROCESS

An Introduction

Trust the Process

In schools, most consultation services begin with someone having a problem or a concern that calls for additional support or a desire for collaboration. The problem-solving process has, in fact, been adapted to the schools, both in direct service through behavior analysis models and in indirect models of consultation. Before further overviewing the problem-solving process, take a moment to reflect on your own assumptions regarding this process in Activity 5.1.

ACTIVITY 5.1 (INDIVIDUAL)

Warm-Up Questions: The Consultative Problem-Solving Process

Write down responses to the following questions. You can write sentences or just key words.

1   Problem-solving is described as a *systematic* process. What do you think this means?
2   What do you think are the consultant's roles and responsibilities during the problem-solving process? What about the consultee's roles and responsibilities?

In the School Consultation (SC) model we have developed here, the process begins with an understanding of the context (school culture), a commitment to building relationships with consultees, and developing effective communication

DOI: 10.4324/9781032622330-5

skills to be used during the problem-solving stages in order to enable the consultant and consultee to have a more productive experience. We now move on to the problem-solving process.

Scan QR code 5.1 to view Dr. Janet Graden describe the application of a problem-solving process in schools and its relationship to SC.

QR CODE 5.1 Janet Graden Video

It is imperative to stress that effective problem-solving is not an informal process. According to D'Zurilla and Goldfried (1971), applied psychologists adopted problem-solving methods from basic research and theoretical literature, as those methods came to be viewed as having real-life relevance. Many problem situations are complex, ambiguous, or have conflicting demands, making obvious or usual solutions often ineffective. Student concerns fit this pattern of *messy* real-world problems, where the information needed was not obvious and the directions for solving them were unclear to those working with them. D'Zurilla and Goldfried stressed the importance of inhibiting the impulse to respond quickly to solve the problem when it was important to define the situation in operational terms and distinguish relevant from irrelevant information, identify primary goals, and specify the issues and conflicts. As we shall see, this is the very purpose of the critical initial Problem Identification and Problem Analysis stage we present in Chapter 7.

The benefits of problem-solving also include that the process *"(a) makes available a variety of potentially effective response alternatives for dealing with the problematic situation and (b) increases the probability of selecting the most effective response from among these various alternatives"* (italics in original; D'Zurilla & Goldfried, 1971, p. 108), which we will explore in Chapter 8 in the section on intervention planning. However, D'Zurilla and Goldfried (1971) also sounded a warning: most people do not approach problems systematically without training. So, our purpose in the following chapters is to present the skills necessary for effective, systematic problem-solving and to help you develop those skills through activities.

The SC model is clearly structured as a stage-based process, originally described by D'Zurilla and Goldfried (1971). Given appropriate implementation, the process holds the consultant and consultee accountable for the outcome. The chapters that follow provide a stepwise view of the stages of problem-solving in the SC model. All prevalent models of problem-solving consultation follow similar stages of problem-solving, with overlapping work to be accomplished within these stages (Kratochwill et al., 2014). Irrespective of the model, these questions are answered during consultative problem-solving:

- What is the problem (Problem Identification)?
- Why is it happening (Problem Analysis)?
- What can we do about it (Intervention)?
- Is the intervention working (Evaluation)?

The SC problem-solving stages we define here build specifically upon two consultation models: Behavioral Consultation (BC; Bergan, 1977; Kratochwill & Bergan, 1990; Martens et al., 2014) and Instructional Consultation (IC; Rosenfield et al., 2014). We illustrate how SC compares to BC and IC in Table 5.1. We also include rationales for our alternatives to traditional BC and IC stage names and features. In Table 5.2, we overview the purpose of each SC problem-solving stage, and in Table 5.3, we overview the components of each stage in depth. The features of each stage are largely informed by Gravois et al.'s (2011) *Training in Instructional Consultation, Assessment, and Teaming*. All the stages and stage components of BC are subsumed within the SC stages. Our purposes in reworking this process are: (a) to further clarify the stages and (b) to account for the relationship variable in consultation (Rosenfield, 1991).

Big Ideas for Problem-Solving

Consultation work is guided by the specific purposes and work tasks of each problem-solving stage but also by several overarching big ideas or principles. Inspired by Schein's (1999) description of Process Consultation principles, these big ideas can be considered "a philosophy and methodology of the helping process" (p. 22) developed during our years working as consultants, consultant educators, and supervisors. We introduce and revisit six Big Ideas during the subsequent chapters, with explicit connections made to the work and processes comprising each problem-solving stage (see Appendix D). We begin here with three overarching Big Ideas that help us think about the problem-solving process in its entirety:

1. **Complex problems, such as those found in schools, rarely have simple or linear solutions.**
2. **The problems school consultants attempt to solve are situated within a school-based context and should be defined accordingly.**
3. **Everything we do is an intervention, beginning from the earliest consultation interactions and including the establishment of a shared problem conceptualization occurring during PID.**

Big Idea #1: Complex problems, such as those found in schools, rarely have simple or linear solutions. Consultees often request consultation in

TABLE 5.1 The Problem-Solving Process in School Consultation, Behavioral Consultation, and Instructional Consultation

School Consultation (SC)	Behavioral Consultation (BC)	Instructional Consultation (IC)	Summary and Rationale of Differences of SC and BC	Summary and Rationale of Differences of SC and IC
1. Contracting	——	1. Contracting	Additional stage because: • SC views a consultant's understanding of school culture as a prerequisite for effective consultation; this is learned during entry and discussed with the consultee during contracting • SC is embedded with distinct assumptions, which are clarified up front during contracting • Contracting accounts for the initiation of the consultation relationship with clear relational expectation	• No differences
2. Problem Identification and Analysis	1. Problem Identification 2. Problem Analysis, including Treatment Design	2. Problem identification and analysis, including Instructional Assessment	Stages are combined because: • Treatment design not considered part of problem analysis • Problem identification and problem analysis occur concurrently in practice • Identifying and defining the problem precedes intervention planning	• Instructional Assessment is part of this stage, as well as other stages of problem-solving, but the full training process is beyond the scope of this text. Readers are referred to Gickling et al. (2016) for an extensive treatment of Instructional Assessment
3. Intervention Planning	——	3. Intervention Planning	• Stage separated from BC's Problem Analysis stage to be a distinct stage because intervention planning is a distinct process • "Treatment" re-termed "intervention" because "treatment" implies a medical model while "intervention" does not	• No differences

TABLE 5.1 (Continued)

School Consultation (SC)	Behavioral Consultation (BC)	Instructional Consultation (IC)	Summary and Rationale of Differences of SC and BC	Summary and Rationale of Differences of SC and IC
4. Intervention Implementation, Monitoring, and Performance Feedback	3. Treatment Implementation 4. Treatment Evaluation	4. Intervention Implementation, including Evaluation	• Stages are combined because intervention implementation and evaluation occur concurrently in practice • "Treatment" re-termed "intervention" because "treatment" implies a medical model while "intervention" does not • "Monitoring" added to stage because progress monitoring is a common term in contemporary educational practice • "Performance feedback" added to stage because performance feedback is a research-based component of school consultation practice	• "Monitoring" added to stage because progress monitoring is a common term in contemporary educational practice • "Performance feedback" added to stage because performance feedback is a research-based component of school consultation practice
5. Post-Intervention Planning and Closure	——	1. Resolution/ Termination	Stage separated from BC's Treatment Evaluation stage to be a distinct stage because: • Post-intervention planning is a distinct process, including planning for generalization and maintenance of behaviors • Post-intervention planning includes redefining the consultant-consultee relationship	• "Resolution/termination" re-termed "Post-Intervention Planning and Closure" because: • The consultation relationship might continue after a case closes • The consultant and consultee plan for intervention fading, behavioral maintenance, and/or generalization as part of case closure

TABLE 5.2 Purposes of Each School Consultation Problem-Solving Stage (Adapted from Gravois et al., 2011)

Stage	Purposes
Contracting	• Introduce consultee to the school consultation model, including assumptions, expectations, and process • Gain agreement to work together
Problem Identification and Problem Analysis	• Create shared perception of consultee concerns • Define problem in observable and measurable terms • Establish baseline of current performance • Establish goals
Intervention Planning	• Collaboratively develop instructional and/or behavioral management strategies targeting goals
Intervention Implementation, Monitoring, and Performance Feedback	• Ensure intervention adherence/accurate implementation of intervention • Evaluate progress toward goals
Post-Intervention Planning and Closure	• Formally conclude the consultation relationship regarding the targeted concern

TABLE 5.3 Business of Each School Consultation Problem-Solving Stage

Stage	Business to be Accomplished
Contracting	• Discuss consultee expectations and prior experiences consulting • Explain stage-based problem-solving process • Clarify school as the context for problem-solving, including the concept of instructional match • Explain potential application of problem-solving for multiple tiers in addition to individual students • Clarify shared ownership of the problem and the consultation process • Clarify non-evaluative nature of the consultation process (only if true) • Explain the parameters of confidentiality • Check for consultee agreement and commitment to participate • Schedule follow-up meeting/ongoing schedule
Problem Identification and Problem Analysis	• Create shared understanding of consultee's concern(s) using collaborative communication skills • Define concern(s) in observable terms • Define concern in the context of the school/classroom, and consider the role of instructional match/mismatch • Follow up with additional data collection such as record or work sample review, observation, or instructional assessment • Prioritize concerns • Establish a plan to measure current performance (i.e., Baseline) • Establish baseline measurement of performance • Set performance goals based on baseline data

(Continued)

TABLE 5.3 (Conitinued)

Stage	Business to be Accomplished
Intervention Planning	• Elicit consultee's ideas/strategies • Discuss: *What* classroom-based strategy will meet goals? *Where* will strategy be implemented? *When* can strategy be implemented? *How often* will strategy be implemented? *Who* will be responsible? • Consider conditions to create/maintain instructional match • Consider if multiple students can benefit from the intervention • Document specifics of what, when, how often, and who
Intervention Implementation, Monitoring, and Performance Feedback	• Continue meeting while intervention is being implemented • Elicit consultee's perception of progress toward client goals • Collaboratively review and discuss data • Compare progress with goals • Clarify what's working and what needs refining • Provide performance feedback regarding level of adherence to intervention and client progress, with consideration given to implementation changes as needed
Post-Intervention Planning and Closure	• Close if (a) goals are met; (b) consultee can implement independently if needed; (c) strategies are fading/faded • Elicit consultee's plans to maintain student progress • Determine documentation of efforts • Consider addressing other priority areas not yet addressed (and return to PID/PA for new priority concern) • If case is explicitly closed, let consultee know how support can be accessed in the future • Communicate with parents, colleagues, teams as needed

search of a "magic wand" or a "silver bullet" to make the problem they are facing (or the student, through special education referral) instantly disappear. This is not surprising in school settings, given the tremendous demands associated with classroom instruction and management. Simultaneously, CITs are eager to learn as many interventions as possible, hoping to fill up their toolboxes with "quick fixes" to prescribe to teachers requesting assistance. Although occasionally, a simple problem and solution do occur, it is not the norm. Consistent with Schein's (2013, 2016) work on process consultation and humble consulting, there are several flawed assumptions associated with a failure to recognize this complexity.

First, there are instances where consultees may know that something is not working in the classroom but not know why it is not working, perhaps because the correct problem has not yet been identified. Imagine a consultee describing an impression of the problem (e.g., "Dave is not putting forth effort") and a consultant prescribing an intervention from this initial description (e.g., a motivating sticker chart with opportunities for Dave to earn stickers). However, what if the problem is that Dave is frustrated or bored with the material? Thus, the intervention may not be well-matched to address the root of the problem.

Second, sometimes consultees are looking for the consultant to diagnose the problem and offer a solution. This presumes: (a) an accurate diagnosis from the consultant, who may not be familiar with the problem, (b) that the consultee will accept the diagnosis, and (c) that the consultee will accept, implement, and adhere to prescribed solutions. A breakdown at any of these steps is possible. The consultant's diagnosis may be incorrect, as in the previous example. Even if it is correct, the consultee may not agree with the diagnosis or may not want to or be able to implement the solution – even if it is an excellent, evidence-based intervention. Schein (2013, 2016) suggests that collaborative assessment and intervention design will support a problem-solving process that promotes professional learning for the consultee, which is especially important in the complex setting of schools.

We live in a world where problems are solved on TV shows in an hour or less, making the notion of complexity in problem-solving seem like a flawed assumption. Further, there is some growing evidence that our capacity to focus and attend in-depth to issues has been stolen by our constant internet and cell phone usage (Hari, 2022). Often in problem-solving sessions or meetings, some members are paying as much attention to their phones as to the discussion, even though evidence that we can multitask has been largely debunked as a myth (Hari, 2022). Big Idea #1 serves to remind us that not all concerns brought to the problem-solving table are as simple and easy as they may first appear, that classrooms and school interactions are more complex than they may seem to be on the surface, and we need sustained and well-directed attention to address them. The intricacies of the problem-solving stages detailed in this book are designed for that purpose.

Big Idea #2: The problems school consultants attempt to solve are situated within a school-based context and should be defined accordingly. When defining problems, consultants and consultees sometimes get distracted with *red herrings*, issues that are peripheral to the problem-solving task. Red herrings include storytelling about students or students' familial contexts and labeling within-child pathology without connecting to concrete behaviors on which to focus intervention within the classroom. This is also sometimes referred to as *admiring the problem*. Knotek (2003), for example, described the irrelevant talk about the homes of students from low-income and economically marginalized families in his qualitative study of problem-solving consultation teams. Similarly, Sherry (2012) found in her school "a lot of storytelling at the meetings . . . there was talk about students' family homes and behaviors unrelated to the concern on the agenda" (p. 100). In a study of Response to Intervention, Sabnis et al. (2020) found that even when enacting a policy intended to support ecological problem-solving, educators "made sense of the student's data by drawing on dominant discourses of deficit – both individual and cultural deficits" (p. 303), thereby perpetuating rather than mitigating systemic inequities.

Scan QR code 5.2, in which Dr. Sujay Sabnis, a faculty member in the school psychology program at Miami of Ohio, discusses the crystallization of perspectives on problem-solving teams. We will revisit the functioning of consultation problem-solving teams in Chapter 10.

QR CODE 5.2   Sujay Sabnis Video

Problems should be defined with reference to the school-based context in which they are situated so that consultants and consultees avoid lingering on red herrings (Rosenfield, 2022). This is true even when problems inherently stem from the student's external context or experience of trauma and their reactions to it (e.g., grief after losing a parent to COVID-19); educators cannot change those circumstances but can think about how to respond within the context of school (e.g., trauma-informed approaches; Ridgard et al., 2015). For example, it may be helpful for a consultant to bond (recall the *bond and move strategy* in Chapter 4) with a teacher who expresses frustration about a student, but dwelling on this information may be detrimental to moving forward in problem-solving. Instead, focusing on what we can do to support the student within the classroom context should be of primary concern. To provide another example, we have observed successful consultations in schools supporting students with severe and profound disabilities, where the focus was not on students' internal deficits but rather on what could be adjusted in the environment to support their academic or behavioral growth (e.g., see Tsakiris, 2012).

Consulting ecologically or with an ecobehavioral lens means thinking about the student but also their interactions with the curriculum, the teacher's instruction and management strategies, and the broader school culture. When problems are operationalized with instructional factors in mind, problems become *solvable* within the classroom setting. Behavioral problems are also initially considered within an instructional context, as misbehavior may result from things like unclear instructional expectations, insufficient motivational techniques, or an instructional match that is too easy or frustrating for the student. And some behaviors result from inadequate classroom management strategies.

Big Idea #3: Everything we do is an intervention. When we discuss interventions, we tend to think of large-scale Evidence-Based Interventions (EBIs) such as universal, targeted, or intensive reading or behavior programs, or intervention components such as increasing praise for appropriate behavior, providing additional opportunities for accurate practice, or clarifying task expectations.

However, as argued by Schein (1999), everything we do as consultants can be considered an intervention, beginning with our earliest interactions with consultees. We call these small interactions with the potential to make large impacts *process interventions* (*ProInts*). One example of a *ProInt* is clarifying the consultation process up front during the *Contracting* stage of problem-solving; this helps you and the consultee get on the same page regarding how you will approach the problem-solving process and what it will mean to work collaboratively. Another example of a *ProInt* is demonstrating support for the consultee by listening and perspective-taking, rather than moving forward with your own agenda without acknowledging the consultee's concerns.

ProInts stimulate ripples in the problem-solving pond. For example, how consultees think about (representation) and talk about (presentation) problems may shift as a result of *ProInts*, which in turn alters the way an intervention will be designed, implemented, and evaluated in subsequent problem-solving stages. Hylander (2017) describes the process of a *turning* in her work in Sweden, the idea that how a problem is conceptualized and presented needs to change through the consultation process into a concern that can be resolved.

Moving on to the Stages

In the following chapters, we will introduce each of the stages and provide you with information on the process as well as activities to support your development of knowledge and skills. In Appendix E, we provide a tool to measure adherence to the SC problem-solving stages, which is aligned with the business described in Table 5.3 and repeated for that stage in each chapter. This tool can be used for self-assessment while reviewing your own recording of a consultation meeting or to assess another consultant's adherence to the SC process.

6

CONTRACTING

Making the Invisible Visible

It takes both sides to build a bridge.

(Fredrik Nael)

The School Consultation (SC) problem-solving process begins with *Contracting*, when an agreement, usually verbal, between the consultee and the consultant is reached that makes the process of consultation transparent to the consultee. It is essential that the consultee have the opportunity to provide informed consent to participate in the process. Transpiring *prior to* tackling the problem, contracting is a systematic process through which consultation assumptions and expectations are explicitly discussed so that the consultee (or consultees – the process can include more than one consultee) can make an informed decision regarding entering the consultation process. The process of contracting should not be so overly rigid as to stifle the relationship, but, at a minimum, a verbal discussion of expectations for the consultation should occur and should include the consultee's verbal agreement to work with the consultant on the concern. When contracting is neglected, or components of contracting are ignored, challenges detrimental to problem-solving may subsequently arise. In contrast, when implemented well, contracting serves as the foundation of trust and honesty on which the consultation relationship and successful problem-solving efforts are built. This is consistent with the first part of Big Idea #3, originally introduced in Chapter 5: **Everything we do is an intervention, beginning from the earliest consultation interactions.**

In this chapter, we consider: (a) the *necessity* of establishing a consultation contract, (b) the *content* that should be included in a consultation contract, and (c) *process* issues related to effectively contracting. As in other chapters, multiple real examples of contracting interactions are provided along with activities,

DOI: 10.4324/9781032622330-6

allowing you to learn and practice this stage of problem-solving. We will spend considerable time on this stage, as understanding contracting will also familiarize you with the subsequent problem-solving stages themselves. Before further exploring the components and process of contracting, take a moment to complete Activity 6.1.

ACTIVITY 6.1 (INDIVIDUAL)

Warm-Up Questions: Contracting

Write down responses to the following questions. You can write sentences or just key words.

1   In what ways do you think the contracting stage of problem-solving relates to school culture?
2   In what ways do you think the contracting stage of problem-solving relates to building relationships?
3   Why do you suppose it is important for the consultant and consultee to clarify their expectations prior to beginning a consultation case?
4   What should a consultant do if a consultee does not wish to work together in the consultation process?

Why a Consultation Contract Is Necessary

Consistent with our definition of competent consultation in the introduction to the text, contracting adds some structure to informing how a consultant *talks* to someone about a problem. The consultee's *informed consent* to participate in consultation is obtained via contracting. Obtaining informed consent is an ethical responsibility delineated in APA's (2017a) Ethics Code and should be done "as early as is feasible" (p. 7), consistent with other psychological services. Achieving transparency regarding the consultation process is likely to enhance the effectiveness and satisfaction of consultants and consultees and their working alliance (Barnett, 2020; Thomas, 2010). In a study synthesizing data from 38 qualitative consultation research studies, data from 12 of the studies suggested that a combination of understanding school/organizational culture (i.e., processes of entry) and establishing clear expectations and procedures for consultation (i.e., process of contracting) made positive differences for how consultation relationships developed and problem-solving ensued (Newman et al., 2017). Several examples from Rosenfield's (2012) compilation of school consultation case studies also evidenced the importance of contracting; for example, Pas (2012) demonstrated, as explored later in this chapter, that when expectations of the consultation process are unclear, it may negatively impact the problem-solving process.

Consultation contracts are embedded within the contexts of psychological contracts and visible contracts (APA, 2017b). Psychological contracts are *invisible* expectations regarding work obligations, efforts, and remuneration. Norms and regularities of school culture, in addition to individual preferences, affect implicit role expectations, such as how a school consultant's work schedule is divided (e.g., time engaged in assessment versus time engaged in consultation) and how much responsibility a teacher owns for supporting students outside of school hours. *Visible contracts* are written/signed contracts between employers and employees. They explicitly specify salaries, hours, and other job expectations. External school consultants might sign a written contract with a school for their work. However, internal consultants and consultees do not often sign a written contract; therefore, expectations for the consultation process, relationship, and roles can, by default, become *implicit unless there is a specific process to clarify them*.

Thus, the *consultation contract* offers an opportunity for the consultation dyad to begin problem-solving with *explicit*, clear assumptions, expectations, and roles. In other words, the *invisible* expectations hidden in psychological contracts and school culture can become *visible, although not written down as with visible contracts*. The contract should be negotiated with the person who brings the problem to the table and who will be responsible for carrying out any planned interventions (Barnett, 2020); sometimes, this involves more than one person.

If there is a misalignment between the consultant's and consultee's assumptions or expectations, this is best clarified before problem-solving begins. Here is an activity that demonstrates the value of a consultation contract.

ACTIVITY 6.2 (INDIVIDUAL, GROUP)

Clarifying Expectations Early in Consultation

Read the following example. Answer the subsequent questions individually and, if possible, compare responses with a partner or in a small group.

Imagine you start consulting on a case for a first-grade student named Yusaf. You believe consultative problem-solving efforts will support Yusaf's reading fluency and comprehension in the general education classroom. The teacher believes that Yusaf has a learning disability requiring intervention support outside of the general education setting and that the purpose of consultation is to document Yusaf's need for specialized instruction.

Questions for Reflection:

1   What are the implications of this misalignment of assumptions?

2 How might clarifying expectations upfront support more effective consultative problem-solving?

3 What else would you want to consider about the teacher's expectations for consultation?

The Nuts and Bolts of Contracting

The SC Model of consultation described in this text has embedded assumptions, as listed in Table 6.1, that are clarified during the contracting stage of problem-solving. A checklist for contracting with these components, as well as examples of how these may be discussed in contracting, is provided in Figure 6.1. In short, contracting provides an opportunity for you to introduce the assumptions, expectations, and process of SC.

Previous Consultee Experience With Consultation

However, before you offer too much information, it is advisable to inquire about the consultee's prior experiences and expectations. Information provided by the consultee may contrast with your own assumptions and expectations as a school consultant. For example, many consultees have primarily engaged in "on-the-fly" consultations, been on the receiving end of advice without feeling their perspectives were considered, or engaged in storytelling about students or families without really problem-solving. Unearthing such prior experiences can stimulate an excellent introduction to how this consultation process will be similar and different. Activity 6.3 provides an additional opportunity for you to think about how you might approach discussing prior experiences when consulting with a teacher.

TABLE 6.1 Purposes and Business of the Contracting Stage of Problem-Solving

Contracting	
Purposes	• Introduce consultee to the school consultation model, including assumptions, expectations, and process • Gain agreement to work together
Business	• Discuss consultee expectations and prior experiences consulting • Explain stage-based problem-solving process • Clarify school as the context for problem-solving, including the concept of instructional match • Explain potential application of problem-solving at multiple tiers in addition to individual students • Clarify shared ownership of the problem and the consultation process • Clarify non-evaluative nature of the consultation process (only if true) • Explain the parameters of confidentiality • Check for consultee agreement and commitment to participate • Schedule follow-up meeting/ongoing schedule

Contracting Task	Example of Language	Observation (Tally and/or Comment)
☐ Discuss consultee's expectations, prior experiences	"What expectations do you have for our work together?" "Tell me about what prior experiences you have had consulting/problem solving."	
☐ Explain stage-based problem-solving process	"The stages of problem solving include…" "The problem-identification and analysis stage will be the 'heavy lifting' for us, so we're sure to intervene on the correct problem"	
☐ Clarify school as the context for problem solving, including concept of instructional match in problem solving	"By attending to instructional match, we'll consider the fit of the student, their cultural background, and their prior knowledge with the instruction in the classroom, and expected tasks"	
☐ Explain potential application for other students	"Sometimes we find that other students can benefit from the intervention we are working on for one student"	
☐ Introduce the collaborative consultation process	"In this process we will work shoulder-to-shoulder through a series of steps to identify, define, and intervene on concerns"	
☐ Clarify shared ownership of problem and process	"We will co-construct the problem, and work step by step together to solve it"	
☐ Clarify non-evaluative nature of process (only if true)	"This is a non-evaluative process – none of the information will be shared with the principal, or be connected to evaluation of your performance"	
☐ Explain parameters of confidentiality	"This process is confidential – we will not need to share what we are working on except…(with the team, with the students' parents, etc.)"	
☐ Check for agreement/ commitment to participate	"Does this sound like a process you'd like to work on together?"	
☐ Schedule follow-up meeting/ongoing schedule	"When would be a workable, regular time for us to meet?"	

FIGURE 6.1   Checklist for Contracting in Consultation

ACTIVITY 6.3 (INDIVIDUAL, GROUP)

Contracting Transcript: Prior Experiences Consulting Example 1

The following is an excerpt from an actual contracting session between a consultant and consultee. Review the transcript and answer the subsequent questions individually and, if possible, compare responses with a partner or in a small group.

> **Consultant-in-Training (CIT)**: Tell me about your prior experiences with consultation.
>
> **Teacher Consultee (TC)**: It was very sporadic and different being in the city because they don't have the same services that are available at this school. It was a team-based approach . . . the caseworker would come in and observe before the whole team got together. Or sometimes, the school psychologist would come in and do an observation. I had a behavior checklist that I had to fill out, and one was sent home to parents to fill out as well to see if the behaviors were consistent across school and home. That's what I remember.
>
> **CIT**: Okay . . . was it that you were working with somebody, or was it that each person had his or her own part to do?
>
> **TC**: Each person had their own part to do, and then the team would meet and come up with the plan that would work . . . it was more so only done when it had to do with Special Education.

Questions for Reflection:

1   How might the consultee's prior experiences influence her expectations of the current consultation process?

2   Imagine you are the CIT. Use the following sentence starters to: (a) paraphrase the consultee's prior experiences, and (b) contrast those experiences to what she might expect in her work with you:
   a.   "It sounds like your previous experiences with consultation included . . ."
   b.   "Our process will look a bit different. We'll . . ."

Some prior experiences may not be explicitly or immediately shared by consultees, particularly those related to bias or racism. For instance, some consultees will have previously experienced power differentials with consultants due to differences in race, gender, and age, as well as other variables and their intersections, or have experienced microaggressions from consultants or others within the school.

Consultants, too, may bring such prior experiences into the consultation relationship. Although such issues will likely not be the focus of early consultation discussions, it is important to be mindful of how prior experiences and current identities may affect the consultation relationship. Demonstrating cultural humility from this initial stage, including an openness to and value of cultural diversity, can help establish a culturally responsive problem-solving process.

Description of Consultation Process

As you get a sense of the consultee's prior experiences and expectations, you can also offer information about your own experiences, assumptions, and expectations. For example, you'll want to clarify that consultation is an indirect, collaborative, and systematic process with specific stages. Problem-solving should be described without using too much jargon. Laundry listing the problem-solving stages or describing stage business in too much detail is likely to *lose* the consultee or inadvertently create a *one-up* power dynamic antithetical to the collaborative dynamic you are trying to establish. The consultee should be clear that the process is ongoing and will involve meeting on multiple occasions over time. Sandoval (2014) suggests that the consultant make it clear that an immediate solution will not be provided until sufficient information is obtained, referencing the importance of the *Problem Identification and Problem Analysis (PID/PA)* stage, which alleviates expectations of an expert dynamic.

Given the school-based context of problem-solving (see Big Idea #2, introduced in Chapter 5), it is important to specify that you are interested in the student's instructional match or the alignment of the student's prior knowledge and cultural background, the curriculum or task they are engaged in, and the instruction being provided. Doing so makes it clear that this is an ecological rather than child-deficit-focused process. It may also be helpful to illustrate the instructional triangle heuristic, originally developed by Bloom (1976) as the learning triangle (see Figure 6.2). We return to the concept of instructional match in Chapter 7.

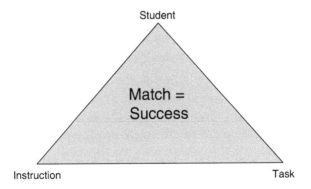

FIGURE 6.2 Instructional Match Triangle

Also relevant to the school-based context is the assumption that problem-solving is viewed through a multi-student lens, namely that the work the consultee does in the consultation for a single student may be relevant for multiple students in the classroom or future students with similar concerns. Multiple students may benefit from assessment strategies and the many interventions that are discussed, and it is helpful to make this possibility explicit to the consultee early in the process. We have not yet considered each of the problem-solving stages in-depth, but the information provided in Chapter 5 and here should give you enough information to begin practicing the contracting process.

Discussion of the Collaborative Relationship

It is essential to discuss the nature of collaboration during *Contracting*, as preconceptions of the consulting relationship will vary based on the consultee's prior experiences. During a *Contracting* session, a teacher expressed her concern about previous less-than-positive experiences, particularly when it came to intervention development. The teacher stated: "It's hard when people are telling you [that] you should do this but there's no way with all the other students that you can possibly do it." The CIT, during contracting, saw the need to both validate the teacher's frustration but also to indicate that she would work together with the teacher to create something feasible, knowing that this issue was key to gaining the teacher's trust to engage in the process.

Activity 6.4 provides a contracting excerpt where the dyad discussed the consultee's prior experiences consulting, which revealed some problematic dynamics in collaborating with other teachers. As the example demonstrates, a discussion such as this might be an excellent jumping-off point to discuss that the relationship will be collaborative and what collaboration will consist of in the context of the relationship (e.g., shared responsibility for exploring and defining problems and planning and implementing interventions; mutual value of the consultee's and consultant's expertise, as both help us to understand the problem).

ACTIVITY 6.4 (INDIVIDUAL, GROUP)

Contracting Transcript: Prior Experiences Consulting Example 2

The following is an excerpt from an actual contracting session between a consultant and consultee. Review the transcript and answer the subsequent questions individually and, if possible, compare responses with a partner or in a small group.

Consultant-in-Training (CIT): Have you ever engaged in consultation before?

Teacher Consultee (TC): Well, not with the school psychologist.

CIT: How about anyone else in the school?

TC: Um, I would not say that it was formal consultation, but I talk to the other fifth-grade teachers a lot, but most of the time it ends up that we just complain about our students (laughs).

CIT: So you've had some interactions with the other teachers in fifth grade, but you didn't find much value in your conversations.

TC: Exactly, I am always trying to do new things and get our grade team together, but we always end up just bashing ideas down, and we all leave conversations more discouraged than when we started.

CIT: It sounds like you are really trying to be a leader here. What would be some of the things that you would find value in from consulting with someone?

TC: Well, when you do the same thing day in and day out, year after year, you get stuck in a rut. Each year classes are different, and they should be treated differently. I just feel like I don't know what to do sometimes to help some of my struggling students. It would be nice to hear what other people do or some ideas of what to do.

CIT: That's great that you are seeking out strategies from others and that you recognize the importance of student differences. Hopefully, we can work together and find some things that will work for you in your classroom and for Oliver, but also maybe for some other students.

TC: Great! Finally!

Questions for Reflection:

1 What information does the consultee offer about her prior experiences with collaboration?
  a. What does this suggest about grade-level collaboration?
2 If you were the consultant, how might you use the information provided by the consultee to introduce expectations of the consultation relationship?
3 What might this say about the culture of the school regarding collaboration?

Evaluation and Confidentiality

The topics of evaluation and confidentiality (and limits therein) should be covered during the contracting process. Consultation is presumably a non-evaluative process in which the consultant's role is to support rather than to evaluate the consultee's work performance (e.g., a teacher's instruction or classroom behavior management). A non-evaluative process allows the consultee to ask for assistance; state that something is not working; or acknowledge being stuck without fearing negative consequences, such as receiving a poor performance evaluation or losing a job.

The process being non-evaluative intertwines with it being between the consultant and the consultee to the extent possible; the consultant does not generally share with others what is discussed during consultation interactions unless safety concerns for a student or students should arise or the process is part of a school problem-solving team. There is no legal confidentiality right for the consultant or consultee. Moreover, the consultee is not held to the same expectations of confidentiality as the consultant (Sandoval, 2014) and is free to discuss the content of the consultation sessions. If the consultation is part of a team problem-solving process, as is true in the Instructional Consultation Team Model (Rosenfield & Gravois, 1996), there should be no expectation of confidentiality, as much of the information is shared with the team. As a CIT, you may be required to audio- or video-record your consultation interactions; if so, when discussing confidentiality, you should be clear about who will listen to recordings (e.g., self, university supervisor, field supervisors, peers in your cohort during peer supervision) and that recordings will be deleted after review, if that is the case.

Although the non-evaluative, confidential, and voluntary aspects of consultation have long been assumed to be part of the process, their precise boundaries have never been complete and have become even more blurred in contemporary consultation practice (Erchul, 2011; Newman et al., 2018). For example, an evaluative authority such as a principal may ask you to consult with a teacher, with implications for whether the process is truly evaluative, confidential, or voluntary. Problem-solving teams as settings for consultation also do not provide a confidential setting for teachers to share their concerns. With the implementation of Multi-Tiered Systems of Support (MTSS) in schools, a consultee may be expected to share the results of consultative problem-solving with a data team and with parents to demonstrate a student's progress in areas of concern. Although some exceptions exist with respect to these features of consultation, the key is being clear and explicit about them up front during contracting. Violations of the contract would undermine trust with the consultee and potentially mitigate your effectiveness as a consultant within the larger system.

Informed Consent

The contracting process concludes with the consultant checking for consultee agreement and commitment to participate in the process. Consultation is a voluntary process, and though it may feel awkward confirming the consultee's readiness to consult when they already had requested your assistance, securing the consultee's informed consent to participate confirms you are on the same page with *how* the consultation process will proceed. Before formally asking for agreement, asking an open-ended question such as "Before proceeding, what questions do you have?" (in contrast to "Do you have any questions?"), may elicit any concerns, such as the time commitment for the process. Finally, you can openly ask the consultee if they want to participate in this process and when would be a good time to meet next.

Once the consultee agrees to participate, it is time to move to the *PID/PA* stage of problem-solving. Often, this happens immediately after confirming an agreement to work together. If there is not sufficient time to begin the process, scheduling the following session is the next task. If the consultee does not wish to participate in consultation, that is acceptable, too. Again, the process is voluntary, and consultees may not view the structure as fitting their needs. It is better to know this before the process begins.

Process of Contracting: Tips for Success

Although we offer a checklist of items to discuss during contracting (Figure 6.1), this stage of problem-solving is more nuanced than checking items off a list. Following are some considerations to promote a successful contracting stage.

Make It a Dialogue

Since you will be offering a lot of information about the problem-solving process, your assumptions, and your expectations, it is easy for contracting to become a monologue. This contrasts with the communication skills we have discussed thus far as well as the bi-directional nature of the consultation relationship and inter-actions you are trying to build. As described earlier, asking about the consultee's prior experiences and expectations for consultation begins the process as a discussion. Demonstrate genuine interest and active listening and use the points brought up by the consultee as a starting point to compare or contrast the SC process. For example, a consultant might provide the following statement:

> It sounds like your grade-level team shares a lot of resources, but you don't always work together when interventions are put in place in your class-room. During our process, we will continue to meet as the intervention is in place to check in about Evan's progress.

Still, the consultant, who has a lot of information to share, may inadvertently dominate the contracting session. Therefore, at times it is useful to stop and make a statement such as, "I've been going on for a while. Let me stop and ask you what questions or thoughts you have about the process I just described?" Doing this will break up the monologue to help make it more of a conversation. In total, the contracting dialogue usually is approximately five to ten minutes in length, unless specific issues, such as those around previous experiences need to be resolved.

Don't Apologize for the Process

It is likely that the teacher you are consulting with has never had someone contract with them prior to consultation or consulted in a systematic way, such as what you are proposing. This leads some CITs to be self-conscious or even apologetic in how they describe the process (e.g., CIT: "We'll work through a formal process, which can be time-consuming – sorry about that"). Apologizing for the consultation process before it even begins can undermine your ability to be an effective consultant. Instead, realize that although this process is different than what the consultee (or you) may have experienced in the past, it is structured this way for a reason.

Relatedly, since consultees may not be used to contracting, they might be ready to dive right into *PID/PA* before contracting is complete. We have discussed several of the challenges with glossing over the Contracting stage of problem-solving. If a consultee should try to move ahead before the stage is complete, it is okay to demonstrate that you heard the consultee's concern and then refocus back to contracting. For example:

> **Consultant-in-Training (CIT):** It sounds like Ellen's been a real handful. I am eager to talk more about your concerns. Before we dive too far into the problem, I just want to make sure we're on the same page about this process. If it's okay with you, can we finish up the contracting discussion before moving to discussing the problem?

Consultant Student Status

For CITs, a frequent concern is that the consultee is working with the CIT as a favor (i.e., helping to get a graduate school assignment completed) rather than genuinely in need of consultation assistance. A CIT reflected this very concern in a supervision process log:

> I think it will be interesting to see how our working relationship develops. Currently, Mrs. King sees me more as a student than as a professional. In our conversation, she kept referring back to how she understands that I need to get my work done, referring to this consultation case, because she remembers what it's like to be a student. So, I am hoping that through my professionalism and working together on this case, our relationship will develop into more of a professional relationship rather than a teacher/student relationship. It may also be necessary to address directly (e.g., "I am a student, but I hope that you find this to be a good use of your time – it is not just for me to complete an assignment").

This is an issue that can be addressed during contracting by making an explicit statement such as the one proposed by the CIT. Although it is kind of a teacher to use their time to support a graduate student, the process should ultimately be beneficial to the consultee and their students. Even when a consultation starts off as a favor, CITs should bear in mind that, although they are learning to consult, they have more to offer than they might think – especially if they are receiving ongoing supervision of their consultation work.

Revisiting the Contract

As you are getting to the end of this chapter, we hope that you are thinking that contracting is more involved than you had initially thought. Indeed, there are several components of contracting and nuances in how they are discussed with the consultee. Sometimes, consultants forget to discuss something during the contracting stage. Do not fret. Rarely is something missed that cannot be brought up later, for example, at the beginning of the next session in an opening summary.

Sometimes, though, even when all the contracting components are covered, a dyad begins the consultation with misaligned assumptions. In a compelling example provided by Pas (2012), the consultee, based on her prior experiences, assumed that Pas would take a prescriptive approach to consultative problem-solving, providing solutions for the consultee to implement. This perspective was inconsistent with Pas' collaborative approach, which had not been sufficiently clarified during contracting. As the consultation progressed, the divergent perspectives became more evident in consultation interactions, which Pas discussed with her consultation instructor/supervisor. Therefore, Pas decided to address the relational dynamic by revisiting the contracting discussion:

> This is actually a good opportunity to revisit some of the stuff that we talked about in the first week. I hear you apologizing to me and feeling badly about [not collecting data] and I am wondering if we can kind of go back to where we quickly skimmed through the process and talk a little bit about our relationship. You don't have to feel bad about this; a really essential part about the type of consultation that I would like to do is a little different from what I understand the [Team] process may be like. I don't want this to be an expert mode, like "I'm the boss" and that I will come in and say "this is what you should to do" and if you don't do it that I will [think or say] "That bad teacher didn't collect data." I really want to work – I guess a good phrase is shoulder to shoulder – with you about this concern.
>
> *(Pas, 2012, p. 201)*

Revisiting contracting, in this case, led to a return to the *PID/PA* stage of problem-solving and subsequent stages, all with additional consultee input.

In addition to misaligned relational expectations, other symptoms may indicate a need to revisit contracting. These include a consultee being frequently late or absent to meetings or distracted in meetings, not adhering to the intervention, presenting with negative verbal or nonverbal behavior, or even talking with you differently when the recording device is off (e.g., "Here's what's really happening …") due to fear of evaluation. In such instances, revisiting relevant aspects of contracting can be useful. For example, for a consultee who seems to have lost interest in meeting with you, inquiring about the behavior can be helpful: "I noticed we haven't been able to get together for a couple of weeks. I just wanted to check in and make sure this process is still something that you want to do." Most often, consultees still do want the consultation support and will be responsive to your reminder about the expectations of ongoing meetings. This falls into the category for many CITs as a difficult conversation. And, indeed, sometimes the consultee really does want to stop, as in one case where the teacher's daughter was getting married and the consultee was feeling too overwhelmed to continue meeting with the CIT. Both accepting that and leaving the door open for the future is important to making this a positive experience for both the CIT and the consultee.

As with all stages of problem-solving, *Contracting* is best learned through practice with opportunities for feedback. Activity 6.6 is a lab activity intended to help you practice contracting skills in a simulated environment.

ACTIVITY 6.6 (GROUP)

Contracting Lab

1   If possible, in a group of three or four, divide up roles: One or two observers, one consultant, and one consultee.
2   The **consultant's goal** should be for the consultee's agreement to consult with the components of the contracting stage. The practice can be audio- or video-recorded, especially if there is no observer.
3   The **consultee** should act as you think a consultee might in this situation: Curious, agreeable, have sought out assistance in advance, but haven't consulted in this way before. Following the practice session, the consultee should provide this feedback to the consultant:
    a.   How did it feel to be on the consultee end of contracting? Did it feel conversational or robotic?
4   The **observer(s)** should use the contracting checklist (Figure 6.1) to take notes while observing regarding content and process. Following the practice session, provide this feedback to the consultant:
    a.   Was the contracting you observed a monologue or dialogue? What evidence do you have for your argument?
    b.   Provide critical feedback in writing, using the checklist, and verbally with examples of consultant statements.

Summary

Consultation is a bi-directional process built on trust and happens *with*, rather than *to*, the consultee. Therefore, a consultee should be able to make an informed decision about whether to participate in consultation. *Contracting* provides an opportunity to establish transparency about the systematic consultation process, including clarifying consultant and consultee assumptions and expectations regarding collaboration, evaluation, and confidentiality; ownership of the problem and intervention; and the consultee indicating their explicit agreement to proceed with problem-solving. Even though the contracting stage is brief, it sets the tone for the consultation relationship and problem-solving process and requires a nuanced application (e.g., making it a dialogue rather than a monologue). By completing the activities in this chapter, including observing and practicing contracting, we hope you begin to appreciate the complexity and centrality of this problem-solving stage.

7

PROBLEM IDENTIFICATION AND PROBLEM ANALYSIS

Look Before You Leap

> *Given an hour to solve a problem on which your life depended, I would use the first 55 minutes to ensure I was answering the right question.*
>
> *(Attributed to Einstein)*

In this chapter, we overview what we view to be the keystone stage of problem-solving: *Problem Identification and Problem Analysis (PID/PA)*. Before considering the components and processes of this stage, we would like you to explore your own assumptions and beliefs about this early stage of problem-solving.

ACTIVITY 7.1 (INDIVIDUAL)

Warm-Up Questions: PID/PA

Write down responses to the following questions. You can write sentences or just key words.

1   When you think about solving a problem, what do you view as the most important steps?
2   How might your own assumptions and beliefs as a consultant influence how a problem is defined?
3   How might your communication skills, as discussed in prior chapters, influence how a problem is defined?
4   If a consultee wants help with more than one problem, how should problems be prioritized?
5   Defining and analyzing problems is considered a critical prerequisite to developing an intervention plan. Why do you suppose this is the case?

DOI: 10.4324/9781032622330-7

Given the historical centrality of evidence-based practices in psychology (APA, 2006) and school psychology (e.g., Kratochwill & Stoiber, 2002), and the ongoing relevance of these issues (e.g., Barrett et al., 2020; Sanetti & Collier-Meek, 2019; Shaw, 2021; Slavin, 2020), we would not be surprised if your thoughts first went to consultants needing to move quickly from referral statements to identifying powerful interventions, and then to support intervention implementation. Our knowledge of and access to evidence-based academic and behavioral interventions designed for struggling students is more robust than ever before in the history of education and psychology. Indeed, we can identify research-based strategies with a high likelihood of success and provide these interventions to students with identified needs, such as those falling below certain curriculum-based measurement (CBM) thresholds or engaging in problematic classroom behaviors.

We agree that identifying and implementing research-based interventions is critical and that there are often pressures, both real and imagined, to move forward quickly in problem-solving. *However, we also believe the most high-leverage stage of problem-solving is the PID/PA stage, which occurs prior to designing and implementing interventions.* The first half of the chapter offers an overview of key components and aims to provide conceptual knowledge and tools for consultants to engage successfully in *PID/PA.* Thus, the first part of the chapter focuses primarily on the *content* of *PID/PA.* The second part of the chapter briefly reviews three Big Ideas from Chapter 5 and introduces three new Big Ideas for consultants to keep in mind during this critical consultation stage. Each Big Idea is paired with examples from actual consultant-consultee interactions in schools. In essence, these Big Ideas are focused on the *process* of *PID/PA.* Activities are provided throughout the chapter for you to continue to develop your skills in identifying, operationalizing, and prioritizing problems.

The Nuts and Bolts of PID/PA

PID/PA is the second stage of problem-solving, following entry and contracting. Often *PID/PA* occurs *immediately* after the consultation is contracted, even within the same meeting, as consultees and consultants alike are eager to dive into the referral issue (being cautious here, as stated in the last chapter, not to shortcut the contracting process because of this pull into solving the referral problem). The importance of *PID/PA* cannot be overstated because what happens within this stage determines what will be done in subsequent problem-solving stages. As has often been stated in various terms, even an evidence-based intervention will not be effective unless the right problem is identified. The purposes and components of *PID/PA* are highlighted in Table 7.1.

The culture of the school can interfere with this stage of the process. In many schools, teams and consultants operate on what Little (2007) called help and assistance. Teachers tell the helper their concern, and the team or consultant provides

TABLE 7.1 Purposes and Business of the Problem Identification and Problem Analysis Stage of Problem-Solving

Problem Identification and Problem Analysis
Purposes • Create a shared perception of consultee concerns • Define the problem in observable and measurable terms • Establish a baseline of current performance • Establish goals
Business • Create shared understanding of teacher's concern(s) using collaborative communication skills • Define concern(s) in observable terms • Follow up with additional data collection, such as record or work sample review, observation, or instructional assessment • Consider student's instructional match • Prioritize concerns • Establish a plan to measure current performance (i.e., Baseline) • Establish baseline measurement of performance • Set goals based on baseline data

multiple interventions, some even evidence-based, which may or may not apply. As one consultant-in-training (CIT) explained:

> This school culture was observed within my first consultation session with the teacher. The teacher showed me this "chart intervention" that she has been using for over a month that was recommended to her at the team meeting. The student gets points deducted when he is bad and gets to keep the points and then receives a positive reinforcement at the end of the week when he is good. After viewing the chart intervention, I tried to help the teacher see how inappropriate the intervention was regarding the student's problem by asking the teacher what the student's concern is, how she is measuring the concern with this intervention, and whether it is effective. The teacher is not only frustrated and overwhelmed with the complexity of the intervention, but she states that it is not working. She cannot look at the chart intervention and tell me how any of the student's problems are recorded. As a result of the obvious ineffectiveness of the intervention, the teacher was not applying it with integrity. It was clear that the intervention did not fit the student, teacher, and classroom. More importantly, the problem was never identified or analyzed. [This is] a good example of problem-solving that does not follow best practice guidelines.

Our experience is that *PID/PA* often requires multiple consultation meetings to appropriately identify and define problems with the right data, sufficient specificity, and shared understanding to move forward to the intervention stage. Even then, problem-solving in the consultation process is often recursive, and *PID/PA* may need to be revisited if an intervention is unsuccessful, additional problems arise, or one problem is solved and then another is prioritized.

A good way to think about the kinds of problems that bring the consultee to the process was developed by Caplan (1970) in his classic text on mental health consultation. He defined four different types of problems in working with consultees: **Lack of knowledge, lack of skill, lack of self-confidence, and lack of professional objectivity.**

We have seen each of these reasons bring a consultee to ask for help. Sometimes the teacher simply lacks information. One case involved a child with seizures, and the teacher needed information about what to do if the child had a seizure in class. Many teachers need additional information on the impact of bilingualism on students' classroom performance (see Ortiz & Melo, 2017 for a good summary of what teachers should know about the impact of language issues on student outcomes). Often the consultee lacks skill, such as in classroom management strategies or assessment of entry-level skills to determine if the student has the skill to succeed in each lesson. In these cases, working with the teacher to develop the skills can provide a meaningful source of professional learning. In cases where there is a lack of self-confidence, consultant support to the consultee can be a productive intervention. For instance, a first-year, second-grade teacher appreciated a consultant observing and affirming that students seemed very engaged during a math lesson. Finally, there are cases in which the consultee lacks objectivity, such as in a case where the teacher had developed negative assumptions about her students (Berger, 2012). In another example, a consultee described to a consultant her concern about a 6-year-old first-grade girl. The student was described as extremely social, chatty, and a distraction to her peers. The teacher went on to report, "She is doomed academically. It reminds me so much of myself when I was that age." Therefore, one thing the consultant needed to consider in the consultation case was how to help the consultee overcome this theme interference (Caplan, 1970) and focus on the needs of the student.

Sometimes a lack of objectivity is related to issues of diversity in the classroom. We have found multiple examples where teachers perceived students of color as unable to learn or as exhibiting subjective problematic behaviors (e.g., disrespect), which, when observed objectively, were at similar or lower levels than White peers. Gustafson (2012) describes her consultee teacher's initial presentation of the student as one "who could not learn" (p. 78), but through the consultation process, the child made all his goals, showing steady progress over time. Similarly, students labeled with a learning disability may also be perceived by teachers as unable to respond to classroom activities.

Aguilar (2018) provides a similar problem typology for consultants, calling them gaps that identify learning needs. She specifies the need for developing cultural competency, which she defines as "the ability to understand, appreciate and interact with people from cultures or belief systems different from one's own: the skill to navigate cross-cultural differences" (p. 230). Such a lack of cultural competence is seen in the Gustafson case described previously, where the lack of objectivity is compounded by the implicit bias of the teacher. But consultants also need to be aware of the need for cultural competence.

Implicit bias may indicate a lack of knowledge or information about other cultures. For example, in interviewing bilingual school psychologists regarding their consultations with teachers of English-learning students, O'Bryon and Rogers (2016) found that nearly all teacher referral concerns related to students' academic difficulties, especially distinguishing between typical rates of second language acquisition and learning problems (e.g., a reading disability). The participants suggested that school consultants should seek out language and culture resources, ongoing professional learning in English language acquisition, and peer consultation from bilingual school psychologists (see, e.g., Ortiz & Melo, 2017). Such ongoing learning in tandem with the consultee can: (a) enhance the effectiveness of problem-solving, (b) demonstrate cultural humility ("Let's learn more about this together"), and (c) bolster consultant-consultee collaboration, which participants reported as their most needed consultation skill. In Chapter 12, we will address the learning and development needs of consultants from this framework as they begin to address what is needed to become a skillful practitioner.

Initial Problem Definition

During *PID/PA*, problems are collaboratively defined between the consultant and the consultee. Using the communication and relational skills described in previous chapters, the problem becomes *our problem* to work on *shoulder to shoulder* rather than *the consultee's problem* or a problem observed and dictated by the consultant that is not shared or owned by the consultee. Problems are defined in observable and measurable terms, including attention to *who* is the focus of the problem, *what* the problem is, *when* the problem occurs, and *where* the problem occurs.

Definitional Red Flags

Overly simplistic, subjective, high inference, or ill-defined problems will not get you and your consultee very far in problem-solving. Poorly defined problems will also increase the possibility for bias, implicit or explicit, to have an unknown impact on the discussion. In Chapter 4, in Table 4.1, we provided several examples of such terminology we have heard used by consultees to describe students early in the problem identification process. Such utterances provide *red flags* alerting consultants of the need to clarify in order to assist the dyad in moving toward observable and measurable problem identification, where bias is likely to have less impact and for an effective intervention to be achieved. Here is where the Ladder of Inference, also discussed in Chapter 4, becomes useful. If a consultant inadvertently affirms high inference problem definitions (e.g., "You're right, she is quite sassy," or, "It sounds like he is quite hyperactive"), the dyad risks admiring rather than solving the problem or focusing on only the student's behavior rather than any aspect of context. Alternatively, the consultant might clarify: "Tell me what you mean by sassy," or, "What does hyperactive look like in your classroom?" thereby moving down the Ladder of Inference toward observable and measurable statements of the behavior. As you develop competence in consultation, *red flags* in need of clarification will begin to stick out more clearly than might be the case as you first begin to practice consultation.

Prioritizing

Multiple concerns may surface in a flash flood of information during *PID/PA*, and you may feel drowned in details, unsure of where to direct the consultation. For example, when asked, "Can you just give me some ideas of what the problems are in the classroom that you are facing?", a teacher responded:

> Okay, at this point, the child is functioning somewhat below grade level . . . There are disciplining problems and work habit problems that we are also facing right now. He has problems with self-control, with body contact and staying on-task, attending to what he's supposed to be doing, and following directions . . . There were language differences and different expectations . . . And he is also trying to make an adjustment between that, which he has been having some difficulty doing. These are some of the problems we're facing right now.

As previously described, all the key consultation communication skills, particularly active listening, clarifying, and paraphrasing, are critical during this stage. Once the dyad has discussed initial concerns in sufficient depth, it makes sense to prioritize a single problem to focus on more closely, which is exactly what the consultation dyad did in the situation described previously. Prioritizing a single problem allows the dyad to home in like a laser on the most pressing or pivotal issue rather than juggling several at once, risking all "balls" falling to the ground. Concerns that are not the first priority can be revisited later in problem-solving or after the priority concern is mitigated (see Gifford, 2012, for an example of how this process was conducted by a CIT). Teacher consultees are often relieved to hear they can focus on one issue in a complex case, as it makes the problem they are working on more manageable and approachable. In a way, prioritizing can be viewed as an intervention in and of itself.

From a behavioral perspective, Zins and Erchul (2002) suggest that problem-solving priorities could be

> ranked based on: (a) behaviors considered to be physically dangerous to self or others, (b) positive low frequency behaviors in need of strengthening, (c) behaviors that can be naturally reinforced in the environment, (d) behaviors viewed as essential for development, and (e) behaviors that maximize functioning in a variety of settings.
>
> (p. 632)

If the issue is an academic problem, attending to how well the student's entry-level skills are matched to the classroom curriculum materials is required (Gickling et al., 2016). Even if the problem is a behavior, we believe that the academic context in which the behavior occurs always requires careful consideration (Rosenfield, 2022). The consultant and consultee must consider whether the behavior problem is a result of a poor instructional match. In that case, the problem might be resolved if instructional or task variables are adjusted in light of student variables, such as what the student knows, enabling the teacher to find the right point in the curriculum sequence for effective instruction (Gickling et al., 2016). Instructional match creates the point where both teaching and learning will be maximally successful. If a poor instructional match is indeed the issue, an instructional intervention may be an appropriate focus instead of, or in conjunction with, a behavioral intervention. Examples of instructional match variables for consideration during *PID/PA* and subsequent problem-solving stages are illustrated in Figure 7.1 (see Gickling et al., 2016, for additional information about instructional match). Barrett (2012) describes a case that shows how instructional match was helpful in producing progress for a group of students.

In sum, a variety of interrelated problems will likely arise in *PID/PA*, and it is up to you and the consultee to collaboratively determine which problem or problems to tackle first. As a dyad, you must move beyond surface-level and high-inference descriptions of problems. Examining the school context within which the difficulty is embedded is critical, whether the concern is an academic one (e.g., reading fluency, early numeracy, math calculation accuracy, completing homework, study skills) or another type of behavior (e.g., following multi-step directions, active off-task behavior, poor attendance, limited social interactions). In addition, you and the consultee will want to think about which behaviors are: (a) most *salient* (e.g., consuming most of the consultee's time or attention) and (b)

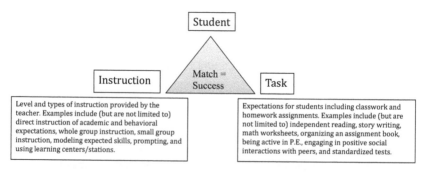

The prior knowledge and experiences the student brings to the instructional match. Examples include (but are not limited to) sight word knowledge, vocabulary, multiplication facts, previous experiences in the content area, prior school attendance, and cultural background.

Student

Match = Success

Instruction

Task

Level and types of instruction provided by the teacher. Examples include (but are not limited to) direct instruction of academic and behavioral expectations, whole group instruction, small group instruction, modeling expected skills, prompting, and using learning centers/stations.

Expectations for students including classwork and homework assignments. Examples include (but are not limited to) independent reading, story writing, math worksheets, organizing an assignment book, being active in P.E., engaging in positive social interactions with peers, and standardized tests.

FIGURE 7.1   Examples of Student, Instruction, and Task Variables in Instructional Match may be *pivotal* in their influence on other behaviors (e.g., enhancing reading skills would likely increase on-task behavior during reading activities) and therefore are likely to have the most generalizable impact for the student or students.

Activity 7.2, an excerpt from an actual consultation session, provides an opportunity to help you think through early problem identification and prioritization.

ACTIVITY 7.2 (INDIVIDUAL, GROUP)

Prioritizing Problems

The following is an actual excerpt from a *PID/PA* session in which a consultant and consultee prioritized concerns to address for Libby, a first-grade student. Review the transcript and answer the subsequent questions individually and, if possible, compare responses with a partner or in a small group.

> **Consultant-in-Training** *(CIT):* Okay, so what I think I'm hearing you say is that there are four main concerns for Libby. Let's try to prioritize these four areas of concern.

> **Teacher Consultee *(TC):*** I would say first the impulsivity, where she is shouting out or impulsively coming up to me without raising her hand. Second, the self-regulation. I would like to work on when it comes to structural changes and she cries because she is confused. Third, ridding her of her obsession with one peer and making more friends. Fourth, the pencil in mouth problem.

> **CIT**: That sounds like a good prioritization to me.
> **TC**: Yes, I am concerned because the impulsivity is affecting other students' work and distracting during class.
> **CIT**: Yes, and as we are prioritizing these concerns, this just means we will start with the first behavior that you would like to see change in or improve on first. From there, we can move to the other behaviors.
> **TC**: Yeah, I think this would be a good place to start because she will be able to be less egocentric and start thinking about herself and others in the classroom. Hopefully, this will help with the other issues as well.
> **CIT**: Yes, and it seems that you and Libby have developed a good relationship. But some of the concern is, how will Libby be in the future? It is important that Libby is equipped with strategies so that she can be self-aware and regulate her behaviors on her own. So hopefully, we can think of interventions that address Libby's learning.
> **TC**: Yes, it is very concerning about her future. I hope that I can help with teaching and learning and providing supports for Libby.

CIT: Well, that is very nice to hear from you. Many educators forget that they have such a large impact, and the environment can play such a large role.

TC: Right, and I worry because in a few years, she is going to have a more compartmentalized education. She will go to science class, social studies, math, reading . . . and there won't be the time to develop that sort of relationship that you can develop in primary school.

CIT: Yes, so I think now would be a great time to start putting in some strategies and trying some different things to help her. I think we have identified a great place to start.

Questions and Activities for Reflection:

1   Identify the four behaviors being discussed by the consultant and consultee.
    a. How well-operationalized are these behaviors?
2   How well did they determine which behaviors to prioritize?
    a.   In your opinion, are the "right" behaviors prioritized? Why or why not?
    b.   Should academic issues be examined? Why might you want to include those?
3   What would be your next steps as a consultant now that a behavior has been prioritized with the consultee?
    a.   How would you bring these behaviors down the "Ladder of Inferences"?
    b.   How might these behaviors be situated within the school-based context in which they are occurring?

Record Review, Ecological Observation, and Ecological Assessment

Imagine that you get to a point where you have talked about several problems on a surface level for about 15 minutes, and your meeting time is nearing its scheduled end. Again, you might perceive pressure to offer solutions (i.e., interventions), although the problem that needs to be addressed remains murky. At this point, it is a common experience for CITs to feel *stuck*, unsure of how to proceed. We propose that you and your consultee discuss what additional information is needed and decide on the next steps, such as reviewing student records, observing the instructional environment, and/or conducting an instructional assessment.

Reviewing Records, Work Samples, and Curriculum Materials

You may dive into a consultation with limited knowledge or information about a student. It makes sense to gather more information before the consultation begins and/or immediately after the first meeting when you have a better idea of the consultee's concern. One source of helpful information will be relevant work samples. For example, if an initial concern expressed by a consultee is that a third-grade student is "struggling with math," it would be helpful to learn more about the scope and sequence of the curriculum, classroom instruction, and how the teacher assesses student mastery. Following that, you may wish to look at in-class assignments, the student's patterns of performance (e.g., error analysis), and, if possible, normative comparisons with peers.

More global records may also be helpful, such as looking at the student's prior school history, including attendance, report cards, performance on state tests, and school-level benchmarking data such as CBMs. Cultural issues might also surface in this review, such as a bilingual background, in which vocabulary or prior knowledge necessary for comprehension is limited. For example, if a student is already in a remedial reading program, based on a screening test at Tier 1, but not making progress, the particular reading program in which they are placed may not be appropriate; the screening test may not have identified the student's specific concern and additional instructional assessment information may be required before the lack of progress triggers a special education referral. In fact, using screening data without additional instructional assessment of a student's knowns and unknowns within the curriculum can lead to poor decisions about intervention that delay the student's progress. In addition, some data may be misleading. For example, just because a student is performing well on standardized or norm-referenced assessments, it does not guarantee they are well-matched instructionally within the classroom (Gickling et al., 2016). Therefore, a record review in conjunction with information related to the classroom and provided by the teacher may be appropriate.

Ecological Observation

In addition to reviewing records and permanent products such as work samples, you may wish to observe in relevant settings during the times in which the problems are occurring. Observations should focus not only on the student or students of concern but the larger instructional context. Imagine attending a baseball game and only focusing your observations on first base. While you would observe the ball come and go occasionally, you would miss the rest of the action on the field. Similarly, it is beneficial to consider how the student is situated within the classroom or other settings (e.g., lunchroom, transitions, recess) rather than just observing the student.

It is beyond the scope of this chapter and book to go into depth regarding observational techniques and foci. Ysseldyke and Christenson's (2002) functional assessment of academic behavior (FAAB) provides several areas for consideration in observing instruction. We continue to find its ecological and qualitative coverage of assessment to be pertinent. Areas for potential observation described in the FAAB are listed in Table 7.2.

TABLE 7.2 Observational Targets Identified in the Functional Assessment of Academic Behavior Tool (Ysseldyke & Christenson, 2002)

Area for Observation	
	• Instructional match (material is not too easy and not too difficult for the student(s) referred)
	• Instructional expectations (high but realistic for amount and accuracy, and clearly communicated)
	• Classroom environment (positive, supportive classroom management)
	• Instructional presentation (clearly presented; sufficient information in directions; teacher checks for understanding)
	• Motivational strategies (techniques are included to enhance student interest)
	• Relevant practice (several opportunities for accurate practice)
	• Informed feedback (immediate, specific feedback, including corrections as needed)
	• Academic engaged time (active engagement/responsiveness to content)
	• Adaptive instruction (curriculum is reasonably adjusted/differentiated to meet individual students' needs)
	• Progress evaluation (direct, frequent, formative assessment of student progress, which informs future instruction)
	• Student understanding (accurate understanding of what to do and how to do it)

In addition to the FAAB, several other observational techniques may be relevant, such as the Classroom Check-up (https://www.classroomcheckup.org; Reinke et al., 2008) and the behavioral observation of students in schools (Pearson, 2013). Regardless of which tool is used, we believe problems are best understood within a nested ecological context, including consideration of the instructional environment.

Observation discussions can focus on the student as situated within the classroom context. Cultural considerations can also be explored here. Care needs to be taken in communicating observational data to the consultee during this stage for the results to be well-received. Clear agreement on the focus in advance of the observation is essential, although sometimes the observation uncovers some unexpected findings. It is always useful to provide the raw data so that the analysis can be conducted together with the teacher; this is even more essential if the data have some unexpected surprises for the teacher. For example, in one case, a CIT's observation in a kindergarten classroom during centertime (where students worked independently at activity areas set up around the classroom) clearly indicated that many students were engaging in inappropriate behavior and that both the quality of the activities and classroom management of the centers were inadequate. The teacher had brought up one student in the consultation, but it was clear from the observation that the problem behavior was widely shared. At times in such instances, the referred student is from a marginalized racial or ethnic background, and implicit bias may play a role in the referral concern. Reviewing observation data alerts the consultation dyad of potential inconsistencies that can be discussed and addressed within the context of a collaborative relationship. In the case described, the shared discussion of the observation data guided the teacher toward considering broad-based classroom management strategies rather than a single, intensive behavior intervention for one child. The communication skills of clarifying and reflecting feelings became useful adjuncts to this consultation session as the implications of the observation became apparent to the teacher.

Ecological Academic Assessment

A third way additional data may be gathered is through processes of academic assessment to determine instructional match. The Instructional Consultation (IC) model requires an ecological academic assessment in almost every case of a classroom concern. Consultants without a strong background in academic assessment and instruction often focus on classroom behavior rather than a connection between behavior and academic frustration of students.

Ecological academic assessment strategies include instructional assessment (Gickling et al., 2016) or curriculum-based assessment by instructional design (Burns & Parker, 2014). Although a full review of these techniques is beyond the scope of the chapter and book, readers are referred to these resources for details on working with consultees to implement ecological academic assessment practices. The idea is that we can assess students within an ecological academic framework that accounts for students' prior knowledge and experiences, task expectations, and instructional practices with a focus on questions illustrated in Figure 7.2, originally articulated by Gickling et al. (2016). These questions are helpful conceptualizers during *PID/PA*, as well as throughout the entirety of the problem-solving process.

This type of instructional assessment has taken on increased relevance with the ongoing disruption of schooling due to the Covid pandemic. Kuhfeld et al. (2020),

FIGURE 7.2   Instructional Assessment Questions

projecting the academic impact of disrupted schooling, stressed the importance of being able to pinpoint each student's academic level within the curriculum, which is not possible with screening tests. They also noted that there would likely be strong differences among students because of the highly variable conditions encountered by students during the pandemic. Being able to determine growth rates and set learning goals are also skills needed by school staff. Such issues are more pressing with many students of color, whose school disruption has been even more severe. Consultation support in this domain to teachers and school specialists becomes an even higher priority than previously.

Baseline

After a concern is prioritized, whether an academic or behavioral issue, and some additional information is gathered through records, observation, or ecological instructional assessment strategies, you and the consultee will continue to work to achieve an observable and measurable definition of the problem (including who, what, where, and when). When it is clear that the problem is operationally defined, the identified problem can be measured precisely and becomes the statement of current performance, or the baseline. Once the baseline is measured, this level of performance can be used to set goals for improvement. During the intervention evaluation stage of problem-solving, goals can be considered in conjunction with this baseline to determine if the intervention is working and, if not, what can be done about it.

Setting Goals

Goals stem directly from the baseline data; they specify an aim line for closing gaps between a student's current performance and expected performance in the problem area that you have prioritized. Goal statements focus on alterable, measurable behaviors; set benchmarks for a standard of comparison; specify target dates for completion; and set standards or social comparisons to consider progress (Kratochwill et al., 2014). Whenever possible, desirable performance should be the focus of a goal, even when the problem is maladaptive behavior (Pluymert, 2014). For example, in one consultation case (Pas, 2012), a CIT and consultee agreed to focus on *increasing* a target student's verbal requests to peers as a replacement behavior for invading the peers' space, and they set goals on the former behavior rather than the latter.

Knowledge of the scope and sequence of the curriculum is essential to academic goal setting as it indicates formative and summative expectations for student progress in that grade level and classroom. It is also essential to know the teacher's expectations for students, both academically and behaviorally, as there is sometimes misalignment with the curriculum. One teacher expected all kindergarten students in her high-achieving school to be able to read upon entering school, and indeed, many did; however, it was beyond the curricular expectations for kindergarten. It is not difficult to imagine the challenges a non-reader would have in this class despite not technically beginning the year below grade level, particularly if the students who entered as non-readers were from a different cultural or socio-economic background or were younger in chronological age.

Goal-Setting Methods

Several approaches can be used for goal setting. For now, let us consider three approaches that CITs in our classes have found helpful in their cases: the use of norms, splitting the difference, and the 25% rule. Irrespective of which of these approaches (or if another approach) is used, remember that goals should be established collaboratively with the consultee, consistent with the entire collaborative problem-solving process.

Normative data provide consultants and consultees information regarding typical rates of students' academic or behavioral progress and expected levels of performance. National norms, such as those established by CBMs, are appropriate to use when these data are aligned with the target behavior (e.g., reading fluency) and the local curriculum's scope and sequence (e.g., sometimes the order of curricular objectives can differ between reading programs). However, local norms (e.g., classroom, school, district) have the advantage of providing estimates of typical performance specific to your setting, curriculum, or a particular population (e.g., students learning English as a second language in your school). For example, in one case, a teacher consultee collected weekly brief written responses from all students in her class. When one student was struggling with writing, the teacher worked with a CIT to analyze writing samples according to a scoring rubric (Fuchs & Fuchs, 2011). The permanent product data acted as both a baseline measure and a way to assess student progress over multiple weeks for all students in her class. Typical rates of progress could be used to estimate short-term (e.g., four to six weeks) and long-term (e.g., 12 weeks) goals for the student. The use of local norms also allows the consultant and consultee to consider if other students they had not initially targeted would also benefit from an intervention.

Another way to set goals is the split-the-difference method. The dyad begins by estimating short-term and long-term goals, which are informed by available information such as norms, the curriculum, or teacher expectations. The short-term goal can then be subtracted from the long-term goal, and the difference between them can be divided in half to estimate an interim goal. Once the intervention is implemented, the dyad will determine the ongoing rate of progress made by the student and readjust the interim goal as needed.

The 25% rule posits that for many problems, a short-term improvement of 25% would demonstrate strong initial progress. Therefore, after measuring baseline data, the dyad takes 25% of the baseline and adds that number to the baseline to create a short-term goal. For example, if a student is reading 30 words per minute,

30×0.25 is 7.5, and therefore the short-term goal would be 37.5 words per minute in approximately six weeks. Given the student's progress over those first few weeks, the consultant and teacher can estimate a rate of improvement. Again, the long-term goal is established based on where the dyad ultimately would like to see the student perform. While it is easy to calculate the short-term goal using the 25% method, it is possible to over- or underestimate the short-term goal.

Documenting PID/PA

One tool that has been developed to document the problem-solving process, including PID/PA and subsequent stages, is the Student Documentation Form (SDF; see Appendix F). Although the tool was developed specifically for the implementation of IC and IC Teams (Gravois et al., 2011; Rosenfield, 2012), we find its features are relevant to any model of consultation, including the SC model presented in this book. Although additional training on the SDF would be helpful, at a minimum, a consultant can use this tool to write out and prioritize problems with the consultee, as well as document the intervention upon which the consultation dyad has agreed. The use of the graph is a tool to help monitor progress and is linked with enhanced problem-solving outcomes for students (Shapiro, 2011). The school in which you are doing your consulting work might have its own tool or process to document problem-solving. Regardless of which tool you use, it should: (a) clearly document and guide the entire problem-solving process, including the identified concern with baseline data, description of the intervention, and the implementation schedule (who, what, when, where), (b) include a graph documenting student progress, and (c) be used in a collaborative manner with your consultee.

PID/PA Big Ideas

Up to now, we have focused on describing the nuts and bolts of the PID/PA stage, or the *content* of PID/PA. Next, we turn to six Big Ideas with relevance to this stage. Big Ideas #1, #2, and #3 were originally introduced in Chapter 5, and Big Ideas #4, #5, and #6 are new to this chapter. Readers should refer to Appendix D for the full list of Big Ideas, which will help prime you for the subsequent activities. We urge you to keep these Big Ideas in mind as you engage in the PID/PA stage, as they should inform the *process* of interactions during this stage.

Big Idea #1: Complex problems, such as those found in schools, rarely have simple or linear solutions. As described in Chapter 5, despite our genuine desire to provide immediate help when a teacher or other consultee is struggling, providing a singular, simple fix that will alleviate concerns is not the norm. Solving complex problems require active listening, genuine curiosity, and mental flexibility for perspective-taking; content expertise (e.g., having an intervention in your back pocket to offer the consultee) in and of itself is not enough.

Activity 7.3 contains a transcribed excerpt from a *PID/PA* session and demonstrates Big Idea #1. Read through the transcript and consider the subsequent questions.

ACTIVITY 7.3 (INDIVIDUAL, GROUP)

Big Idea #1

The following is an actual excerpt from a *PID/PA* session in which a consultant and consultee were identifying concerns for several first-grade students, beginning with Kyle. Review the transcript and answer the subsequent questions individually and, if possible, compare responses with a partner or in a small group.

Teacher Consultee *(TC)*: Okay. When are we going to start something in the class and get something going, because I really need it?

Consultant-in-Training *(CIT)*: Well, that's part of what the [Evidence-Based Intervention] is about, which is why I think it's important to go through because it's basically going through . . .

TC: Is there any way that you could maybe do a small group, too? Like sooner, so we can start them on trying to do something.

CIT: Yeah, about? So, you are not clear what this group is intervening about, are you?

TC: You know, shouting out even, that would be fine. Being disrespectful. Kyle's very disrespectful, to me, to his classmates, to whoever the teacher is.

CIT: That's obviously an issue.

TC: And the opposite is another student, Deanna: she sucks her thumb and hides in her shirt, doesn't look at you . . . walks away, doesn't answer. So maybe even if you put them together [in an intervention group], they're together on other things. If you put them together, they could learn how to get in the middle . . . And then I have this other one, Marjorie . . . She's okay, she's pretty quiet, and she could probably benefit from it too.

CIT: A small group is definitely something we can get going separately. I just really wanted to have something in place in your classroom that we can collaborate on.

TC: Yeah, I just wanted to . . . That's fine too, but I need Kyle to get started on something because Check In Check Out does nothing.

CIT: And that's something, too . . . looking at the match between the student, the instruction, and the task, so when you set up the student for success in the classroom, it really . . .

TC: I mean, he needs instant praise 24 hours a day. I always have feathers; I try to give him feathers. I try to call on him, but I can't call on him every single time. I try to call on him, and then I call on someone else two seconds later, and he gets upset because he is the world. And I can't . . . because then if you call on him all the time, then Deanna starts crying, and then she doesn't get a feather, and then multiple other things happen . . .

CIT: And that's something that we can really work on too. It seems contradictory, because when you have students displaying these problem behaviors, what [the Evidence-Based Intervention] suggests is that you promote frequent positive interactions with them. They need more. An average student maybe needs a "great, good job," but the students who misbehave so much need that ratio to increase, which is kind of counterintuitive.

TC: So if there's any way you can do anything with those three [students]. . . Or maybe you can even do something with Kyle.

Questions for Reflection:

This is not a simple issue to address, is it?! But let's begin with the most basic issue, operationally defining a complex situation.

1   What problem or problems(s) are the consultant and consultee working on?
    a.   In your opinion, are the problems sufficiently defined? Why or why not?
    b.   How would you move forward to define behaviors?
2   The consultant has an evidence-based intervention in mind. Identify some problems with offering this intervention at this point in the process.

Big Idea #2: The problems school consultants attempt to solve are situated within a school-based context and should be defined accordingly. As introduced in Chapter 5, for effective problem identification and analysis, it is essential to remember that problems are situated within a school-based context. Rosenfield (2022) emphasized, for "SCHOOL [consultants], the ecological context of schools and schooling is key. The school is an organization that can support academic and personal growth or contribute to the opposite outcomes" (p. 7). The best school consultants avoid irrelevant or red-herring variables (e.g., an overemphasis on unalterable variables such as intelligence) and focus on the student's match within the instructional environment within which they are situated. Consider how you might respond to the teacher or social worker in the next activity if you were the consultant.

ACTIVITY 7.4 (INDIVIDUAL, GROUP)

Problem-Solving Within an Ecological Context

Look at the following actual interaction between a teacher consultee and a social worker consultee about an academic problem during a consultation about a first-grade student. Answer the subsequent questions individually and, if possible, compare responses with a partner or in a small group.

Teacher Consultee: I still don't think we really understand what the problem is up here (points to head). There is something wrong.

Social Worker Consultee: And we are not neurologists.

Questions for Reflection:

1   If you were the consultant, how would you respond to these comments?

As described earlier in this chapter and in Chapter 1, consulting ecologically or with an ecobehavioral lens means thinking about the student and his or her interactions with the curriculum, the teacher's instruction and management strategies, and the broader school culture. When problems are operationalized with instructional factors in mind, problems become *solvable* within the classroom setting. Behavioral problems are also initially situated within an instructional context, as misbehavior may result from things like unclear instructional expectations, insufficient motivational techniques, or an instructional match that is too easy or frustrating for the student. And some behaviors result from inadequate classroom management strategies.

The following transcribed excerpt demonstrates how a CIT worked with a second-grade teacher consultee to move from storytelling to a more focused, school-situated problem definition over the course of one *PID/PA* session. We have included *italicized written reflection* by the consultant regarding the transcription, which demonstrates her struggle to help move the dyad toward a focus within the consultee's classroom setting in which they could realistically intervene.

Consultant-in-Training (CIT): In addition to the Reading Mastery [pullout intervention], what kind of support would you expect her to get [in your classroom]?

Teacher Consultee (TC): I almost feel like maybe we need to have some kind of meeting with mom, the nurse, and me. And say, "These are the expectations. She needs her medicine." I wonder if either the medicine is not right or she is not getting it. Because her being out of her seat . . . something is wrong with that. And then from there, maybe seeing how that goes if her medicine is changed. Because I know the Reading Mastery teacher is seeing the same behaviors where she is totally not focused, she is worried about "what's in your lunch"; I guess is something she says a lot, because the other teacher's lunch is on her desk . . . she is unfocused.

CIT: So how could that meeting happen? Could you arrange it? Who needs to arrange it?

TC: Well, the problem is that mom doesn't have a working phone . . .

CIT: So getting a hold of her is a problem.

TC: Yeah.

CIT: So, does a letter need to be sent home? Have you been able to communicate with her that way?

TC: Yeah, and she expects that packet to be filled out, and I've started, but that's a process in itself; it is like 11 pages . . .

CIT: So maybe that is an opportunity where she could get the packet, and you could also meet . . .

TC: Well, the packet has to be mailed to the Social Security office.

The teacher continued to express obstacles to meeting with [the student's] mom. I think this piece of our conversation is an example of our different agendas in the conversation. I was "solution-focused," while the teacher was interested in venting. It got us into a back-and-forth without ever reaching a solution. The discussion led back to the student and special education, so I tried to rephrase the original question:

CIT: What would those minutes be? What would that support look like?

TC: First of all, she would have to be tested. So I guess that would be the start to see how low she really is, and then from there, I could say, "Well, she should get support in this and this . . ." definitely math. Well, definitely reading, but I would think math too.

CIT: Okay, so she is getting reading support, and you would think that she would need additional to that, and also some support in math?

TC: Yeah. Here is her report card.

Again, I felt that the conversation veered off from my goal. So, I tried to restate my question a third time:

CIT: What additional support would you want her to get in addition to Reading Mastery?

TC: Sight words . . . blending. I know Reading Mastery is blending, but I think she needs more of it, consistently.

CIT: So I'm just thinking if we could take what is already going on in Reading Mastery. So, if we are focusing on one thing at a time, which would be that reading is your biggest concern, she is getting Reading Mastery; she does probably need a little more time to see progress. What could we do in the classroom to reinforce what she is doing with Reading Mastery? Like sounds and blending. Maybe she is not getting that sight word component, and she needs that also.

Following this interchange, the dyad went on to define the student's current reading skills and needs more clearly, and eventually planned an intervention focused on streamlining and supplementing the supports she was already receiving. Notably, over multiple subsequent sessions, the conversation did not return to a focus on medication or familial context, two issues that were outside of the dyad's immediate control.

Big Idea #3: Everything we do is an intervention. We initially introduced Big Idea #3 in Chapter 5 and revisited it in Chapter 6 with respect to Contracting. Early interactions, including attaining consent for consultation and laying out clear expectations, may be considered interventions in and of themselves. The processes of problem-solving embedded in the *PID/PA* stage may also be considered interventions.

For instance, the following is an example of a consultee's changing frame of a problem, again from a real example as described by the consultant in a final reflection, demonstrating a turning in one teacher's problem representation and presentation:

> After 18 weeks of working together, the teacher was still open to share what she's been working on with the student and how things are going. On my part, I think I offered a lot of support through listening, sharing my representation of the problem, and simply keeping the process going. A couple of weeks after being asked to reflect on what would change when her student would meet eligibility criteria for special education, the teacher told me that she knew that special education eligibility won't change the fact that Amalia would still be her student, and the teacher would be looking for ways to include her in the general curriculum because she felt confident in that and in knowing what Amalia can do. For me, this was the greatest metamorphosis and turning in my teacher's perception about the student that began from the "student can't do" attitude to being empowered to do more things with the student on her instructional level. This turning had an impact on how the teacher was engaged in implementing our interventions.

You can further reflect on the process of conceptual turning by completing Activity 7.5.

ACTIVITY 7.5 (INDIVIDUAL, GROUP)

Big Idea #3

The following are actual excerpts from a teacher consultee over the course of multiple *PID/PA* sessions in which a consultant and consultee were identifying concerns for a first-grade student, Amalia (the same case the CIT reflected upon previously). Review the examples and answer the subsequent questions individually and, if possible, compare responses with a partner or in a small group.

Initial Presentation Statements	Subsequent Presentation Statements
• She has forgotten how to act in school – not that she was doing great with that – but she was catching on to a few things, and I moved a few desks because they were all irritated with each other. • Yes, it is a new group and somebody she gets along with, but she cannot sit down, she can't pay attention, she's talking all the time. • I'm not sure if here is the best placement. I don't make those decisions, and I understand the least restrictive [environment], but I also look at her come and go, and she needs a lot of attention. There is no classroom teacher with 26 kids who has time to do that. If there were two teachers and 20 kids, maybe.	• And there are workbook pages that go with that, too, that have the same characters in it, and we'll have the same sounds, so I'll be working on that. She did more when we were doing worksheets, so when there is one word that starts with the letter B, she can usually find it, but if there are two that start with the letter B, we have to start looking at. Maybe I can look at the end of the word because yesterday we had *boot* and *book*, and she wasn't sure which one was which, so she is still looking at the beginning of the word. It's a huge improvement from where she was. • There is a lot of improvement and a lot of things to do. She is a little more independent in a sense . . . she says "I can do that" or . . . even when we started telling time and she wasn't sure about how to do. But we've only done a little bit, and once I showed her how to do it, it was like, okay!

Questions for Reflection:

1   What differences do you notice between the earlier *PID/PA* sessions and the later *PID/PA* sessions in terms of how the teacher consultee represents the problem?
2   What are the implications for the differences in problem solvability?
3   What process interventions (*ProInts*) can you think of that might have shifted the course of problem-solving, including a teacher's representation and presentation of a student problem, in the ways demonstrated by this example?

Big Idea #4: Problem operationalization stems from listening and seeking clarification, not from asking scripted questions; communication skills are critical. During all problem stages, especially the *PID/PA* stage, the most foundational communication skills you can apply are paraphrasing and clarifying the information offered by the consultee. As you listen carefully to the consultee's presentation of the problem, you can begin to see the problem through the consultee's eyes.

Listening can be difficult, especially for CITs. Bringing a script of pre-packaged questions to the consultation session without knowing what information the consultee is going to offer can make it even more difficult for you to be mindful or fully present in a consultation meeting. It is easy to become too focused on what to ask or say next rather than what the consultee is saying. In turn, you may not accurately hear the consultee's concerns or, worse yet, respond in a manner that is far removed from how the consultee is conceptualizing the problem. Such interactions can be detrimental to: (a) building a relationship based on a genuine interest in the consultee's problem and (b) co-conceptualizing the right problem to solve.

This is not to suggest that you should arrive at the consultation session unprepared. In advance of a meeting, you can take actions such as gathering appropriate background case information and thinking through pertinent points for clarification and discussion. However, such an agenda should be flexible and adapted based on the emergent needs of the consultee and the student or students of concern.

Following is an example of a consultation with an art teacher consultee. After the teacher shared some information, the CIT asked a scripted question without clearly having listened to the teacher:

> **Teacher Consultee** *(TC)*: They have a lot of free time in here, and it really backfires on us. It's the constant noise level. They do get out of their seats a lot, they make excuses to sharpen their pencils, and they get up to use the hand sanitizer 300 times a day. So, they want to do everything opposite of what I'm telling them to do.
>
> **Consultant-in-Training (CIT)**: Do you notice a time of day when . . . is this happening at the beginning of the period with them?

Although it is appropriate for the CIT to be thinking about what time of day the behavior was occurring, the question was poorly phrased and did not stem directly from information provided by the teacher. Instead, the CIT might have used a clarifying statement such as: "Tell me more about the free time," or paraphrased and clarified: "It sounds like you have expectations that are not being followed. What are some of those expectations?" Arguably, such communications would have been more successful in demonstrating that the CIT was listening and then moving to clarify the consultee's information, which was too broad to specify patterns (e.g., "300 times a day").

Given the CIT's question, here was the consultee's response:

> **TC**: It's the whole hour. Sometimes they walk in noisy, and I have to get them to line up in the hallway. I say, "Okay, guys, when I have to start the day like this . . ." I try to be really calm. Sometimes they walk in and they're so loud it's ridiculous. It's tricky because when we start off the day on the wrong foot . . . and there is a good group of kids – they're amazing. And they are irritated because we're starting five minutes later. They yell at each other, like, "Stop talking! We're going to get in trouble!" You hear a lot of that, and you feel bad because . . .

Although more information was offered, it didn't get the dyad much further in terms of operationalizing the problem.

Next, the CIT took a more flexible approach in her communication, offering information that she had noticed in a recent classroom observation, which was related to what she heard the teacher describe. The observation description affirmed some of the teacher's positive instructional practices. This interaction moved them forward in problem-solving more effectively and led to more specific behavioral descriptions. Activity 7.6 is a good opportunity to practice the communication skills presented in Chapter 4.

ACTIVITY 7.6 (INDIVIDUAL, GROUP)

Big Idea #4

Read the following excerpt from an actual consultation session. Based on the underlined pieces of information from the teacher consultee (TC) in this transcript, answer the subsequent questions individually and, if possible, compare responses with a partner or in a small group.

Consultant-in-Training (CIT): When I was here [observing], I felt like they did a really good job with putting effort into their masks and following the directions you were giving. You're always doing hands-on activities.

Teacher Consultee (TC): I haven't thought about that, really. I'll have to pay closer attention to that. They'll go in waves. If they're engaged in their activity, the noise level sometimes does get louder. Then I'll break and say, "freeze," and sometimes it works. Sometimes I'll turn off the lights, or I'll redirect them to the carpet. It's okay to talk . . . you'll have the kids that are talking but are doing what they're supposed to be doing shouting at the kids that aren't, and it'll take more minutes out of art. My guess is that when they're more involved in the activity, [they'll get louder].

Questions and Activities for Reflection:

1   How would you respond to demonstrate you heard the teacher? Write a response and identify the communication skill(s) you are using.
2   How would you respond to continue to move forward in identifying observable and measurable problems? Write a response and identify the communication skill(s) you are using.

Big Idea #5: Accurate problem operationalization precedes well-matched intervention planning. Before selecting and then implementing an intervention, it is necessary to first operationalize the problem clearly. This is a consistent theme throughout the text and is logical, considering *PID/PA* precedes intervention. However, consultants still often fall into the trap of offering solutions prior to the dyad adequately understanding the problem. Educational researcher Anthony Bryk (2015) termed this issue "solutionitis," as school leaders are often guilty of quickly attempting solutions without sufficient insight into the problem(s) that are being addressed. Activity 7.7 compares two transcriptions in two different consultation cases. Review the transcriptions and answer the questions.

ACTIVITY 7.7 (INDIVIDUAL, GROUP)

Big Idea #5

Read the following excerpts from actual consultation meetings. Answer the subsequent questions individually and, if possible, compare responses with a partner or in a small group.

Actual consultation excerpt from a meeting between a consultant and a kindergarten teacher for a student named Charlie	Actual consultation excerpt from a meeting between a consultant and a kindergarten teacher for a student named Javier
Consultant-in-Training (CIT): So last week, when we met, we started talking about how Charlie is impulsive in class, and he does things like not raising his hand and shouting out. Could you give me more examples of that impulsivity in the classroom?	**TC**: I would say defiance. Like defiance, if you ask him to do something, he will look at you and walk away. Or he will escape and find something else that he . . . he'll go and talk to a different teacher. We have two teachers in here. So he'll go and try and talk to me. If I give him a prompt to go do something, he'll go and talk to the other teacher, and he's constantly just avoiding doing tasks.
Teacher Consultee (TC): He doesn't sit still very well on the carpet, and I don't know if that's because he's bigger and he's not comfortable . . . his legs are always out, and he's hitting people. He tries, you know, and he's always apologizing, but I don't think he's aware he's moving so much until a kid looks at him like, "You just bumped me!" So that whole . . ."this is my space, and I should stay in it" isn't always working for him . . .	**CIT**: So it seems that Javier has trouble following through with instructions, and he is avoiding it by either going and talking to other students or teachers. Is that distracting in the classroom to other students?
CIT: Tell me a little more about the carpet and how that works with the kids.	**TC**: Yes. Especially when we're on the carpet, and we're all so close together, and he'll constantly try to talk to other kids or turn his body around or laugh or make jokes. And that gets the rest of the kids around him off-task.

TC: They each have a square that they sit in, so sometimes I have noticed that he does have a hard time because the squares . . . I mean, they're not little, but . . .

CIT: And he's not exactly a little kid . . .

TC: He takes up the whole square because he's not a little kid . . . so there have been times when I've moved him: "Okay, you can sit in this square because there's no one in front of you, and then if you have to put your feet out you can put your feet out . . . but you can't do that if you want to sit in the middle of the carpet because that's someone else's space in front of you." Sometimes he doesn't like to move away from the class, and he tries, you can see he's thinking, "sit still, sit still," but then he might not always be paying attention as much to what we are doing . . .

CIT: So I guess next time we could discuss possible interventions for that. Is that something that sounds good to you?

TC: Yes, I would love to have something to implement in the classroom to help him.

Questions and Activities for Reflection:

1 For each column, write down an observable and measurable problem with the information that you have.
2 Of these two excerpts, which one do you believe demonstrates a more clearly defined problem?
3 Of these two excerpts, which would be easier to intervene upon now?
4 For the less well-defined problem, what information would you need to get closer to a clearly operationalized problem?

The dialogue on the left shows how in a brief interaction, a dyad may move from a problem definition that is high on the Ladder of Inferences and internal to a child ("impulsivity") to a more clearly defined problem, in this case, Charlie's carpet square is too small for his body. We can surmise that the carpet setup was an antecedent to the student's behavior, whether the behavior was defined as impulsive, off-task, disrespectful, disruptive, or anything else. Indeed, once an intervention was implemented to adjust Charlie's carpet square, he experienced dramatic behavioral improvement. Meanwhile, the dyad on the right side of the column had more difficulty determining appropriate next steps for an intervention because the problem was not yet well-defined.

Following is another example, an actual excerpt from a *PID/PA* session in which a consultant and consultee discussed concerns to address for a third-grade student named Logan following a classroom observation by the consultant. Review the transcript and answer the subsequent questions individually and, if possible, compare responses with a partner or in a small group.

ACTIVITY 7.8 (INDIVIDUAL, GROUP)
Big Idea #5

Consultant-in-Training (CIT): Yeah, and I noticed a pattern at the end of each of the independent tasks. If it was something he finished before everyone else, that's when he'd start being, I guess, not off-task because he was done with the task, but it was disruptive, like movement or noise, something like that. That can be something we could focus on.

Teacher Consultee (TC): Great.

CIT: Then these tasks that he didn't finish early, like he was working until the end, then he didn't do that.

TC: Right. That's great. I'm glad that you were able because now it makes sense looking at the data. But like, in my head, I would never have been able to process that at the end of each independent session.

[later in the same session]

TC: Yeah, it was a review sheet, which actually makes sense because he would have already known it.

CIT: Okay, so review sheet, and he was extra noisy. So maybe on days like that when he doesn't need the review as much as other students . . . and then January 8. . .

TC: January 8 was the beginning of the unit, so we really hadn't done much of it. It's higher-order numbers, writing numbers into the millions, which is pretty challenging for kids because they can't read it.

CIT: And he wasn't very disruptive. Aha!!!

TC: And also, it might be interesting; we're doing another review sheet next week. It might be interesting to calculate the review sheet day again just to see if it's consistent. All right, great, thank you, that's exciting to see a pattern; that's kind of cool!

Questions and Activities for Reflection:

1   How did data help the dyad identify a pattern that was important for identifying the "right" problem to work on?
2   How might other data have been misleading?

Big Idea #6: More data aren't necessarily better data when it comes to understanding and solving problems. Consultative problem-solving is akin to solving a mystery, with the consultant in the role of detective. Therefore, let's take some advice from the great Sherlock Holmes about solving problems:

> "The principal difficulty in your case," remarked Holmes in his didactic fashion, "lay in the fact of there being too much evidence. What was vital was overlaid and hidden by what was irrelevant. Of all the facts which were presented to us we had to pick just those which we deemed to be essential, and then piece them together in their order, so as to reconstruct this very remarkable chain of events."
>
> *(Conan Doyle, 1894, p. 236)*

Indeed, consultants and consultees are often awash with data, some of which is vital to the case and some of which is irrelevant or distracting. For example, one consultation dyad was unsure how to proceed when a fifth grader's nationally normed CBM data indicated reading fluency to be comparable with peers, but the student struggled to read fluently in the classroom setting. Although both pieces of data were relevant to understanding the problem, the CIT needed to refocus the consultation on the student's and teacher's experience of the problem in the classroom setting and the context of a high-achieving school culture. In another instance, a teacher consultee frequently referenced data from a student's special education evaluation, including cognitive assessment scores, in trying to define the problem. The frustrated CIT did not believe these data were relevant to their problem identification or intervention planning but was unsure how to redirect the consultation focus.

Activity 7.9 is intended to help CITs think through the common challenge of discussing data with a consultee when the data differ from the consultee's description of the problem.

ACTIVITY 7.9 (INDIVIDUAL, GROUP)

Big Idea #6

Sometimes it can be difficult to share observation data with a consultee, particularly if what you observe is different than what the consultee reports is happening. Read the following case study and then answer the subsequent questions individually and, if possible, compare responses with a partner or in a small group.

As part of a consultation case, you observe in the classroom to support a student named Lucinda, whom the teacher reports is having behavioral difficulties. You observe a chaotic classroom lacking one or more of the evidence-based classroom management practices identified by Ysseldyke and

Christenson's (2002) FAAB, as described earlier in this chapter. The teacher also discusses Lucinda's family background, including that she lives in a single-parent family currently relying on food stamps. Lucinda is the youngest of seven siblings, and two of her brothers were suspended from school during the prior school year due to truancy. Lucinda is no more "off-task" than others in the class.

Questions and Activities for Reflection:

1   What information do you think is relevant?
2   How might you approach this conversation with the teacher consultee?
3   What challenges do you predict might arise in this conversation?
4   What would you do if you suspected issues related to implicit bias may be involved?

Summary

PID/PA is considered the most pivotal stage in the SC model, an essential prerequisite to successful intervention. During *PID/PA*, the consultant and consultee create a shared understanding of the problem(s) to be solved through discussion, observation, and data collection; they prioritize a concern to be addressed first; define the problem in observable and measurable terms; measure baseline performance; and establish goals to close the gap between current performance and expected performance. Since consultation is an indirect service, consultants attend to consultee needs (i.e., knowledge, skill, self-confidence, and professional objectivity) in addition to student needs during this stage.

There are numerous challenges that emerge during the *PID/PA* stage. Consultants must clarify high-inference consultee language, including guiding the problem-solving beyond surface-level problem descriptors, and avoid the temptation to prematurely intervene or prescribe solutions. By working through the numerous activities provided in this chapter, and bearing in mind the chapter's six Big Ideas, we hope you will feel more prepared to accurately identify and understand problems in collaboration with your consultee, thus boosting your chances for subsequent intervention success.

8

DESIGNING AND IMPLEMENTING INTERVENTIONS

It's Not Magic – It's Planning, Monitoring, and Performance Feedback

Those who plan do better than those who do not plan, even should they rarely stick to their plan.

However beautiful the strategy, you should occasionally look at the results.

(Winston Churchill)

In this chapter, we overview two stages of problem-solving related to interventions: (1) *Intervention Planning*, and (2) *Intervention Implementation, Monitoring, and Performance Feedback*. Before moving too far along, consider your own prior experiences with interventions in schools.

ACTIVITY 8.1 (INDIVIDUAL)

Warm-Up Questions: Intervention Stages

Think about an intervention that you have designed and implemented or observed during any school-based experience you have had thus far in your professional training or in practice. Write down reflections on your prior experiences with interventions in schools. You can write down sentences or just key words.

1   Was the intervention successful? Why or why not?
2   What did you learn about designing, implementing, and evaluating interventions?
3   Did you consider the empirical evidence for the intervention?

DOI: 10.4324/9781032622330-8

One lesson we have learned over our combined years of consulting and supervising consultation is that *interventions are not magic, and consultants are not magicians.* Careful planning is necessary for implementation to occur with fidelity. It is essential for the consultant and consultee to continue to work together during this stage (Noell et al., 2017). First, as stated in Big Idea #1 in Chapter 5, complex problems such as those that arise in schools rarely have simple solutions. Even interventions that boast an excellent evidence base will not work for every child in every context and may not work instantly or may lose their effects over time. Secondly, interventions are not implemented with the flick of a magic wand. It takes effort, time, flexibility, and collaboration to put an intervention into place, to keep it working successfully, and to achieve behavior maintenance and generalization. This is even truer when the intervention is designed to impact more than one student, a group, or a school. Even in baseball, according to the former New York Mets' President Sandy Alderson, "What differentiates teams now is not the ability to comprehend new ideas . . . but the ability to implement those new ideas throughout an organization." Whether in schools or in baseball, effective implementation is the holy grail of consultation.

During the *Intervention Planning* stage of problem-solving, the consultation dyad establishes an appropriate intervention to implement, one based on the identified problem from the *Problem Identification and Problem Analysis (PID/PA)* stage. As part of the process of implementation, it is necessary to determine who will implement the intervention as well as when, where, and how often it will be implemented. Subsequently, through ongoing data review and discussion during the *Intervention Implementation, Monitoring, and Performance Feedback* stage of problem-solving, the consultant and consultee consider what is working and what is not working with the intervention and what steps to take next. This chapter overviews more specifically what is to be accomplished during each of these two related problem-solving stages. Consultation processes that facilitate successful stage navigation are also highlighted. Several real examples and activities are integrated throughout the chapter to enhance your knowledge and skills during these two stages.

The Nuts and Bolts of Intervention Planning

In the *Intervention Planning* stage of problem-solving, the consultant and consultee select an intervention that matches the baseline problem established during *PID/PA*. The purpose and business of the intervention planning stage is described in Table 8.1.

Scan QR code 8.1 to view a video of Dr. Elise Pas discussing the implementation process and its intersection with the problem-solving skills we have been presenting.

QR CODE 8.1   Elise Pas Video

TABLE 8.1 Purpose and Business of the Intervention Planning Stage of Problem-Solving

Intervention Planning	
Purpose	• Collaboratively develop instructional and/or behavioral management strategies targeting goals
Business	• Elicit consultee's ideas/strategies • Discuss: *What* classroom-based strategy will meet goals? *Where* will strategy be implemented? *When* can strategy be implemented? *How often* will strategy be implemented? *Who* will be responsible? • Consider conditions to create/maintain instructional match • Consider if multiple students can benefit from the intervention • Document specifics of what, when, how often, and who

Selecting the Intervention

Select Research-based Interventions When Possible

Interventions may be selected from several pre-existing academic, behavioral, or social-emotional programs with manualized curricula and strong foundations of evidence. We term them here Evidence-Based Interventions (uppercase EBI). Alternatively, the consultant and consultee may collaboratively design an intervention based on strong evidence-based principles underlying effective prevention or treatment, that is *kernels* of behavior management (e.g., Embry & Biglan, 2008) or instruction (e.g., Ysseldyke & Christenson, 2002) targeted to match student needs, and the consultee's classroom context and instructional needs. We term these interventions evidence-based interventions (lowercase ebi). Both EBIs and ebis are informed by empirical data, making them research-based interventions that can be appropriate to incorporate in consultative problem-solving. The evidence base behind EBIs and ebis suggests they are interventions with a high likelihood of success when implemented as intended; therefore, they are an appropriate starting point during intervention planning as opposed to low-value practices without evidential support (Shaw, 2021). Some examples of consultation interventions implemented by consultants-in-training (CITs) and teacher consultees during a recent semester of consultation training are provided in Table 8.2.

Intervention Flexibility

Table 8.2 contains both EBIs and ebis and mentions modifications made to interventions when they were implemented. When interventions are adapted to fit

TABLE 8.2 Examples of Interventions in Consultation Cases During a Recently Instructed School Consultation Course

Interventions

- Pre-teaching and reviewing vocabulary from an evidence-based reading curriculum
- Incremental rehearsal to teach sight words
- Incremental rehearsal for letter sounds and sound blends; adapted to include speed naming for known sounds, teacher-made stories, and more direct instruction
- Planned Discussion with the student regarding disruptive behavior, combined with verbal praise from the teacher, self-monitoring, and reward motivator
- Supporting the teacher to implement an evidence-based classroom management program
- Coordinating carpet space for a "bigger" kindergarten student so he wouldn't bother peers, discussion with the student about boundaries, teaching behavior through examples/non-examples
- Classroom setup rearrangement (e.g., no kids seated behind teacher)
- Sticker reward, with immediacy and frequent review, to combat refusal behavior/reward compliance
- Point system with rewards
- Stickers to promote on-task behavior
- Online math intervention for practicing basic math facts to promote fluency
- Behavior Intervention Plan with "mini-interventions" at Antecedents, Behavior (e.g., Instructional strategies), and Consequence stages
- Clarifying step-by-step oral directions (the original problem was "too many redirections") by providing a written list on a whiteboard at the student's desk
- Visual checklist as a reminder of things to take home from school/bring to school
- Previewing vocabulary with individual students, and as intervention progressed, with the whole class

the individualized context of implementation, they achieve "*flexibility within fidelity*" (Kendall & Beidas, 2007), thereby enhancing the likelihood of intervention acceptability, adherence, and success. Flexibility within fidelity also can increase cultural responsiveness within school consultation problem-solving (Parker et al., 2020; Sander et al., 2016). Modifying evidence-based intervention protocols to be compatible with the needs of students and families, including matching with their language, culture, and context, is called *cultural adaptation* (Bernal et al., 2009).

For example, the *Positive Behavioral Interventions and Supports Cultural Responsiveness Field Guide* (Leverson et al., 2021) supports coaches and trainers who work with teams implementing Schoolwide Positive Behavioral Intervention and Supports (SWPBIS) to culturally adapt practices to enhance educational equity. Though a full review of the guide is beyond the scope of this chapter, important components with broad relevance include:

- Promoting *identity awareness* (e.g., of self, students, caregivers, community)
- Soliciting, valuing, and incorporating the *voices* of students, families, and community partners in design and implementation

- Establishing a *supportive environment* across cultures rather than solely focusing on dominant cultures
- Understanding that *situational appropriateness* may inform behaviors with school and community expectations that are sometimes at odds (e.g., some cultures value overlapping discussions, while in school, this may be viewed as interrupting or calling out)
- *Using data for purposes of equity*, including disaggregating data to understand patterns related to inequities and to inform problem-solving.

In addition to EBIs such as SWPBIS, ebis can also be designed and adapted to be culturally responsive. For example, in an intervention targeting the math problem-solving skills of four second-grade Latinx English-learning students, Luevano and Collins (2020) incorporated evidence-based instructional techniques and culturally relevant practices. Procedures such as schema instruction (mapping word problems to numerical problems), video modeling with a comprehension check, and vocabulary instruction were enhanced with culturally responsive practices such as reading word problems in English and Spanish in person and within video models and personalizing word problems based on information gathered in a preference assessment, which included questions about culture. Multiple baseline data indicated improved math problem-solving skills for all four student participants.

We acknowledge that it is tricky to balance between being flexible and staying true to an EBI protocol (Simon, 2016). In one vocabulary intervention adopted by a school, teachers had students keep a word box on their desks for new words but did not correctly implement the recommended number of new words per week that students were required to learn, leading to a lack of progress for many of them (Rosenfield & Rubinson, 1985). In the intervention stages of problem-solving, school consultants need to be critical thinkers rather than overly rigid, robotic, or prescriptive, but it is also essential to be mindful of the critical design element(s) when adapting an intervention to the context in which implementation will occur.

Social Validity

In addition to being flexible, interventions should be socially valid. Social validity refers to the social significance of the intervention goals and outcomes as well as the acceptability and feasibility of implementation (Bailey & Burch, 2017; Wolf, 1978). Questions for consideration regarding social validity include:

- How valuable is this intervention to those involved (e.g., teachers, parents, students)?
- Are the target variables important to these partners?
- Are the target variables meaningful?
- Is the intervention acceptable to the consultee?

Social validity may be assessed via consumer ratings (e.g., interviewing or survey-ing consultees) and by comparing student performance to peer norms (e.g., is the intervention helping the student perform more like typically performing peers?).

A social validity issue is the popularity of certain interventions that do not have empirical support. The concept of needing to de-implement has recently received additional attention (Wilcox et al., 2021). Suspension and expulsion are common interventions that lack empirical support and proliferate inequi-ties. Such zero-tolerance practices can stunt academic achievement (e.g., through missed instructional time), increase dropout rates, and reinforce the problematic behaviors they were intended to address, all without improving student behavior or promoting safety (NASP, 2020a; Skiba et al., 2006). Data consistently indicate that minoritized students are the most affected by these problematic practices (U.S. Department of Education, Office of Civil Rights, 2018). The NASP (2020a) *Framework for Effective School Discipline* provides an outline of socially valid alterna-tives to suspension and retention, such as SWPBIS, Social-Emotional Learning frameworks, and Restorative Justice. Of course, as with other interventions, con-sultants and consultees will need to consider the fit of such practices within their own contexts as these are large-scale practices requiring systems-level investment.

Another example of a widespread intervention with limited empirical evi-dence is the use of retention to remediate academic concerns (NASP, 2022b). Pickering (2012) found that the experienced kindergarten teacher with whom he was consulting was less interested in academic interventions for the child because she assumed he would be retained and would repeat kindergarten the following year. As a student consultant, it became an issue for Pickering to de-implement the teacher's belief in retention in a school culture that supported it. Wilcox et al. (2021) stress the need for school psychologists to become knowledgeable about the evidence underlying interventions in common use in schools. However, this might also be a good example of where intervening at the school level would be appropriate, with an opportunity to impact a larger number of students. The NASP (2022b) position paper on retention should also assist school psychologists in making a commitment to respond to this intervention at the systems level.

Designing the Intervention Together

The process of selecting or designing an intervention should be collaborative. The notion of collaborative intervention design is introduced in consultation during *Contracting* (see Chapter 6) and is further catalyzed through the establishment of a shared problem definition during *PID/PA* (see Chapter 7). It is appropriate for you to bring to an *Intervention Planning* consultation session some ideas for poten-tial interventions. You likely will have ideas given your specialized knowledge base as a school consultant. However, in our view, providing a list of interven-tions and saying "choose one" is not the best approach to intervention design; nor is prescribing an intervention without eliciting sufficient consultee input.

The intervention you think is best may not be feasible within the classroom context; it may be too time- or other resource-consuming; or the teacher may have attempted the intervention previously and found it to be ineffective.

Teacher input into intervention selection increases the likelihood of intervention adherence, meaning the plan is more likely to be implemented as designed. For example, Dart et al. (2012) investigated outcomes when teachers "test drove" interventions, that is, tried them out for a brief duration during behavioral consultation. The researchers found that intervention plan adherence increased when preferred interventions were selected, as did student academic engaged time. An excerpt from an actual *Intervention Planning* dialogue is provided in Activity 8.2, along with some questions for consideration to help you reflect on the role of collaboration during this stage of problem-solving.

ACTIVITY 8.2 (INDIVIDUAL, GROUP)
Intervention Acceptability

The following is an actual excerpt from an *Intervention Planning* session in which a consultant and consultee discussed a second grader's lack of instructional match in math assignments, which also seemed to be problematic for several other students. Review the transcript and answer the subsequent questions individually and, if possible, compare responses with a partner or in a small group.

Teacher Consultee (TC): She is in here for afternoon math. It's hard to give her any individual attention. We do as much as we can.

Consultant-in-Training (CIT): Yeah, during their math worksheets, you are typically walking around a little bit, right?

TC: Right, right.

CIT: And you discuss if the students have any questions and things like that.

TC: Right.

CIT: And I know that when you are assigning the work to the students, you ask them to take out their notebooks and rip out a page. Is that right?

TC: Yeah.

CIT: So how do you think we can make [packets aligned with their instructional level in math] something that we can make simple enough to do in the classroom and on a daily basis?

TC: It's so hard . . . And maybe [the students] get 30 seconds of me saying, "Go back and correct this problem or that." Then they go back to their seat and copy off someone else's paper, then bring it back up, and oh, okay, now it's right.

CIT: I'm hearing what you're saying because you're saying that you don't have a lot of time.

TC: Yeah, and I know it's my job . . .

CIT: Yes, that's why we are sitting here and trying to brainstorm what we can do here in the classroom for these students. I'm just wondering how much time it would save if you were able to pull them aside for a couple of minutes and just give them a quick rundown of what they, as a small group, would be going over. Versus them each coming up individually and you giving them each individual feedback . . . and it is sporadic and disjointed, and then they don't even do the work as you described. Does that make sense?

TC: Yeah.

CIT: Is that something you'd be willing to try?

TC: Who's going to put the packet together? Me?

CIT: Well, that's something that we can do together and obviously with the special education teacher.

TC: And when? Everyday? What time?

CIT: I understand you feel you don't have a lot of time.

TC: It just becomes hard to be consistent . . .

CIT: So here's the thing with the packets: I would be willing to work with the special education teacher to put these together if you would be willing to discuss it with them for a couple of minutes after you give the whole group math lesson.

TC: Sure, yeah.

Questions for Reflection:

1   Given this brief excerpt, how acceptable do you think this intervention idea is to the teacher? How do you know?
2   How would you guess intervention acceptability demonstrated through this excerpt relates to the *PID/PA* process the dyad had previously engaged in?
3   What consultant and consultee actions might be useful to increase intervention acceptability?

Detailing and Documenting the Intervention

Intervention details requiring attention include:

- *What* (i.e., a strategy to meet goals),
- *Where* (i.e., intervention setting),
- *When* (i.e., time of day for implementation),
- *How often* (i.e., frequency of implementation), and
- *Who* (i.e., person or persons responsible for implementation).

Each of these aspects of the intervention can be documented on a tool such as the Student Documentation Form (SDF) referenced in Chapter 7 (Appendix F).

However, in practice, we have found discussions of interventions are often vague, relying on one or a few of these details without the others or not fully specifying a protocol for implementation. Plans such as, "She can go with Carole [the reading specialist] during that time," or "he gets reading help during homeroom – that should be sufficient," are unclear intervention plans. Describing the intervention in detail allows the consultant and consultee to work out logistical kinks, thereby enhancing the likelihood of intervention adherence and effectiveness. Further, students who are discussed in consultations often have other interventions in place to support them, and communication with other resource providers about intervention details, including schedules, can help streamline intervention strategies. A real example of a poorly defined intervention plan is provided in Activity 8.3, with a chance for you to reflect on the consequences of this plan.

ACTIVITY 8.3 (INDIVIDUAL, GROUP)

The Homework Club

Read the following case example. Answer the subsequent questions individually and, if possible, compare responses with a partner or in a small group.

Sophia is a school psychologist intern participating on a middle school problem-solving team. Many of the students that are discussed by the team are assigned to an after-school homework club in lieu of other interventions. Although it is primarily geared toward students struggling academically (in any subject), the team sometimes prescribes the homework club for students with non-academic issues. Although it is clear the group meets at 4:00 PM after school, other details, such as what instructional support strategies are applied, which personnel support which students, and other logistics, are unclear. Additionally, the homework tutors rely on students to indicate which assignments/academic areas they need support with, even though many of these students are struggling with problems such as poor organization and not logging assignments in their homework agenda books. When Sophia asked some teachers "off the record" about their perceptions of the homework club, all reported the group wasn't effective in increasing students' academic skills.

Questions for Reflection:

1   What are some of the problems with the homework club intervention?
2   How might this intervention be redesigned to be more effective?

Who Will Implement the Intervention?

Detailing who will implement the intervention is particularly important. Traditional descriptions of consultation put the consultee in the roles of plan designer and executor (e.g., Kratochwill & Bergan, 1990), roles consistent with the indirect nature of consultative service delivery. However, consultees may enter the consultation relationship with a mistaken assumption that the consultant will shoulder the responsibility for direct services, such as assessing the student as part of a special education eligibility decision or providing a pull-out intervention for the student without the consultee's involvement. Sometimes consultants inadvertently reinforce this perception through frequent usage of "I" language (e.g., I will assess, I will observe, I will determine, I will provide) or through actions such as prescribing interventions or taking full ownership of intervention implementation. Activity 8.4 provides an example of an implicit struggle over intervention ownership between a CIT and a consultee about a seventh-grade student.

ACTIVITY 8.4 (INDIVIDUAL, GROUP)

Who Owns the Intervention?

The following is an excerpt from an actual consultation session focused on intervention design between a consultant and consultee about a seventh-grade student named Luis. Read this interchange and answer the subsequent questions individually and, if possible, compare responses with a partner or in a small group.

Consultant-in-Training (CIT): Okay, so one of the things I was thinking might work for Luis, and this, again, I want to keep this as collaborative as possible, is having some sort of self-monitoring tool for him, so you know we can have the definition of what it means to follow teacher directions, classroom directions, what it means to follow through with directions and also have some sort of rewards, structured reward plan, as well as consequences that are embedded in the plan. And when I say consequences, I mean things that you can easily implement within the classroom that wouldn't take time, and it wouldn't be distracting, and something that you know, we can even start off with it being during his 20-minute warm-up you know for a week and leave it at that. And if he's self-monitoring, we can set a criterion for how many points he would have to earn either that week or that day in order to get some sort of reward. And if he was not doing it, what kind of consequence would be part of that, and you know, you can agree, disagree, you know if you have any thoughts on how that might work.

Teacher Consultee (TC): I'm just not good with papers and contracts, I'm really not good – and I'm open for anything, but I . . .

CIT: Okay, well, this is kind of what I was thinking about, okay? And I can talk to him, pull him or teach him, but if it was something along the lines of this [I'm showing her a self-monitoring graph example], you know that he can have, if they were half sheets of paper he can have in his room or on his desk, we can laminate it, Velcro it, you know have it be dry erase; it doesn't matter – something that he can easily keep track of it himself and be able to see, so it's not necessarily you watching him, it's him watching him.

Questions for Reflection

1   How did the consultant attempt to be collaborative in this brief interchange? Was it successful? Why or why not?
2   In what ways might the consultant have approached this conversation differently?
3   If the consultee agreed to a version of this intervention, what would you predict about the eventual implementation process?

In contemporary school settings, it is likely that the consultant has some sort of direct contact with the student (Gutkin & Curtis, 2009). However, it is essential to remember that consultation is provided with the intention of giving psychology away (Miller, 1969) to the consultee, teaching them how to fish rather than supplying the fish. Therefore, the consultant must strike a balance between providing support to solve the problem and taking full ownership of the problem. The consultant's involvement in intervention implementation should be designed with adult learning principles (Joyce & Showers, 2002) and professional development frameworks (Desimone & Garet, 2015) in mind (see Chapter 1, Figure 1.1), thereby positioning consultation as a form of embedded professional development for consultees.

For example, in one school district, consultation support was provided for teachers regarding the research-based instructional strategies of increasing opportunities for student responding, formative assessment, effective feedback for students, and systematic problem-solving (Barrett et al., 2018). Not only can school consultants discuss the research base of these strategies and an implementation plan with teachers, but they also can support the gathering of baseline data regarding instructional practices, sometimes model the new practices, and scaffold the integration of the instructional strategies within the classroom. Given the collaborative relationship between consultants and teachers, the processes were viewed by the teachers in the district as supportive and helpful, and the data demonstrated increased implementation of research-based instruction (Barrett et al., 2018).

Intervening With More Than One Student

Interventions are often implemented within the context of Multi-Tiered Systems of Support (MTSS) in schools (Burns et al., 2016). As discussed elsewhere in this text, although sometimes an individual student surfaces as the focus of consultation, multiple students can often benefit from the support provided by the teacher. In other words, many Tier 3 concerns can better be framed as Tier 2 or Tier 1 concerns relevant to a classroom, grade level, or even school building. Such reframes often allow you and the consultee to move from a focus on an individual student's pathology toward an ecologically framed problem situated in the school. For example, you might think aloud with the consultee: "I am wondering if some of the other students in Noah's reading group would also benefit from previewing the vocabulary. What do you think?" Asking the consultee directly about broader intervention applicability would also be appropriate, for example: "Are there other students who might benefit from re-teaching the expectations of the morning meeting?"

The Nuts and Bolts of Intervention Implementation, Monitoring, and Performance Feedback

Following *Intervention Planning*, it is time to put the plan into action during the *Intervention Implementation, Monitoring, and Performance Feedback* stage. An overview of the purposes and "business" of this stage is provided in Table 8.3. Several steps can be taken to ensure that the plan is delivered completely and appropriately.

TABLE 8.2 Purposes and Business of the Intervention Implementation, Monitoring, and Performance Feedback Stage of Problem-Solving

Intervention Implementation, Monitoring, and Performance Feedback
Purposes • Implement intervention • Evaluate intervention adherence/accurate implementation of intervention • Evaluate client progress toward goals • Provide performance feedback on adherence and client progress
Business • Continue meeting while intervention is being implemented • Elicit consultee's perception of progress toward client goals • Collaboratively review and discuss data • Compare progress with goals • Clarify what's working and what needs refining • Provide performance feedback regarding the level of adherence to the intervention and client progress, with consideration given to implementation changes as needed

Ongoing Meetings

The consultation dyad should continue to meet during this stage of problem-solving (Noell et al., 2017; Rosenfield, 2014). Although this might seem like an obvious point, we have observed time and again consultants or problem-solving teams prescribing interventions for teachers to implement and then leaving the teachers for multiple weeks without providing further support. This lack of support helps to explain why glaucoma patients do not take their prescribed medicine and risk blindness. Too often, doctors, as is true of consultants and teams, assume their task is completed when they recommend a solution and are not available to problem solve the normal problems of implementation. Then, when the intervention is not implemented as intended, the consultee may be unfairly labeled as "resistant" or "disinterested" when "unsupported" would be a more appropriate descriptor. Research has confirmed that "in the absence of effective programming to support implementation, implementation is often poor and deteriorates over time" (Noell et al., 2017, p. 525). There is also evidence that quality implementation, as one would suspect, is related to positive outcomes for students (Noell et al., 2017).

But what happens during the meetings is the critical factor. Continuous contact between the consultant and consultee allows for discussing any necessary tweaks to the intervention or implementation plan (i.e., performance feedback; Fallon et al., 2022) and for reviewing data (i.e., progress monitoring), assessing what is and is not working for the consultee and student via collaborative data review. These features of the meetings are essential to implementation quality. Different consultees may require different types and levels of implementation support (Collier-Meek et al., 2019; Sanetti & Collier-Meek, 2015), further indicating the need for ongoing contact and evaluation during implementation.

Meetings during this stage may occur less frequently than in earlier stages of problem-solving and tend to be briefer in nature, as they focus on "fine-tuning" the intervention as needed. We recommend beginning this stage of problem-solving by meeting with your usual frequency (e.g., weekly or more frequently) and thinning the meeting schedule (biweekly and then monthly) consistent with data indicating the intervention's continued success *and* the consultee's comfort with receiving reduced support.

Progress Monitoring

Two types of monitoring occur while the intervention is being implemented: Monitoring the student's progress and monitoring the plan's implementation (Kratochwill & Bergan, 1990). With respect to monitoring student progress, intervention outcome data can be compared to baseline data and goals established during *PID/PA*. Consistent with descriptions of goal setting in Chapter 7, consultation interventions will ideally result in both student growth and a reduction in the performance gap between the student or students and typically performing peers. Although beyond the scope of this chapter, single case design methods are applicable to monitoring consultation outcomes given the focus on individual or small groups of students; interested readers are referred to Kazdin (2020) for more information on single case designs.

With respect to monitoring the intervention plan, gathering data on intervention adherence is essential because if a plan is not implemented as intended, it is a non-event, and it is impossible to conclude whether a student is responsive to the intervention. A checklist of intervention steps may be helpful to measure adherence and as a reference tool to support implementation (e.g., see Schussler, 2012; also, an example of an intervention script and adherence checklists can be found in Appendix G). Direct observation, permanent products, and self-report provide useful approaches to gathering data regarding intervention adherence.

Performance Feedback

A robust research base focused on performance feedback in consultation indicates that ongoing meetings between the consultant and consultee serve to enhance intervention adherence (Fallon et al., 2015). Performance feedback meetings include a discussion of what is going well and what is not going well with the intervention, with reference to intervention adherence and student outcome data (Sanetti et al., 2013). Performance feedback is more easily delivered within the context of a collaborative relationship developed during earlier stages of problem-solving. Feedback could easily be facilitated via virtual meetings with an implementer and incorporated as part of ongoing consultation. Recent evidence suggests that performance feedback can be delivered effectively via virtual means such as videoconference, though research on email-based performance feedback is limited (Fallon et al., 2022).

An additional effective strategy is integrating a commitment emphasis with performance feedback prior to implementation, as described by Noell et al. (2017):

> The consultant described how it is common for us to plan to change our behavior, but fail to follow through due to competing demands and ingrained habits . . . the teacher and consultant discussed proactive steps the teacher could choose to take to support implementation . . . Teachers were free to devise any strategy they thought would be helpful or no strategy at all.
>
> (p. 532)

CITs are sometimes concerned about providing performance feedback, as doing so may seem critical of the consultee if the intervention is not working. This feeling can be exacerbated if earlier relationship issues have not been addressed, including issues about differences between the consultant and consultee in diversity identity.

However, in such instances, performance feedback can be viewed as an opportunity for perspective-taking, including discussing with the consultee what is not working, why, and what can be done to improve implementation. Of course, such a conversation is more easily done within a functioning, collaborative relationship, as mentioned previously. In Activity 8.5, an excerpt from a CIT's supervision process log is provided for your consideration of challenges in providing performance feedback to consultees.

ACTIVITY 8.5 (INDIVIDUAL, GROUP)

Performance Feedback

The following is part of a reflection from a consultant-in-training (CIT) who was consulting with a kindergarten teacher, Ms. Young, to support a student named Sal. She describes challenges faced during progress monitoring and performance feedback and requests supervision advice. Read the reflection and answer the subsequent questions individually. If possible, compare responses with a partner or in a small group.

Consultant-in-Training (CIT) Reflection:
We are progress monitoring and still meeting weekly to see how the intervention is going. I have gone into the classroom many times and have noticed that the interventions are not going exactly how I wish they would. The timer that we were setting for Sal was not working properly, and Ms. Young [the consultee] seemed a little confused about reinforcing Sal. These issues were what we talked about in our meeting . . . It seems as though the intervention addressing latency (getting Sal to start working right away) is not working, according to Ms. Young's data. I think Ms. Young is not implementing the timer intervention exactly how we talked about because the timer is not working correctly, and our data are inconsistent from each other. I also feel as though she is worried about collecting data on Sal that shows that interventions are not working.

She has a team meeting to address Sal's needs next week, and I feel as though she wants to collect as much data about Sal's difficulties and not focus on the intervention. In the consultation session, Ms. Young showed me the idea she had to change one of the interventions. Every two minutes, the timer goes off; if Sal was working, then he gets a sticker. There are four stickers, and then Sal gets to go to the treasure chest. I thought this was a great idea! She explained that Sal has only gotten one sticker, and it is really hard for him to stay on task for two minutes and get a sticker. We talked about how the timer is not working properly, and that may be why it seems the intervention is not working. I explained the importance of making sure Sal is successful and making sure he gets a sticker every two minutes. We decided to try the intervention again. We are going to continue with interventions and see how they go. I plan to go in two days per week to work individually with Sal. If these interventions don't work, I will feel very frustrated and disheartened. I think Ms. Young believes that Sal needs an aide with him at all times to be successful in school and that our efforts are not enough. I definitely feel like a behavior plan would benefit Sal, and I hope to see him stay in the classroom.

We will continue to use our interventions, hoping that the timer will work and that Ms. Young now knows when and how to reinforce Sal's good behaviors. Maybe I can show her how to use the chart correctly with a timer that works. What are your suggestions for how to use communication skills better when Ms. Young says things like, "He laid on the floor for 45 minutes today," or, "He can't even work for two minutes, and I can't keep monitoring him because I have a whole class!"? This is a tough first case!

Questions for Reflection:

1   Summarize the concerns that the consultant has regarding intervention implementation.
2   Given those concerns, how might she provide performance feedback to the consultee?
3   What thoughts would you have as the consultant's supervisor or as a peer support? What additional information might help you provide feedback to support this consultant?

Summary

In this chapter, we have reviewed two stages: *Intervention Planning* and *Intervention Implementation, Monitoring, and Performance Feedback.* The stages are collaborative and systematic. Consultants and consultees work together to select a socially valid intervention matched to the problem(s) defined during *PID/PA*; clarify all details of an implementation plan, including what, where, when, how often, and who; and attend to intervention integrity or adherence, including the potential need for flexibility within fidelity.

As posited earlier, *interventions are not magic* (even EBIs!), *and consultants are not magicians.* Therefore, despite the natural tendency consultants might have to provide immediate help and the reinforcement consultants might receive from consultees to provide a quick fix, doing so might actually derail the consultation process. After reading the chapter and completing the activities embedded within, we hope you feel more prepared to navigate the numerous challenges that emerge during these problem-solving stages.

9

POST-INTERVENTION PLANNING AND CLOSURE

Great is the art of beginning, but greater is the art of ending.
(Henry Wadsworth Longfellow)

In this chapter, we explore the *Post-Intervention Planning and Closure (PIPC)* stage of problem-solving in school consultation. We highlight strategies to facilitate successful case closure, including consideration given to consultation goals both for clients (i.e., students) and consultees. Before we begin, take a moment to consider these questions:

ACTIVITY 9.1 (INDIVIDUAL)

Warm-Up Questions: Post-Intervention Planning and Closure

Write down your assumptions about closing out a consultation case. You can write down sentences or just key words.

1 When is a consultation complete? How do you know?
2 Which variables are important to consider when closing out a consultation?

These questions are trickier to answer than they might first appear. First, even if a problem is technically solved according to the data (i.e., long-term goals are met and gaps between students and typical peers are closed), the consultant and consultee need to determine which aspects of the intervention will remain in

DOI: 10.4324/9781032622330-9

place, which will be eliminated or faded as the consultation comes to a close, and how behavioral generalization and maintenance will be achieved. Second, consultees may also have an additional problem they wish to work on with the consultant that has not been directly addressed through this initial consultation. Third, a consultation may end abruptly even if the problem is not solved. For example, the school year may have ended; a student may have moved; the teacher may be taking a maternity leave; a teacher may have lost interest in the consultation or not have further time to devote to it; or the student has not made academic or behavioral progress despite ongoing consultation efforts. Fourth, even after meeting consultation goals for an individual or group, broader systemic issues may persist, suggesting a need for a shift from a secondary or tertiary to a primary prevention lens. Finally, school consultation is also more than a series of problem-solving steps. It is a complex process with embedded interpersonal interactions at its heart. Therefore, closing out a consultation requires attention to the consultation relationship. Once again, this ties back to the notion that **Everything We Do is An Intervention, Big Idea #3**.

The Nuts and Bolts of Post-Intervention Planning and Closure

Scant conceptual literature or empirical research has focused on the final stage of consultation (Dougherty et al., 1996). When it is referenced, the formal conclusion of consultation has been called closure (Rosenfield, 2014); disengagement (including four phases: evaluating, post-consultation planning, reducing involvement and following up, and terminating; Dougherty, 2013); post-intervention planning (Kratochwill et al., 2014); and termination (Gallessich, 1982). We term the stage as *PIPC*, a title that indicates consultation: (a) does not end with intervention selection, implementation, or evaluation, (b) needs to be systematically rather than haphazardly resolved or left hanging, and (c) has at its core a formal relationship that needs to be concluded. The purpose of the *PIPC* stage and its "business" are outlined in Table 9.1.

Assessing Student Goal Attainment

The first consideration regarding closing out the consultation is whether consultation goals are met. Progress monitoring during the previous problem-solving stage served the purpose of formative assessment. In *PIPC*, the consultant and consultee engage in summative assessment by measuring present levels of performance on target variables compared to long-term goals. Graphic representations of the data are helpful in analyzing progress and making decisions regarding goal achievement.

TABLE 9.1 Purpose and Business of the *Post-Intervention Planning and Closure* Stage of Problem-Solving

Post-Intervention Planning and Closure	
Purpose	• Formally conclude the consultation relationship regarding the targeted concern
Business	• Close if (a) goals are met; (b) consultee can implement independently if needed; (c) strategies are fading/faded • Elicit consultee's plans to maintain student progress • Determine documentation of efforts • Consider addressing other priority areas not yet addressed (and return to *PID/PA* for new priority concern) • If the case is explicitly closed, let the consultee know how support can be accessed in the future • Communicate with parents, colleagues, and teams as needed

Assessing Consultee Goal Attainment

In addition to student goals, you and the consultee may have goals for the consultee regarding intervention ownership and knowledge and skill development; this is a second consideration in closing out a consultation. As articulated elsewhere in this text, consultee professional learning is part of the purpose of School Consultation (SC). Consultees can gain new knowledge, skills, confidence, and objectivity to support their future work (Kaiser et al., 2009). Therefore, assessing the consultee's professional learning as well as efficacy in implementing the intervention now and in the future are part of the *PIPC* stage. This can take the form of a verbal report during a consultation interview or ratings of social validity. Open-ended questions can help stimulate discussion regarding the consultee's professional learning and overall experience in consultation. Examples of such open-ended reflection questions are provided in Table 9.2. The consultee's willingness to reflect on the consultation process may be facilitated by your own willingness to share your experiences as the consultant. You should genuinely reflect on any challenges faced but also emphasize positives such as student progress made because of the consultation and things you learned from working with the consultee.

Planning the Future of the Intervention

A third consideration in closing out the consultation is if, when, and how to fade intervention strategies that are currently in place. For example, a school psychologist consultant worked with several eighth-grade teachers to more frequently acknowledge positive peer-to-peer interactions in the classroom. The consultant and consultees planned how to thin out the reinforcement schedule over time yet continue to acknowledge student behaviors in the future. Some interventions may remain fully intact after the consultation ends, such as added instructional techniques supporting multiple students in a third-grade classroom (e.g., previewing unfamiliar vocabulary before reading a new story). Others may be

TABLE 9.2 Examples of Open-Ended Reflection Questions a Consultant May Ask During *PIPC*

- What are your thoughts on this consulting experience?
- What changes, if any, have you noticed with the student since we started working together?
- Have we accomplished what we set out to do?
- What, if anything, have you learned from working together?
- What will happen after our consultation ends?

fully removed after goals have been accomplished, such as a planned discussion with a student about homework completion that immediately solves the problem. Regardless of whether intervention strategies remain as they are, are altered, or are eliminated, a discussion of how student progress will be maintained should occur.

Documenting the Outcomes

Since consultation encompasses a data-based problem-solving process, the consultation efforts and their results, positive or not, should be documented. Visual representations of baseline data, goal setting, progress monitoring, and summative results provide strong evidence of the process. It may also be helpful for you to create a format for documenting your collaborative efforts or to write an email to the consultee containing the details of the intervention and highlighting the progress made by the student(s) (see Figure 9.1 for an example of such an email). A written document can be particularly useful before a disruption in the school calendar, such as prior to winter or summer break. The Student Documentation Form (SDF), found in Appendix F and described earlier in this text, provides another example of a tool that documents most of the aspects of the problem-solving process described here. The school in which you are consulting might have its own system to document consultative problem-solving efforts. If so, you might consider whether that procedure documents all components of the process.

Sometimes intervention efforts that were successful with a student during one school year are not implemented at the beginning of the next school year, or efforts that were unsuccessful are futilely repeated the following year. Providing information about the intervention to parents, next year's teachers, colleagues who will work with that student, and/or school problem-solving teams can increase the likelihood that support for the student will be jumpstarted in the future. Documenting successes and sharing that information with key partners can also act to increase support for future consultative service delivery in the school.

Continuing the Consultation With a New Priority Concern

In the *Problem Identification and Problem Analysis (PID/PA)* stage of problem-solving, you and the consultee may have prioritized one problem, putting other issues

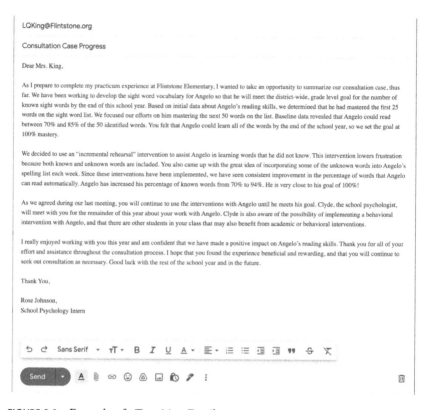

LQKing@Flintstone.org

Consultation Case Progress

Dear Mrs. King,

As I prepare to complete my practicum experience at Flintstone Elementary, I wanted to take an opportunity to summarize our consultation case, thus far. We have been working to develop the sight word vocabulary for Angelo so that he will meet the district-wide, grade level goal for the number of known sight words by the end of this school year. Based on initial data about Angelo's reading skills, we determined that he had mastered the first 25 words on the sight word list. We focused our efforts on him mastering the next 50 words on the list. Baseline data revealed that Angelo could read between 70% and 85% of the 50 identified words. You felt that Angelo could learn all of the words by the end of the school year, so we set the goal at 100% mastery.

We decided to use an "incremental rehearsal" intervention to assist Angelo in learning words that he did not know. This intervention lowers frustration because both known and unknown words are included. You also came up with the great idea of incorporating some of the unknown words into Angelo's spelling list each week. Since these interventions have been implemented, we have seen consistent improvement in the percentage of words that Angelo can read automatically. Angelo has increased his percentage of known words from 70% to 94%. He is very close to his goal of 100%!

As we agreed during our last meeting, you will continue to use the interventions with Angelo until he meets his goal. Clyde, the school psychologist, will meet with you for the remainder of this year about your work with Angelo. Clyde is also aware of the possibility of implementing a behavioral intervention with Angelo, and that there are other students in your class that may also benefit from academic or behavioral interventions.

I really enjoyed working with you this year and am confident that we have made a positive impact on Angelo's reading skills. Thank you for all of your effort and assistance throughout the consultation process. I hope that you found the experience beneficial and rewarding, and that you will continue to seek out consultation as necessary. Good luck with the rest of the school year and in the future.

Thank You,

Rose Johnson,
School Psychology Intern

FIGURE 9.1 Example of a Transition Email

to the side. During *PIPC,* you can revisit the previously defined problems to see if any are still in need of attention or if any new issues have arisen. Often the focus on a pivotal issue during the consultation eliminates the other problems that the teacher initially experienced, such as when gaining academic skills increases academic engagement, work completion, and mitigates problem behavior. Sometimes additional problems remain to be addressed. In such instances, revisiting the *PID/PA* stage of problem-solving will be necessary, cycling back through the full problem-solving process for the concern to be addressed.

Closing Words on Closure: Leaving an Open Door

Just as entry and *Contracting* set the stage for how consultation will ensue, *PIPC* determines how it will conclude *and* how it will be accessed in the future. Therefore, a final key component of the *PIPC* stage is making sure consultees know the door is open for future consultations and are aware of how to access future support (Dougherty et al., 1996; Rosenfield, 2014). This is particularly important for internal school consultants, given that relationships with consultees such as teachers are ongoing. Therefore, although the *consultation case* may be closed, the *consultation relationship* remains open for future collaborative problem-solving.

Scan QR code 9.1 to view a video in which Dr. Arlene Silva summarizes the issues around this stage.

QR CODE 9.1   Arlene Silva Video

To end this chapter, we offer some final thoughts on the importance of this under-studied and under-emphasized consultation stage. You may be thinking that engaging in closure could be awkward. However, just as in romantic relationships, closure in consultation may be considered a form of respect. Leaving a consultation hanging without a formal conclusion (i.e., ghosting the consultee) is disrespectful to the consultee and may deter their future willingness to access consultation support (Dougherty et al., 1996). Instead, explicit closure acknowledges your joint work and sets the stage for future consultations with this consultee as well as with other consultees in the system. In other words, closing the door on one consultation opens the doors to others.

10

COLLABORATION AND CONSULTATION ON TEAMS

The magic to a great meeting is all of the work that's done beforehand.

(Bill Russell)

When you step into a meeting, you're entering a shared space for collaboration, decision-making, and exchanging ideas. Treasure this space, and it will turn into a source of joy.

(Marie Kondo and Scott Sonenshein)

Teams present an organizational structure where consultation with school staff and caregivers occurs. In this chapter, two roles of consultants on problem-solving teams will be presented, although there will be some overlap: enhancing the functioning of the team and improving team problem-solving processes. Skills that have been described earlier in this book will continue to be relevant in this new context of teaming. We will consider how an individual consultant who is working either as a team facilitator or team member can apply the core skills from this book with a team. We will also provide some background on the context, that is, the role of teams in schools over time. But please note that there is considerable literature on teams (e.g., Aguilar, 2016; APA, 2015; Benishek et al., 2016; Rosenfield & Gravois, 1996; Rosenfield et al., 2018), and this chapter is limited in its scope.

Why Teams

Over the past decades, the number of teams serving multiple purposes in schools has grown and become part of the organizational culture of schools. Teams have become more common in schools, as in other organizations, given the increased recognition that organizations need to integrate across departments and functions (Gravois,

DOI: 10.4324/9781032622330-10

2013). With the incorporation of Multi-Tiered System of Supports (MTSS) into schools, teams have become even more prolific. As described in Chapter 2, collaborative cultures have become a major feature in schools, and teams might be considered synonymous with collaboration. However, it might be more accurate to view teams as structures that have the potential to facilitate collaboration.

Indeed, schools have not always been a comfortable home to teams, as historically, teachers were viewed as "independent artisans" (Huberman, 1993). Yet, from the start of the special education law in the 1970s, special education decisions were required to be made by a multidisciplinary team (MDT). Early on, critics questioned the effectiveness and cost of the team model, as well as its place in the organizational structure of schooling (Yoshida, 1983). Many of the questions raised then have continued to plague teams in schools, including problem-solving teams and the MDTs associated with special education on which school psychologists and other education staff serve. Further, the idea that teams can function effectively and efficiently without training has been consistently debunked (Delise et al., 2010). The question of how to enhance team development and monitor outcomes continues to be relevant.

Teams can be mandated by law or district policy, but a functional team is one where it is expected that the members can accomplish a shared goal, and achieve more together than individually. Delise et al. (2010) remind us that while the competency of the individuals on the team is obviously essential, it is still not enough for the team to be effective. Teams are more than the sum of the individual contributions of the team members, and supporting team members to learn how to work together is essential if the structure is to maximize its utility. Sitting in the same space and being called a team is not sufficient.

A high-performance team shares certain common traits. To maximize the value of teams, leadership and member skills for effective teams are required. Given the purpose of this book, we will examine how communication and relationship skills, as well as problem-solving, can be integrated into team functioning by consultants.

To begin, consider these warm-up questions regarding collaboration and consultation on teams.

ACTIVITY 10.1 (INDIVIDUAL)

Warm-Up Questions: Teams

Write down your own responses to the following questions. You can write sentences or just key words.

1   What do you believe are the advantages of teams over individual work?

2   What kinds of teams have you observed, worked with, or do you know
    are present in the schools? Did you think these teams were effective?
    Why or why not?

3   What, in your view, makes teams function effectively or ineffectively?

Creating Better Teams

In Chapter 2, we presented the rationale and background for the emergence
of collaboration and teams in schools. Although we may pay lip service to collaboration and teamwork, developing the skills to maximize the benefits of collaboration remains a work in progress (Hargreaves, 2019; Rosenfield et al., 2018).
While the power of collaboration has been acknowledged, several authors have
reflected on the difficulty of moving to an effective culture of collaboration (e.g.,
Hargreaves, 2019; Hargreaves & Fullan, 2012). Early on, Kruse et al. (1994) concluded that structural elements (e.g., time) in reform proposals were receiving
more attention than social and human resources (e.g., interpersonal relationships).
Several authors have raised the larger issue of whether schools as organizations are
conducive to teams (e.g., Doll et al., 2005; Pugach et al., 2011).

However, while there is an assumption in the development of teams that we
are more capable together than when we are apart, whether this is true depends
in large measure on our skills in creating effective teams and being team members. The relevance of the purpose for which the team has been created is also
key. Recently, for example, Geller (2021) cited research studies showing that
team reviews of student data were often not productive. Teachers did not receive
impactful instructional advice from these data-focused meetings, yet they were
using up precious time.

Teams are not always the best structure to get a job done, and in some circumstances, they detract because they drain off resources that could be better
used otherwise. The Instructional Consultation, Assessment, and Teaming model
(Gravois et al., 2011; Rosenfield & Gravois, 1996) takes these issues seriously. The
model combines individual consultation with teachers and a problem-solving
team. Given the importance of accurate problem identification, relationship and
trust building, as well as communication skills, the team members are trained in
individual consultation processes as well as how to have productive team meetings. Given that teachers bring concerns to problem-solving teams that often
result from lack of skill, lack of knowledge, lack of self-confidence, and lack of
objectivity, the team members consult individually with the referring teacher
in a setting far more conducive for exploring concerns that are related to those
issues rather than child deficit oriented. In other words, allowing space for individual consultation in conjunction with team consultation may allow consultees
to express vulnerability about their professional needs ("I am not sure how to do
this") – vulnerability that may be difficult to express on or to a team – potentially

resulting in deeper professional learning and change. The team itself, which requires training to perform its own functions effectively, supports the individual team members in their consultation efforts, examines more systemic issues related to teacher and student concerns, and conducts evaluations of its functioning.

Team Training

Considerable evidence exists that training impacts the effectiveness of teams (Rosenfield et al., 2018). Delise et al. (2010) compiled a meta-analysis examining the relationship between team effectiveness and team training, defined as "acquiring new information, skills, and attitudes essential to effective performance in a team environment" (p. 55). They found that team training works to "foster improvement in affective, cognitive, and skill-based . . . team-level outcomes" (Delise et al., 2010, p. 76). Rosenfield et al. (2018) suggest that teams focus first on transportable competencies, that is, those applicable to all teams and tasks, including good communication and relationships. Other types of competencies relate more specifically to tasks and knowledge of context within the school needed to understand and intervene in the types of problems and issues brought to the team.

Identifying Effective Team Processes

Effective problem-solving teams are concerned with two types of processes: processes for effective team functioning (team development and maintenance) and processes for effective problem-solving, similar to those used in consultant-consultee problem-solving work. We will begin with some basic processes of effective teams that are relatively easy to assess and implement.

Effective Team Functioning Has Multiple Components

As a facilitator or consultant to a team, there are some key elements that have been identified as essential to team success. Awareness of these processes and commitment to their presence are marks of an effective team leader or member.

Common Understanding of the Mission or Function of the Team

A basic process to any functioning team, similar in concept to contracting in individual consultation, requires all members of an effective team to understand and agree on the function or mission of the team as well as their own role within the team. For example, sometimes, on problem-solving teams, there are differences in understanding between members about the mission and their own role regarding labeling and special education, with some members believing their role is to find the underlying student deficit based on the teacher's presentation of the problem, some viewing their role as intervention prescribers, and others believing that the role of the team is to work with the teacher to form a different perspective on the problem and address how the problem might be resolved without labeling the student or necessarily requiring specialist support. Failure to at least acknowledge these differing beliefs undercuts the team's work.

Regular Structures of Operation

Just as in individual consultation, teams that function well have regular meetings that are convenient for members, a clear agenda, and a process for documenting their work. Teams where members are chronically late or absent and the failure to record the work of the team are markers for ineffective teams.

Agreement About and Implementation of Problem-Solving Structures

The problem-solving stages are as relevant to team problem-solving as in consultation between a consultant and consultee. Consistent with the problem-solving process articulated in earlier chapters of this book, a well-trained team also has systematic, shared approaches to: a) establishing shared expectations, as in contracting, b) problem identification and analysis, c) how interventions are selected and monitored, and d) how solutions are evaluated, including how data are collected and used for this purpose. Providing follow-up and feedback for teachers who bring concerns to the team is as critical for team consultation as it is when consulting with individuals. These steps or stages of problem-solving need to be clear to team members and adhered to in the way the team functions. Some teams have developed formats for this process and even have placed posters of the problem-solving structure on the wall of the meeting room.

ACTIVITY 10.2 (INDIVIDUAL)

Assessing Team Structure

Select a school-based problem-solving team. First, interview members about their understanding of the mission of the team and their own role on the team. Compare across members whether the mission is the same and whether there is a shared contract about what the roles of others on the team are. Second, observe a team meeting:

1   Is there an agenda for each meeting? Who created the agenda? Is there an agreement on the agenda?
2   Are team members able to attend the meetings, or are only some members regular attendees? How is the work of each meeting documented? How are members held accountable for following through on their responsibilities?

3   Is there a written description of the steps the team uses in problem-solving? Do the members agree on this process? Is the process implemented on a regular basis?

4   Finally, given the information you gathered through interview and observation, how would you evaluate the team's structure?

Incorporating Feedback and Outcome Evaluation Into Team Functioning

Strong teams have a feedback and outcome evaluation system in place and reserve time for team maintenance activities. Some examples of team maintenance activities put forth by Gravois et al. (2011) include the following:

- Temperature taking: Regular sessions using a structured process for sharing and discussing issues and concerns, as well as positive outcomes of the team itself.
- Skills in giving and receiving feedback that allows for team and member growth and development.
- Needs assessment to support designing and planning training.
- Continued professional development based on needs assessment.
- Strategies to cope effectively with intra-team conflict.

Communication and Relationship Skills

How team members communicate with each other is an important factor in how effective a team can be. The same communication skills described in Chapter 4 continue to be of value in teams, with some variations. Garmston and Wellman (2016) describe these dynamics as norms of collaboration or styles of interaction that may positively impact team processes and outcomes. Adapted from Garmston and Wellman, Table 10.1 displays some of the communication skills and examples of how they function as team members communicate with each other.

ACTIVITY 10.3 (INDIVIDUAL)

Observing Norms of Collaboration on Teams

Observe at least two different types of team meetings in a school (e.g., problem-solving, IEP, grade-level team, PBIS team, MTSS team, etc.). For each meeting, refer to Table 10.1. Rate on a scale of 1 (Low) to 5 (High), the level that you perceived the norm of collaboration to be present on the team. Write down examples or non-examples for each norm that you observed occurring or being violated.

TABLE 10.1 Norms of Collaboration on Teams (Adapted from Garmston & Wellman, 2016)

Norm	Definition and Purpose	Examples
Pausing	Team members wait 3–5 seconds before responding or asking a question to allow time for reflection, thinking, and participation and decrease the potential for reactivity and defensiveness.	In a grade-level problem-solving meeting, a teacher asks for support regarding a third-grade student who has low scores on the Fall reading benchmark. The team facilitator requests that the team members pause and write their thoughts and clarification questions for themselves before the larger team dialogue begins.
Paraphrasing	Restating information in your own words to test your understanding of the message, highlight key information from what is stated, and make the concern more observable and measurable. Paraphrasing can be used to acknowledge and clarify, summarize and organize, or shift the level of abstraction in the conversation.	**Acknowledge/Clarify:** "So, you're concerned about how this will look in your class" **Summarize/Organize:** "There appear to be two issues here: One is resource allocation, and the other is the impact of this decision on student learning." **Shift Level of Abstraction Up:** "It sounds like you're saying, a major goal here is for us to determine if PBIS will be a fit for our school." **Shift Level of Abstraction Down:** "From what I'm understanding, implementing PBIS may help with our problem of suspending too many students"
Posing Questions	Exploring perceptions, assumptions, and interpretations of others before presenting and advocating for our own ideas. Includes using non-dichotomous questions and probing for specificity with high inference language with the purpose of making problems solvable.	**Non-dichotomous Questions:** "What are some thoughts you all have regarding incentives for Oliver?" (versus "Does anyone have any other incentives?") **Probing for Specificity:** *Team Member:* We need to improve our MTSS implementation. *Consultant:* What aspects of MTSS implementation are you thinking about?
Putting Ideas on the Table, and Taking Ideas Off the Table	Sharing ideas or information that may be helpful in problem-solving and labeling it as one possibility enhances receptiveness to discussing ideas.	"This is one possible approach …" "I wonder if …" "I'm thinking out loud here …" "Let's set this aside for a second …"

TABLE 10.1 (Continued)

Norm	Definition and Purpose	Examples
Providing Data	Offering qualitative or quantitative data to help the team establish a shared understanding of problems.	At a PBIS team meeting, the school psychologist begins the discussion by sharing: "Our schoolwide behavioral data suggests that Black boys in our school are being referred to the office for issues of 'respect' at two times the rate of all other students. What should we make of these data when thinking about our work?"
Paying Attention to Self and Others	Each team member's awareness of themselves and of others on the team, including verbal (what is said and how it's said) and nonverbal messages, and how messages are received. Awareness promotes team cohesiveness, consideration of purpose (e.g., shared understanding versus decision-making), and allows for clearer roles.	An instructional consultation team assigns roles to team members, including timekeeper, notetaker, jargon buster (clarifying unclear terminology), and process observer.
Presuming Positive Intentions	Shared assumption that others want to do their best and are trying to do so within the team. Presuming positive intentions can help limit defensiveness, reduce negative conflict (about personal issues), and enhance positive conflict (about goals, decisions).	On a fifth-grade teacher team, one teacher commented, "My students are not coming to school prepared." Another teacher asked, "Which students?" beginning a rich discussion about within–child deficit perspectives. The cognitive conflict supported increased team cohesiveness.

Diversity on Teams

Diversity on teams is an intrinsic factor and includes a variety of types of diversity and their intersectionality – but diversity is always there. Diversity, of course, includes what we typically think of when the topic of diversity arises, such as demographic attributes meaningful in our culture, including age, race, ethnicity, and gender. But it also includes the intersectionality among these attributes, making the team an even more complex setting than consultation dyads. On one grade-level team that was having difficulty working together, three of the four teachers were supporting each other, but the fourth teacher was not a functioning part of the team. In supervision, the consultant-in-training (CIT) described the team but did not report that the three teachers working well together were White and the fourth teacher was Black. Once the supervisor asked about the ethnicity of the team members, the CIT's perception of the problem was turned. While a critical first step was alerting the CIT to the possibility of implicit racial bias, as the teachers viewed the Black teacher as less competent, the next step was to build activities that included the Black teacher in team activities and built trust among the four teachers, enabling the team to become more cohesive and effective.

But diversity factors that impact team functioning also include knowledge, skills, and abilities; values, beliefs, and attitudes; cognitive and behavioral styles; and status in the team's organization (e.g., specialty, position). Evidence indicates that diverse teams can hold an advantage over homogenous teams in how they process and weigh evidence, maintain objectivity, and innovate in problem-solving (Rock & Grant, 2016).

ACTIVITY 10.4 (INDIVIDUAL)

Reflection on Team Diversity

Write down your own responses to the following questions. You can write sentences or just key words.

1 How do different types of diversity impact collaboration and team functioning?
2 Can you provide two examples?

Team Leadership/Facilitation

One of the roles that school psychologists and counselors often play on the team is that of leadership or facilitation of the team. However, there are also times that school psychologists, as team members, take on shared leadership functions rather than being designated as the formal leader.

ACTIVITY 10.5 (INDIVIDUAL)

Team Leadership

Leadership on teams can take many different roles. There are designated leaders, sometimes called facilitators, and there are shared leadership roles. In this activity, you will be observing a team to see how that looks on the team.

1   What are some skills you have seen effective facilitators of teams use?
2   Are some team members who do not have a facilitator role demonstrating leadership on the problem-solving teams you have observed? What skills do they demonstrate?

Power has always been an issue on school teams, but there has been a shift from focusing purely on principals, who have legitimate power in schools as leaders, to how team members also have leadership roles depending on the situation and the need. For example, a school psychologist on a team might take the lead on a problem involving a social-emotional issue brought to the team. *TEACH Teamwork* modules (APA, 2015) provides some examples of ineffective leadership behaviors, including arbitrary expectations, mismanaging resources, and treating other team members inappropriately (e.g., not listening). Effective behaviors of team leaders include monitoring the team's processes, openness to the perspectives of other team members, establishing shared expectations and goals, and ensuring resources for team activities (from supplies to bringing needed expertise to the meeting in the form of information or skill related to a problem). While most team members are focused on the problem being addressed, monitoring the team process is a team leadership function – it involves monitoring your own contributions and considering what is going on around you.

More to Know About Teams

This chapter is a brief introduction to how consultants can function effectively as both facilitators and team members. The point of this chapter has been to demonstrate how the skills of becoming a skilled consultant are valuable for team practice; that is, culture and context, communication, relationships, and problem-solving skills are as helpful for working with teams as for consulting with individual consultees.

11

TELECONSULTATION

Navigating Technology in a Relational Model

It's not the tools that you have faith in – tools are just tools. They work, or they don't work. It's people you have faith in or not.

(Steve Jobs)

The area of telepsychology, including teleconsultation, has received significant attention in the psychology literature since the publication of the first edition of this text. Modalities such as videoconferencing have long been considered viable mechanisms for teleconsultation (Frieder et al., 2009). Since the COVID-19 pandemic forced many psychological services, including consultation, to be delivered online, it is likely that engagement in teleconsultation has increased across settings, including schools. Regardless of if the pandemic ends anytime soon, and no matter what becomes the "new normal," it is not controversial to conclude that the application of technology to facilitate consultation and collaboration is here and is here to stay.

As we were writing this chapter, we asked several friends and family members who work in the business world about their perceptions of consulting and collaborating online versus in person. Why do large corporations spend millions of dollars to send their employees on distant trips to meet with clients when technology is more easily accessible and functional than ever before? As the pandemic eases, and after it is over, will such practices renew? One friend from Cincinnati is known to fly to Chicago and back in a day and catch a Cubs game with clients in between. Another friend regularly travels from Cincinnati to China to meet with clients for just a couple of days. A third friend, an executive at Coca-Cola, has successfully built a new team during the pandemic with only virtual meetings. He reported that the "schmoozing" that happens between the meetings is harder to come by online and that learning about organizational culture is challenging for

DOI: 10.4324/9781032622330-11

new employees; he actively elicits interpersonal connections across team members. One family member reported that even when videoconferencing is a viable option, meeting in person before conducting online meetings sets the stage for a successful working relationship in the future. In sum, the consensus from those that we spoke with was that establishing and maintaining relationships best happens in person, and business travel will re-emerge. Online meetings are and will continue to be important, but strategically combining them with in-person contact and connection is critical.

Accordingly, this chapter reflects the assumption that establishing and maintaining strong interpersonal connections during consultation is important irrespective of consultation modality. We begin the chapter by briefly reviewing research on teleconsultation in schools and identifying key constructs and definitions. Challenges and opportunities presented by using virtual modalities are reviewed, and considerations regarding teleconsultation specific to each of the problem-solving stages are provided, beginning with system entry. Consistent with other chapters, our primary focus is on the *application* of teleconsultation, with significant attention given to communication skills and establishing and maintaining the consultation relationship.

ACTIVITY 11.1 (INDIVIDUAL)

Warm-Up Questions: Teleconsultation

Write down responses to the following questions. You can write sentences or just key words.

1 How do you define teleconsultation?
2 In what ways is your definition the same or different from consultation as defined in Chapter 1?
3 What do you view as some advantages of teleconsultation versus in-person consultation?
4 What do you view as communication challenges that may occur in teleconsultation versus In-person consultation?

A Brief Overview of Teleconsultation

The American Psychological Association (2013) defines *telepsychology* as the synchronous or asynchronous delivery of psychological services through telecommunication technologies such as telephone, mobile devices, video conferences, emails, text messaging, and the Internet. *Teleconsultation*, specifically, is "the provision of consultative services through videoconferencing and other technologies" (Fischer et al., 2018, p. 249). The definition suggests that videoconferencing is a primary modality for teleconsultation but that teleconsultation also includes connecting by phone, text, or email with a consultee. Such electronically delivered supports are increasingly considered relevant during consultation, including to provide performance feedback to consultees (Fallon et al., 2022).

Also implied in the previous definitions is that teleconsultation, just like in-person consultation, is informed by a consultant's personal definition of consultation, including their framework or model for consultative service delivery. School teleconsultation research has primarily focused on client-centered behavioral models to support the teachers of students with intensive behavior concerns (King et al., 2022). Therefore, a client-centered behavioral approach may be what comes to mind first when you think of teleconsultation, although teleconsultation is also relevant to other consultation models, including the School Consultation approach described throughout this book.

Overall, school teleconsultation research is limited in quantity (e.g., in a systematic review, King et al., 2022, identified only 13 studies meeting their inclusionary criteria). However, preliminary research suggests teleconsultation can result in positive outcomes for students (e.g., increased appropriate behaviors, decreased inappropriate behaviors) and teachers (e.g., increased treatment integrity). Studies also suggest that teachers are amenable to engaging in teleconsultation (Bice-Urbach & Kratochwill, 2016; Fischer et al., 2017). Teleconsultation takes place across distances and can potentially help provide access to school psychological services for underserved communities (e.g., rural settings; Witte et al., 2022), though additional supports may be needed for students and caregivers to navigate the technology. This is especially important given the shortages of school psychologists nationally (National Association of School Psychologists, 2021). Delivering consultation virtually also saves travel time and other costs associated with travel (Bice-Urbach et al., 2018).

Potential Limitations of Teleconsultation

Although many resources required for teleconsultation are available for free (e.g., basic software), some technology purchases are cost prohibitive (e.g., computers, Wi-Fi access, information technology support, network security, and advanced technology such as telepresence robots). Therefore, a push toward teleconsultation services may inadvertently perpetuate inequities between or within school districts. Several additional limitations of teleconsultation identified by Bice-Urbach et al. (2018) include a lack of reliability (e.g., poor phone or internet connections, including freezing and poor sound), the static nature of most cameras (as opposed to seeing a full classroom for an observation, for example), consultees or clients expressing concerns with technology use (e.g., lack of skill or confidence), and consultants having limited control over the consultation setting (e.g., to reduce distractions). Messages can also get lost, such as when phones cut in and out in a dead zone, a text message or email is not delivered, the tone of a text or email is misperceived, or a smartphone autocorrects incorrectly. The loss of in-person contact is a potential challenge in teleconsultation which may interfere with communication and negatively impact the consultant-consultee relationship, although this has not yet been the focus of school consultation research. We are in the embryonic stages of understanding the parameters of teleconsultation effectiveness, including how technology usage may impact communication and relationship dynamics and how it may be optimized to support consultees and clients.

Considerations for Virtual Teams

Most of our focus thus far has been on individual teleconsultation, though, as described in Chapter 10, school consultation often occurs in the context of teams. Virtual team meetings sometimes occur out of necessity, such as during a school break or closure. Technology can also be creatively leveraged to support team-based problem-solving in schools. For example, Sussman et al. (2022) implemented a group teleconsultation approach called ECHO-MTSS, which provided educators with consultation support that increased their self-efficacy for data-based decision-making. Yet as with individual teleconsultation, when teams meet virtually rather than in person, several potential challenges may emerge.

Morrison-Smith and Ruiz (2020) synthesized several barriers to virtual teaming in a comprehensive literature review. Potential relational issues abound, including the decreased ability to hold informal conversations; increased feelings of isolation; limited awareness of others' roles and contributions; and challenges in establishing trust. Limited trust can be a significant detriment to team coordination, cooperation, communication, and problem-solving. The collaborative work that is presumably needed for effective school-based teaming may be particularly challenging to engage in virtually, given the need for interdependence of team members and reliance on clear communication (Morrison-Smith & Ruiz, 2020). In sum, findings from the Morrison-Smith and Ruiz (2020) review suggest a process-oriented emphasis may be useful in effectively facilitating or participating on virtual teams, including a balance of explicit task management, empathetic style, and attending to interpersonal interactions. The team's history of working together and cultural composition, including team members' perceptions of each other's cultural similarities and differences, are also relevant in navigating virtual teaming, as is an understanding of the broader organizational culture.

Teleconsultation Considerations During the Problem-Solving Stages

In previous chapters of this text, we overviewed various considerations regarding entering a school setting and getting to know its culture (Chapter 2), as well as the content and process of each problem-solving stage (Chapters 5 to 9). In the sections that follow, we propose several distinct issues that consultants may wish to consider when consultative problem-solving takes place virtually as opposed to in person. Table 11.1 overviews the communication skills needed for teleconsultation problem-solving, and Table 11.2 poses several specific questions intended to help you to prepare for and navigate teleconsultation through each problem-solving stage. We begin here by summarizing multiple overarching issues regarding communication that are important for you to consider.

TABLE 11.1 Teleconsultation Communication Skills

Communication Skills Considerations During Problem-Solving
- If videoconferencing, what is the best way to arrange my camera and background?
- How will we communicate between meetings?
- Am I using the communication skills discussed in Chapter 4?
- Am I engaged in active listening, including being free of distractions (e.g., open email)?
- Does the consultee seem free of distractions? If not, how should I address this?
- What is communicated by my non-verbal behaviors?
- What changes do I need to make to communication to make this consultation more effective?

Overarching Communication Considerations During Teleconsultation

Communication Logistics

Consulting in person differs in some ways from consulting virtually. If videoconferences are the primary modality for consultation, you should consider the best arrangement of your camera and laptop or desktop (which are preferable to using a phone or tablet for professional videoconferencing) and you may choose to use a headset to optimize meeting sound quality (Florell, 2022). Arranging the camera to be slightly above eye level can make it appear that you are making eye contact with consultees. If you choose to have a virtual background select one that is not distracting, and if not using a virtual background, try to ensure there are no distractions or opportunities for interference behind you. In one recent teleconsultation session, I (D. N.) attended, a man's head extended out of a slightly ajar door in the background of one of the participant's videos before he quickly bounded across the room in a towel! The event was hilarious and humanizing but also quite distracting.

According to Young (2022), virtual office space, like physical office space, can have implications for how consultees perceive the consultant's cultural responsiveness. You should intentionally consider what messages are conveyed to others by your virtual space, including pictures, art displays, books, religious items, and what pops up on the desktop when sharing a screen. When unsure, it may be preferable to use a neutral or blurred background (Young, 2022). Consultants may also consider displaying preferred pronouns alongside their usernames to demonstrate the value of gender inclusivity.

TABLE 11.2 Teleconsultation Considerations Within the Problem-Solving Stages

Consultation Stage	Stage-Specific Considerations
Pre-Teleconsultation/ Entry	• How will I learn about school culture? • What resources do we have or need to have to make this work? • What technology will we use for communication? What are my preferences? What are the consultee's preferences? • What is my level of confidence in using this technology? • What is the consultee's level of confidence in using this technology? • What ethical issues may arise due to the use of technology, and how will they be addressed?
Contracting	• How do we best establish rapport and trust? • What unique issues may arise in our teleconsultation that I should introduce at this meeting? • How does our teleconsulting arrangement impact shared ownership over the problem, if at all? • Am I sure the consultee is okay with the teleconsulting arrangement (i.e., agreement and commitment to participate in teleconsultation)?
Problem Identification and Problem Analysis	• Do I have sufficient knowledge of the context to understand the problem? • What, if anything, am I missing from not being in the setting? • What are the best ways to receive relevant case data such as records, work samples, observation data, or assessment data?
Intervention Planning	• Do I have sufficient knowledge of the context to consider whether the intervention will fit? • When discussing what, when, how often, and who – which parts will involve remote communication?
Intervention Implementation, Monitoring, and Performance Feedback	• Are we staying true to the process by continuing to meet during intervention implementation? • How should I provide performance feedback? • How can we collaboratively review case data (e.g., shared screens)?
Post-Intervention Planning and Closure	• What are the consultee's plans to maintain case progress if I am not there? • How can I be accessed in the future for other cases? • What additional communication is needed with stakeholders other than the consultee (e.g., parents, colleagues, teams), and what is the best modality?

You and the consultee(s) can also consider logistics regarding how communication will occur between meetings. One lament we have heard about consulting at a distance is that short "pop-in" discussions (e.g., asking a teacher a quick question between more comprehensive sessions) are not possible. In such circumstances, rather than holding a separate meeting to address brief issues, time may be better spent texting or emailing pertinent information between meetings.

Consistent with approaches articulated throughout the book, any plan for communication should be discussed with consideration given to the consultee's preferences (e.g., texting during the day may not be possible for a teacher) and may evolve throughout the consultation process. It should also be recognized that brief communications such as these do not replace the value of ongoing meetings (Augusterfer et al., 2020).

Communication Interactions

Interactions during teleconsultation meetings differ in some ways from in-person interactions. Discussions of the construct called Zoom fatigue (exhaustion felt after spending a good deal of time in virtual meetings) point to some differences in communication between in-person and virtual communication with potential relevance to consultation interactions. Bailenson (2021) suggested that nonverbal behavior is more complex online, both in terms of sending cues and receiving them, which in turn taxes the cognitive load of communicators. When sending nonverbal cues, challenges include positioning and repositioning oneself in the camera; having to exaggerate gestures (bigger movements for longer periods of time) such as head nodding, thumbs ups, and waving goodbye; trying to make eye contact although the camera and eye level of partners do not align; and speaking louder on video than one might do in person. With respect to receiving cues, it is difficult to gauge others' engagement, as nonverbal signals can easily be misinterpreted. Since most videos are focused above the neck, we must rely on facial expressions rather than additional body language (e.g., crossed arms). Plus, we look at faces for longer time periods and closer distances than we would in day-to-day, in-person life. Think about our tendency to look straight ahead or down at the ground when we are on an elevator with individuals we do not know well. Finally, communicators are essentially looking into a mirror throughout videoconferences (Bailenson, 2021), which may be particularly stress-inducing for new consultants who are learning to consult and are made hyperaware of their communication.

In addition to nonverbal behaviors, verbal behaviors likely differ between in-person and teleconsultation meetings. For example, Boland et al. (2022) found that small delays occur when communicating over video, which can disrupt the normal flow of conversations, including conversational turn-taking. A recent survey of therapists (including professionals and trainees) indicated that despite an increased need to provide teletherapy during the pandemic, therapists perceived significantly more difficulty employing therapeutic skills such as empathy, warmth, establishing an alliance, and other basic helping skills when conducting therapy online as opposed to in-person (Lin et al., 2021). Although the study was focused on therapy, these helping skills are also relevant to consultation, as discussed in Chapter 4. The Lin et al. (2021) survey respondents also perceived teletherapy to be less effective than in-person therapy with respect to client outcomes, although actual outcomes were not measured. It is possible that some consultees may be more amenable to teleconsultation than others; therefore, consultants can stay attuned to consultees' modality preferences and adjust accordingly and as circumstances allow. Although in-person consultation may not always be an option, perhaps there are ways to make an online meeting more effective through advanced discussion of needs.

In sum, the same communication skills described throughout this text are pertinent to teleconsultation, but it may be more difficult for consultants to apply them. For example, the skill of gently interrupting a consultee (e.g., with a paraphrase) to make sure you understood them may be more challenging. Active listening behaviors may also be more arduous to engage in when working online versus in person, both for the consultant and consultee. Activity 11.2 demonstrates such a challenge and will help you think through if and how it may be addressed in practice.

ACTIVITY 11.2 (INDIVIDUAL, GROUP)

Addressing a Consultee's Nonverbal Behavior During Teleconsultation

Read the following example. Answer the subsequent questions individually and, if possible, compare responses with a partner or in a small group.

Imagine that you have contracted with a teacher to meet weekly via videoconference to engage in problem-solving and begin working together. You have never met in person and do not yet know each other well, although the first two meetings are cordial and professional. During your third meeting (Problem Identification and Analysis), you notice that the teacher seems distracted and may not be giving her full attention to the conversation. Her email alert rings multiple times, her eyes seem to be darting around, you hear her keyboard clicking, and she loses her train of thought when answering a question. Your previous two meetings took place without these issues.

Questions for Reflection:

1   What concerns do you have, if any?
2   Would it be appropriate to raise your concerns with the teacher? Why or why not?
3   If yes, how would you do so?

Unique Considerations for Pre-Teleconsultation, Including System Entry

In addition to general logistical issues, several issues are pertinent before teleconsultation begins. Effective consultants facilitate problem-solving with a school culture view in mind, including holding some knowledge of the system's norms and regularities. This is as true for teleconsultation as it is for in-person consultation. If possible, it may be easier to learn about a school's culture in person and move to a virtual or hybrid format for consultation after entering the system. At times, consultants may be faced with hitting the ground running with teleconsultation without any on-site contact. Learning about school culture continues to be important and can still occur through some mechanisms described in Chapter 2, such as engaging in conversations with teachers, administrators, families, and students; reviewing school-level data (e.g., in terms of behavioral referrals); and comparing school- and district-level data. Further, the consultant should be clear on the role of teleconsultation at the consultation site, including which technologies are used and which are preferred and how ethical expectations related to confidentiality and sharing sensitive data will be upheld. The alignment of organizational policies and personal preferences regarding technology can be discussed during the *Contracting* stage of problem-solving.

Unique Considerations for Contracting

Contracting, the process for establishing consultation expectations and agreement to work together (see Chapter 6), is as pertinent to teleconsultation as it is to in-person consultation. One initial consideration involves how to best establish rapport and develop trust with the consultee. It is tempting to jump right into problem-solving as, realistically, everyone's time may be short, and online meetings and communication may be more succinct than in person. However, *personizing* the relationship (Schein et al., 2021) is necessary to establish trust so that the consultee can express what is really affecting them and it can be determined what kind of help is needed to solve the problem (Schein, 2016). Personizing requires demonstrating genuine interest for the consultee as a person (in addition to interest in their problem from their perspective). It requires active listening and humble inquiry and prioritizes inquiring before telling, as described throughout this book. Several unique issues may be considered during the *Contracting* stage, including the consultee's prior experiences using this modality for professional consultation or collaboration and the consultee's comfort level with the teleconsulting arrangement.

Unique Considerations for Problem Identification and Analysis

During the critical problem identification and analysis (*PID/PA*) stage, skilled consultants continue to reflect on the potential impact of the teleconsultation modality. Overarching considerations regarding communication skills have already been described in this chapter and are consistent with the description of *PID/PA* in Chapter 7. Further, based on the entry process and subsequent *Contracting* stage, you may reflect on questions such as: "Do I have all the information I need to understand this problem?" and "If not, how can I access the pertinent information without being in person at the site?" The *PID/PA* stage involves reviewing various forms of data to supplement general case discussion, so being thoughtful about how data are reviewed and shared is important. Many consultation dyads and teams prefer the use of shared documents, which hold the potential for enhancing collaboration. Sharing screens, too, can be helpful to make sure you are conjointly looking at the data.

Unique Considerations During the Intervention Stages

The teleconsultation modality also has some unique impacts on intervention planning and implementation that build on the description of these stages in Chapter 8. Again, knowledge of the consultation context is important, including thinking about the conditions needed to create an instructional match for students, knowledge of students beyond those that are the initial focus of the teacher (i.e., can multiple students benefit from this intervention?), and planning to support intervention adherence. When discussing the what, where, when, how often, and who of the intervention, you can address the consultee's preferences for receiving intervention supports for intervention implementation fidelity. Based on an empirical review of the literature, Fallon et al. (2022) provided a helpful overview of prospective electronically delivered intervention supports (EDIS) to address various needs during the intervention stages of problem-solving. Many EDIS are combinable, can be delivered synchronously or asynchronously, and in various electronic formats (e.g., email, text, video). Examples of EDIS include *online training* (with didactic instruction, modeling, roleplaying, and feedback) and/or *video modeling* of an intervention; a consultee's *self-evaluation* of implementation data to support a discussion about implementation; a consultee's *self-monitoring* of their own implementation progress; and *performance feedback*, a brief (<15 minutes) discussion of implementation data, student progress, challenging intervention steps, and overcoming barriers to implementation.

Unique Considerations for Post-Intervention Planning and Closure

Finally, teleconsultation during *Post-Intervention Planning and Closure* requires some reflection. Discussions about how the consultee will sustain and build upon the student's progress in the future and how intervention supports will be maintained or faded are important, just as during in-person consultation. A future check-in meeting may be planned to make sure everything continues to go well; for example, if you and the consultee had been meeting weekly, perhaps scheduling a brief video meeting in a month would be appropriate. Discussing how information about student progress will be provided to others (including through which modality or modalities) is also relevant when closing out a teleconsultation. Finally, you and the consultee can confer regarding how you may be accessed in the future. An on-camera, exaggerated wave goodbye at the end of this meeting need not be your final consultation interaction.

Final Thoughts About Teleconsultation

Teleconsultation is a way to provide consultation with technology, but it is not a framework or consultation model in and of itself; indeed, teleconsultation may be considered a process by which a theory of consultation (behavioral, instructional, etc.) can be implemented with consultees. This chapter has focused on considerations for consultants as they consult online, navigating through the problem-solving stages as a *School Consultant*. Therefore, consistent with the assumptions reflected in this text, teleconsultation requires attending to the nuances of school culture and reflecting on the professional communication and relational dynamics which are mediated by technology. Unique considerations are recommended during each problem-solving stage, which we hope will help you navigate problem-solving in a consultee-centered manner, even when consulting at a distance. Ultimately, as expressed in the chapter's opening quote by Steve Jobs, "Tools are just tools," and knowing who you are as a consultant is essential to being effective at teleconsultation, just as it is for consulting in person. Therefore, in the next and final chapter of this text, we turn our attention to the intricate process of learning to consult.

12

LEARNING TO CONSULT

The Roles of Assessment, Feedback, and Deliberate Practice

You become what you give your attention to.

(Epictetus)

It is not enough to simply engage in consultation experiences as a novice to become competent in the domain. The literature on developing expertise (e.g., Ericsson, 2009; Ericsson & Pool, 2016) helps us to understand why. As is detailed for psychotherapist supervision, training, and professional development (Rousmaniere et al., 2017), we propose that the development of consultation competency and expertise requires a cyclic process of:

- Assessing a baseline of knowledge and skills, including strengths and skills in need of improvement;
- Obtaining systematic, ongoing, and formal feedback from a knowledgeable other (e.g., a supervisor or mentor); and
- Engaging in ongoing application and practice of skills, with an eye toward continuous, incremental improvement.

These components can be thought of as a three-legged stool, each leg essential and reliant on the others to support the development of consultation competency. They also are aligned with features of deliberate practice (Miller et al., 2020; Rousmaniere et al., 2017), which are pertinent to the development of consultation communication skills (Newman, Gerrard et al., 2022; Newman, Villarreal et al., 2022). But it is important to acknowledge that no matter how many hours you work developing your consultation skills, without supervision feedback linked to direct observations/assessments of performance, you are not likely to hone your skills for effective and efficient practice in the complex context of

DOI: 10.4324/9781032622330-12

the schools. This chapter provides points of reflection for consultants-in-training (CITs) being supervised so that they can make the most of the training process, as well as considerations and tools for competent consultants who are teaching and supervising consultation.

In Chapter 7, we presented Caplan's (1970) four types of consultee problems, which we would like to retitle developmental learning needs: increase of knowledge, development of skill, awareness of lack of objectivity, and development of self-confidence. Each of these are also potential problem areas for the CIT. While we have focused on the first two, knowledge and skill, it is important to remember that CITs can also experience issues around self-confidence or objectivity.

In Chapter 6, we alluded to the lack of self-confidence that a CIT might feel when contracting to consult with more experienced staff members in a school and the strategy of "acting as if" one were competent. But this lack of self-confidence can also emerge at later points in the process. Here, supervision can be helpful in providing support (see Vaganek, 2012, for an example of lack of self-confidence and the support of supervision around this issue). Similarly, CITs can experience a lack of objectivity in working on a consultation process, and supervision and feedback are necessary to help the CIT recognize when that is occurring. For example, Pickering (2012), through supervision, came to recognize his loss of objectivity in his work with the teacher. It is critical to remember that along with lack of knowledge and skill, lack of objectivity and self-confidence are also barriers to competent performance as a consultant.

Scan QR code 12.1 to listen to a podcast in which Cyril Pickering discusses his experiences as a CIT and school psychologist engaging in consultation.

QR CODE 12.1 *Cyril Pickering Podcast*

In addition, the ongoing development of cultural competence permeates each of the four areas of learning and development needed by CITs (Ingraham, 2017). For example, *knowledge* of issues related to various aspects of diversity is one element in the knowledge base of school consultants that may not be consistently present for CITs or included in their training (Newell, 2012), although some changes have occurred over the last decade. Even when consultants possess knowledge of relevant cultural variables, they may not discuss these issues due to feelings of discomfort or lack of preparedness (Newell et al., 2013). Therefore, *skill* in consulting with teachers and students from diverse backgrounds and in school cultures that are different from members of the consultation constellation also needs to be part of training. Understanding how *lack of objectivity* due to implicit biases can impact the effectiveness of school consultants is essential and requires developing awareness of one's own cultural assumptions, beliefs, and worldviews (American Psychological Association, 2017a; Ingraham, 2017; Newman & Ingraham, 2020). Finally, gaining self-confidence as new consultants working with teachers, parents, and students in the increasingly diverse context of schooling is critical. CITs can strive to achieve *confident cultural humility* (extended from Grant's [2021] description of confident humility), which involves believing in their capabilities while also appreciating the need to understand others' perspectives and experiences. We can simultaneously be confident in our capability to solve a problem but also appreciate that there is much to learn about ourselves and others and "that we may not have the right solution or even be addressing the right problem. That gives us enough doubt to re-examine our old knowledge and enough confidence to pursue new insights" (Grant, 2021, p. 47).

Scan the following QR code to listen to Dr. Kamontá Heidelburg, a faculty member in the school psychology program at The Ohio State University, discuss multicultural school consultation training and his experiences participating in a cross-university dialogue case study.

QR CODE 12.2 Kamontá Heidelburg Video

Assessing Consultation Knowledge and Skills

The first leg in the stool of consultation competency development is the assessment of your knowledge and skills, including strengths and weaknesses. Consultation is a complex domain to evaluate. Three interrelated areas may be the focus of evaluation: (1) consultation content knowledge, (2) consultation process skills, and (3) consultation outcomes (i.e., what impact you have on the consultees and clients you are serving).

Evaluating Consultation Content Knowledge

There is some agreement as to what the body of school consultation content knowledge consists of, much of which is embodied in this text. The National Association of School Psychologists (NASP, 2020b) specifies Consultation and Collaboration as a key competency domain and provides examples of professional practices (see Chapter 1, Table 1.3). Division 13 of the APA (2017b) has published consultation competency guidelines that are relevant to school consultation competency development and could inform evaluation. Burkhouse (2012) provided a specific example of an evaluation tool that measures both content knowledge and process skills specifically for Instructional Consultation (IC; see Appendix H). In addition, this scale is aligned with the developmental model of training described in Chapter 1 in this text since it includes levels of skill acquisition. Another tool developed and psychometrically validated by Guiney et al. (2014; see Appendix I) can be used to measure self-efficacy for consultation. Consultation content knowledge emerges within a graduate classroom setting, largely focused on awareness or conceptual understanding. To move beyond conceptual understanding toward the application of skills in action requires sufficient exposure to content combined with opportunities for simulated practice, application in real school contexts, and supervision.

There is also burgeoning literature on consultation with diverse consultees and students, as well as on how to approach consultation from a social justice orientation, with important content with which competent consultants should be familiar. For example, Ingraham's classic multicultural school consultation (MSC) framework, referenced throughout this text, helps consultants consider issues such as consultee and client needs, perspectives, and worldviews (Ingraham, 2000, 2017). Recent adaptations of the MSC framework address applications in specific circumstances, such as navigating racial, gender, and sexual identities and their intersectionalities (e.g., Brown et al., 2022; Parker et al., 2020). Miranda's (2016) edited casebook focuses on consultation across cultural contexts, including in urban settings, and provides considerations from the perspectives and voices of CITs. Additionally, several special issues of the *Journal of Educational and Psychological Consultation* provide compilations of relevant readings focused on issues such as social justice (Schumacher-Martinez & Proctor, 2020; Shriberg & Fenning, 2009), increasing educational access and improving conditions for LGBTQ Youth (Fisher & Huchting, 2019), and the overarching development of multicultural competence (Sander et al., 2016).

The development of multicultural competence can be evaluated generally or with specific consideration for consultation. For example, Malone et al.'s (2016) psychometrically validated *School Psychology Multicultural Competence Scale* is broadly relevant for culturally competent consultation practice and contains some consultation-specific items such as "I can recognize prejudice and prevalent obstacles that may affect consultation" (p. 235). The previously referenced Consultation Self-Efficacy Scale (Guiney et al., 2014) also contains several items focused on self-efficacy for culturally responsive consultation (e.g., items 39–45, Appendix I).

Evaluating Consultation Process Skills

Process skills such as strategic communication and relationship building are trickier to evaluate than content knowledge. There are specific supervision strategies that are most helpful to objectively assess such processes. First, live observations or audio or video recordings of consultations provide direct information about the application of skills. Live observations may include a range of supervisor interjections in the session – from no interjection to the supervisor extensively supporting skill development in the moment. Recording consultations has an advantage over live observations in that recordings can be reviewed by you and your supervisor multiple times and paused and discussed after the session is complete.

Recordings and observations are combined with a review of the session by you and your supervisors (e.g., watching the video); your transcription of part or all of the consultation session; directed self-reflection on your own skill development (see Appendix B for a process log format); supervisor written feedback on your reflections and transcription; and discussion in supervision, with explicit reference to observed behaviors and reflections (see Newman, 2012, for a full description of this process). Rubrics are also useful for evaluating the application of basic listening skills such as paraphrasing, clarifying, and reflecting feelings (see Appendix C). Rubrics can be completed by you (self-assessment), your supervisor, you and your supervisor together, or by peers, with subsequent reflection on how you might have said something differently in the case of misapplication. It is important to remember, too, that skills are applied in context – so even if you apply a skill correctly (e.g., a clarification), it is useful to consider whether the timing for that skill was appropriate (e.g., would reflecting feelings have been more appropriate at this point in the conversation?).

An example of how you can analyze a transcript or portion of a transcript is using the left side/right side procedure, demonstrated in Activity 12.1, along with some questions for you to address. Table 12.1 provides a set of reflective analysis questions. Two additional models for analyzing recordings, adapted here from the psychotherapy supervision literature (Gonsalvez et al., 2016) for supervision of school consultation, are delineated in Tables 12.2 and 12.3. Each of these techniques can be flexibly applied to work best for the supervisor and CIT. For example, the five points highlighted in the Give-Me-5 technique could focus on five CIT strengths and needs; five critical incidences; five session themes; five specific consultation skills; or another area relevant to CIT development.

TABLE 12.1 Reflective Analysis Questions

Reflective Analysis Questions
1 What were the essential strengths of your behavior during the session?
2 What, if anything, would you change about your behavior during the session?
3 Do you think the session was successful? Why?
4 Which specific factors were important to the outcome?
5 What issues of culture, if any, were salient in the session?
6 What, if any, unanticipated outcomes resulted from the session?
7 Can you think of alternative approaches to your consultation goals that might have led to a better process?
8 Do you think the content covered was important to the teacher? Why?
9 Did any moral or ethical concerns occur during or because of the session?

TABLE 12.2 The Give-Me-5 Technique for Video Review and Feedback in Consultation Supervision

Step	Description
1	• The Consultant-in-Training (CIT) records a consultation session and selects an uninterrupted excerpt that best captures the meeting
2	• The CIT reviews the recording and composes notes with three columns: time, observation, and inferences/conclusions
	• The CIT writes down a summary of five key points from the session to discuss with the supervisor
3	• The CIT and supervisor review the recording together within a supervision meeting
	• The supervisor writes down a summary of five key points from the session to discuss with the CIT
4	• The CIT and supervisor compare and discuss their notes and five key points
5	• If applicable, roleplaying is used to support consultation skill development
6	• The supervisor summarizes observations and implications
	• The supervisor and CIT debrief
	• If applicable, the next steps for consultation and supervision are determined

TABLE 12.3 The I-Spy Technique for Video Review and Feedback in Consultation Supervision

Step	Description
1	• The supervisor and Consultant-in-Training (CIT) identify a micro skill (e.g., a communication skill) to target for change
2	• The CIT records a consultation session and selects an uninterrupted excerpt that best captures the meeting
	• The CIT reviews the recording in search of applications of the micro skill
	• Occurrences are tagged (e.g., 3 min, 30 sec) and alternative responses, as appropriate, are proposed
3	• The CIT and supervisor review the recording together
	• The supervisor searches for additional opportunities of micro skill application and/or alternative responses
4	• If applicable, roleplaying is used to support consultation skill development
5	• The supervisor summarizes observations and implications
	• The supervisor and CIT debrief
	• If applicable, next steps for consultation and supervision are determined

ACTIVITY 12.1 (INDIVIDUAL, GROUP)

Left–Right Reflection Format

Here is a format to support your analysis of a consultation session transcript. On the analysis side, it is useful to reflect on your understanding of what the consultee stated, as well as what you said as a consultant. You can also use the analysis column to practice providing alternative CIT responses that might have been helpful.

We have provided a model of one CIT's use of this format but would like to encourage you to add to the analysis by providing alternative responses that might have been helpful at different points in the session.

Question for Reflection:

1   What might the CIT have said to obtain more clarity? Write your alternative CIT response in the analysis column.

Transcript	Analysis
CIT: Have you gathered any information?	
TC: When the reading analysis was done in September, he had 94 miscues, which is not like 94%. If your word recognition is 94, that is significant. His comprehension was like a 65%, so his comprehension is on a frustration level, and this was a fifth-grade IRI that was given. The fact that he is going back in the text and is still getting 65%, and that is about what I see. I see better word recognition than comprehension, but, like I said, I can do another IRI this week.	*I'm thinking that I don't fully understand what she is talking about and how I am going to talk to her in reference to this information.*
CIT: You said that he appears to be on frustration level with his comprehension. Have you done any reading with something below grade-level?	*I jumped on the term frustration level and decided to see if she has worked with him on material that was below frustration level.*
TC: Well, the novel he is working on right now, I have two groups, and his is slightly easier than what the other group is doing, and they work in small groups. When he himself is reading independently, we try to make sure it's on – you don't give children frustration level.	
CIT: Okay, so you have been working with him on reading passages that he is not at frustration level with.	*Trying to clarify what she just told me.*
TC: Well, that is something that is hard to say because of decoding. He can read, though, but he doesn't necessarily have the comprehension. That is one of the things I'm seeing. It's really hard with Billy to figure out whether he's comprehending or not; he's not clear in his writing, so it's hard to tell if it's his writing or his reading comprehension. I think this time, when I give him the IRI, I'll give him one, probably start off with fourth grade and do a series of them and see where he leaves that frustration level.	

Transcript	Analysis
CIT: Also, we can take a look at where he is based on your expectations and the curriculum and the instructional level just to make sure if there is a match or anything can be done so that he's not at frustration level, because maybe if he's always at frustration level, then it's not very motivating, because he doesn't know where else to turn.	*At this point, I don't know where I should go with the information I have already obtained, and I don't know what info I still need, so I became uncomfortable and started rambling.*
TC: Yeah, I mean, I'll do the IRI to find out according to that what level he's on. We do what we can; I just don't want you to think I give him work all the time that's at that level.	*Case in point that rambling gets you into trouble. I wanted to disappear after she said this.*
CIT: Oh no, I don't!	

Evaluating Consultation Outcomes

In addition, the effectiveness of the consultation itself can be assessed. This may include a combination of measures: consultee and client change, adherence to the consultation model/process, social validity of interventions, and whether the consultee applies new skills learned during the consultation in future problem-solving efforts (Kaiser et al., 2009). Based on 274 teachers in six school districts, Kaiser et al. (2009) documented several consultee outcomes, including satisfaction with the consultation experience, confidence about handling similar problems in the future, and learning skills that would be useful in addressing similar concerns. Their findings showed congruence between teacher perceptions and student outcomes in a subset of cases. They also provided an example of a teacher survey that could be used with individual teachers or at the school level to assess consultee outcomes. Focusing on a single domain, such as client outcomes alone, does not provide sufficient data for evaluating the development of consultation competency.

Client outcomes are important, although consultants may have less control over that, given consultees usually control intervention implementation and implementation integrity. The Instructional Consultation model has consistently used the Student Documentation Form (SDF) data to evaluate whether consultation goals for the student clients have been met, including goal attainment data, effect on special education placements, and results with racially minoritized students (see, e.g., Rosenfield et al., 2014). Data collected to evaluate progress can be helpful to CITs in evaluating client outcomes. A multi-dimensional evaluation process of consultation competency development can be developed together with your supervisor.

Who Evaluates?

Several individuals may contribute to evaluations of competency development, including self, field supervisors, university supervisors, peers, consultees, and clients. Gathering information from multiple sources on several points of interest allows for data triangulation and bias reduction within the supervision evaluation process (Kaslow et al., 2009).

Self-assessment is a critical skill throughout psychologists' careers and can provide an excellent starting point for supervisor-supervisee interactions. Of course, self-assessments are inherently subjective, and you may inadvertently underestimate or overestimate your skills or simply not know what you do not know. In one study, Newman, Villarreal et al. (2022) found that CITs significantly increased their ratings of self-efficacy for consultation communication from before to after their first consultation course but did not demonstrably change in how they applied the basic listening skills of paraphrasing, clarifying, and reflecting feelings. The Dunning-Kruger effect (Dunning, 2011; Kruger & Dunning, 1999) suggests that students with gaps in content knowledge may not recognize their own deficits and, therefore, may overestimate their performance. Some supervisees may also be dishonest in their self-assessments due to fear of repercussions in supervision. Therefore, self-assessments are best compared with supervisor assessments (field and/or university) completed on the same scale. Discussions of these data can inform goals for your consultation training and directions for future supervision. Peers can also evaluate and provide feedback to one another, for example, through observing each other in course simulations or live consultations during field-based experiences and engaging in peer supervision. Ingraham (2017) and Ingraham et al. (2022) describe a scaffolded peer feedback process used to supplement instructor supervision, which uses consultation session video recordings and attends to cultural variables in consultation. Given potential issues related to the Dunning-Kruger effect (a peer providing assessment or feedback though they may not have more advanced knowledge, and that they might not know what they do not know), supplementing peer processes with support from course instructors or supervisors is recommended.

Consultees might provide ratings about your work, which offers information on how the consultation was received. Though such ratings attempt to measure social validity, some consultees may be concerned about you receiving a poor grade for your consultation assignment and, therefore, might rate the consultation as more helpful than they perceived it to be (Guiney & Zibulsky, 2017). Clients may also provide feedback about the consultation. Since consultation is an indirect service, the feedback would focus primarily on problem improvement based on implemented interventions and may indirectly reflect your contributions to problem-solving, including intervention planning and supports provided during implementation.

Feedback

Evaluation data should be linked to systematic, ongoing, and formal feedback from a knowledgeable other; this is the second leg of the consultation competency development process. Feedback should be timely, frequent, objective, consistent, clear, specific, credible, balanced, collaborative, and occur within the context of a strong supervisory relationship (Heckman-Stone, 2004). Ideally, feedback is also bidirectional, so you will have a chance to report to your supervisors on your perceptions of what is and is not working well in the supervision process (APA, 2015). For example, a supervisor might ask supervisees, "What would be helpful for us to do in this supervision meeting?" at the beginning of supervision meetings and check in midway and at the end of meetings by asking if we are accomplishing what we set out to do. In our experience, this has resulted in supervisees requesting further clarification on points that are unclear and us providing additional strategies (e.g., modeling how to say something in the consultation session) that we didn't initially recognize were needed by the supervisee.

Just as evaluating process skills is challenging, it can be challenging for supervisors to provide feedback on such skills and for supervisees to receive this feedback. For example, imagine you are a supervisee receiving the following feedback in supervision. Which of these would be easier for you to hear and to try and improve upon?

> **Supervisor A**: I am wondering if the consultation relationship is evolving collaboratively. What are your thoughts on how your relationship with the consultee is developing?
>
> **Supervisor B**: It sounds like the intervention may be missing some components that would help it work more effectively. This may need to be revisited with the consultee.

As demonstrated in the first statement, getting feedback on process skills is almost always *personal*; it can be challenging to accept, let alone address in practice. On the other hand, feedback on content such as intervention design, implementation, or evaluation is easier to accept and to address immediately. Therefore, providing supervision feedback about a consultant's process skills is best accomplished by referencing low inference data as may be captured through observation, transcription, and supervisee self-reflection. Further, direct feedback offered by supervisors can be combined with questions that can help stimulate CIT reflection and growth.

Table 12.4 highlights examples of concerns that might present themselves during CITs' early consultation interactions. Such concerns can be subtle but require immediate feedback from a consultation supervisor in support of the CIT's improved professional behaviors. Although *working on the process* is, in many ways, challenging, it is a critical growth avenue for consultees (Newman, 2012).

As we described previously, self-reflection is an important process for new consultants. Consultation courses, including applied practice opportunities, can

TABLE 12.4 Professional Behavior Concerns That May Manifest During Consultation Communication Interactions and Require Supervisor Feedback

Professional Behaviors	
Verbal	*Non-Verbal*
• Talks as a "layperson" rather than as a professional (e.g., use of "like," "um," or other filler language) • Relationship becomes too friendly, preventing professional work (e.g., excessive storytelling or talking about personal lives instead of the problem) • Uses excessive jargon • Asks questions without seeming to listen to responses by pausing, paraphrasing, or summarizing • Ignores or glosses over consultee frustration, emotional expression, or need for ventilation • De-emphasizes collaboration (e.g., "I can …," rather than, "We can …") • Talks too quickly or too much • Asks double-barrelled or vague questions • Engages in advice-giving before the problem is clear	• Dresses unprofessionally • Physical proximity to consultee is too close or too distant when speaking • Avoids making eye-contact • Is over-reliant on supporting materials (e.g., problem-solving checklist) • Nods head, even when disagrees with what the consultee is saying • Appears closed-off or disinterested in the conversation • Default face is dissonant with what is happening (e.g., "thinking face" looks bored or angry) • Appears outwardly nervous or is paralyzed by nerves • Is unprepared for consultation meetings

provide a unique opportunity for supervisors to give feedback on process skills and for you to work on those skills. You, as a supervisee, can be an active guide (versus a passive recipient) in the supervision feedback process by identifying areas in which you perceive the need for additional support. You and your supervisors can also preemptively consider frequently occurring concerns faced by novice consultants, discuss strategies to overcome barriers, and recognize that many concerns you are experiencing are typical for new consultants. For example, Newman (2012) and Cramer and Rosenfield (2004) provided multiple examples of common CIT concerns, including becoming fluent in the problem-solving process, using data, communicating systematically, building relationships, and bridging paradigm differences between training program views of consultation and the enactment of the consultant role in the field. More recently, Hatzichristou et al. (2017) reported that Greek consultation students found many of the same difficulties as those in the US.

Deliberate Practice

The final leg of the stool supporting the development of school consultation competence is applied practice, linked with the assessment and feedback mechanisms already described. Deliberate Practice (DP) is a specific approach bringing together assessment, goal setting, performance, feedback, and continuous skill improvement. DP, often taking place in the early stages of skill development, is a mindful and systematic practice that occurs over time and requires a knowledgeable other (e.g., a supervisor or mentor) to support the learning process via direct instruction, observation, and feedback (Ericsson & Pool, 2016). Several hallmarks of DP put forth by Ericsson and Pool (2016) and Miller et al. (2020) also apply to DP of school consultation:

- Includes pre-established training techniques overseen by a supervisor.
- Is challenging but achievable.
- Is goal-oriented, including short-term and long-term goals.
- Is deliberate, requiring full attention from the consultant trainee.
- Is combined with feedback from a supervisor (or mentor, or teacher).
- Produces and depends on improved mental representations (i.e., structures allowing us to recognize and remember patterns) of trainee performance.
- Involves continuous improvement upon previously acquired skills.

Recent research suggests DP is a viable approach to school consultation training, particularly for teaching and learning communication skills (Newman, Gerrard et al., 2022; Newman, Villarreal et al., 2022). Appendix J provides a sequence of activities derived from this research. The activities can be completed using the four videos of a consultee requesting assistance presented in Actvity 4.10 in Chapter 4 to practice communication skills with support from a course instructor or supervisor.

Stay the Course

DP is hard work and is not necessarily "enjoyable," especially at first, although trainees have rated the DP exercises from the consultation research as valuable (Newman, Gerrard et al., 2022; Newman, Villarreal et al., 2022). One of us (S. R.) experienced that feeling as she learned Tai Chi, where novices are told that it takes months to learn, months to become comfortable, and a lifetime to develop expertise. As Ericsson and Pool (2016) state:

> It's hard to keep going, and even if you keep up your training – you go to the gym regularly, or you practice the guitar for a certain number of hours every week – it's hard to maintain focus and effort, so you may eventually stop pushing yourself and stop improving.
>
> (p. 167)

The same goes for ongoing learning once you enter the field. It is way easier to engage in routine, "on-the-fly" consultation than engage in the process of ongoing deliberate learning and intentional practice of consultation skills. However, consistent with our initial premise in Chapter 1, we believe consultation is worth the effort to teach, supervise, learn, and practice, given the potential benefits that expertise in the process leads to better results for consultants, consultees, clients, and systems. It is worth remembering that many individuals who are at the top levels of their fields, for example, Olympic athletes and professional musicians, receive ongoing coaching toward continuous improvement.

Consultation Research

In this text, we have incorporated the underlying research to the extent possible. However, research in school consultation is ongoing, and there are additional resources of which you should be aware. Two journals that publish school consultation research are the *Journal of Educational and Psychological Consultation* and the APA Division 13 (Society of Consulting Psychology) journal, *Consulting Psychology Journal: Practice and Research*. In addition, much contemporary research in consultation can be found in the chapters of the *Handbook of Research in School Consultation* (2nd ed.; Erchul & Sheridan, 2014), which is currently being updated in a 3rd edition.

There is also a case to be made for practitioners engaging in research. Truscott et al. (2017) discuss opportunities and methods for practitioners to conduct consultation projects as publishable research, encouraging colleagues to present and publish their work on school-based projects as a contribution to the literature. They provide resources and suggestions for conducting such work. They cite earlier authors, such as Stoner and Green (1992), who recommend conducting school-based projects as local experiments, beginning with a scientific basis for the consulting process and interventions, adapting the evidence to the local condition and context, and using scientific methods to evaluate results. Ideas for publishing their results are also provided.

Scan QR code 12.3 to view a video of Dr. David Shriberg, a faculty member in the school psychology program at Indiana University and past editor of the *Journal of Educational and Psychological Consultation*, discussing research in consultation.

QR CODE 12.3   David Shriberg Video

Continuing to Build Your Competence

Consistent with competency in any domain area, building competence in school consultation requires the development of knowledge, skills, and values. But it requires personal commitment, as in the Tai Chi saying: "As your intention, so shall it be." In this book, we have provided a starting point for your development in each of these areas, which we hope will inspire you to continue your development.

Scan QR code 12.4 to view Dr. Markeda Newell discussing the development of school consultation competency.

QR CODE 12.4   Markeda Newell Video

Building Knowledge

Competent consultants possess a clear guiding framework that informs their consultation practice. The School Consultation (SC) model articulated throughout the text is built on research-based features developed from several consultation models and is aligned with the needs of teachers and students in contemporary school settings. We hope you find this framework to be a meaningful and pragmatic guide to your consultation work. Knowledge of culture, relationship-building, communication skills, and the problem-solving stages, and their features, are core to the model. We have offered you detailed nuts and bolts components of the stages and described nuances in their implementation to help you navigate. However, as you have hopefully gleaned from reading the book, the SC model is more than a series of problem-solving stages. The model is situated within a school context and therefore requires you to be knowledgeable about school culture, including *why* the norms and regularities in your school are relevant when initiating and conducting consultation services and *how* best to work in your specific setting. Knowledge of schools as organizational systems and the role of relevant content, such as instructional match, in assessing and intervening in problems are also critical.

Developing Skills

Competent consultants are more than intervention dispensers. Competent consultants are skilled in the nuanced processes of consultation, including building strong relationships with diverse consultees and consultee systems through thoughtful, purposeful communication. Competent consultants are humble consultants who engage in asking before telling and are genuinely interested in understanding the difficulties faced by consultees and supporting changes in the consultees' knowledge, skills, confidence, or objectivity that can ultimately support students. Cultural humility is critical, including being aware of our own limits in cultural knowledge, and seeking out knowledge and skills, sometimes in tandem with our consultees. And competent consultants treat consultation as an ongoing process rather than a short-term event; even when the problem is solved, the door remains open for future consultation. In short, being knowledgeable about problem-solving interventions is not enough to be a competent consultant; the skilled application of consultation processes is also necessary.

Values

We have discussed throughout this book, in some ways explicitly and others implicitly, the values of competent consultants. Competent consultants are ethical consultants, including navigating the intersection of ethics and the consultation relationships (e.g., competence, informed consent, confidentiality, and multiple relationships) and organizational consultation issues (e.g., conflicts of interest, failure to use research science and evidence-based practices, conflicts between organizational demands and ethical practice).

Competent consultants also value the diversity of individuals in the organizational system and are responsive to the needs of consultees and clients from a variety of backgrounds. That requires that they acquire knowledge and skills that support the values that they hold around diversity and social justice. Cultural humility is essential, as issues of lack of objectivity and self-confidence, as well as knowledge and skill, play a role in developing as a culturally competent practitioner. This domain is one where the practitioner is always in the state of becoming competent.

Competent school consultants are also reflective practitioners. Reflection is at the heart of consultation training. The combination of *learning* (e.g., formal coursework, reading), *doing* (e.g., simulated experiences, systematic consultation cases during a practicum or internship), and *reflecting* (e.g., written reflection, recording and reviewing your work) augments the development of consultation competence. Video recording and review, both individually and with a supervisor, are critical components of consultation training. Indeed, this is now standard practice in training for related clinical skills such as counseling (Goodyear et al., 2016). Once you enter the profession, reflection continues with ongoing consideration of your consultation work and how your actions impact consultees, clients/students, and systems.

We hope your developmental journey as a school consultant does not end with your graduate training or upon reading this book. Indeed, several of the video speakers note the importance of continuing the process of learning to be a consultant. To consider your own learning process as a consultant thus far and your starting point for future learning, complete Activity 12.2. Examples of how you might forge a path beyond consultation competence toward consultation expertise are provided in Table 12.5.

You can also scan QR code 12.5, which features three advanced graduate students from the University of Cincinnati, Mary Kate Gerrard, Hannah McIntire, and Julia Villarreal, discussing their own consultation learning skill application during their doctoral training, including their internships. They also offer strategies for you to consider as you consider the role of consultation in your school psychology practice.

QR CODE 12.5   Mary Kate Gerrard, Hannah McIntire, and Julie Villarreal Video

TABLE 12.5 Examples of Actions to Continue Your Professional Learning Focused on School Consultation

Actions

- Seek out additional readings about school consultation, such as some of the materials referenced throughout this book
- Attend presentations focused on school consultation at professional conferences
- Listen to podcasts focused on consultation and related topics, such as *Conversations About Consultation* (https://rss.com/podcasts/conversationsaboutconsultation/)
- Get involved in professional organizations/groups focused on consultation, such as the Society for Consulting Psychology/Division 13 of APA or NASP's consultee-centered consultation special interest group. Consider becoming a member, attending a conference or meeting, or taking on a leadership role
- Engage in ongoing formative self-assessment regarding your consultation knowledge and skills using one or more of the tools provided in this book, and set professional goals based on current performance
- Seek feedback from a coach, mentor, or supervisor on your consultation skills. If possible, have the coach, mentor, or supervisor directly observe your work through live observation or audio or video recording rather than relying solely on self-report
- Coordinate a process of peer support, such as a peer supervision group of professionals in your work setting. If possible, have a peer observe your work through live observation or audio or video recording rather than relying solely on self-report.
- Become an assistant to the consultation course instructor to supervise and receive supervision on your work
- Engage in applied school consultation research

Note: APA = American Psychological Association. NASP = National Association of School Psychologists.

ACTIVITY 12.2 (INDIVIDUAL)

Revisiting Your Consultation Map

At the beginning of this book (Chapter 1), you wrote down your initial thoughts about school consultation, designed a map to diagram your understanding of school consultation at that point in time, and wrote a brief written summary of your map.

Without looking at your first map, design a new map diagramming your *current* understanding of school consultation. Underneath the map, write a brief written summary of your map.

Questions for Reflection:

1 After completing your new diagram, compare it to your diagram from Chapter 1. How do the diagrams compare to each other?
2 What are the similarities and differences in the diagram? What do these suggest about your learning?
3 Which areas that are in your diagram do you believe require additional training and practice to build competency in consultation?
4 What actions do you need to take to continue to build your own competency as a consultant?

Finally, and perhaps most importantly, competent school consultants value the promise of consultative service delivery. Although this might seem obvious, it is easy for school consultants to get wrapped up in delivering other practices, many of which are interpersonally and professionally isolating and perhaps less effective forms of helping. Nearly every aspect of working in schools involves interacting with adults on behalf of students (Conoley et al., 2020; Gutkin & Conoley, 1990). As Julia Szarko (2022), the 2021 NASP School Psychologist of the Year, stated:

> Being a school psychologist is a whole lot more than just working with children, as I initially envisioned when I was in college. There is a lot of working with grown-ups! All types of personalities, all types of strengths and needs, and all types of outside factors influencing how individuals interact with each other.
>
> (p. 27)

Consultation should be viewed as foundational to the practice of school psychologists. Through the provision of indirect services, school consultants can build, support, and enhance the capacity of the school system, its students, and their families.

APPENDICES

APPENDIX A

Assessment of School Climate for Collaboration (Vu et al., 2013)

Please mark the extent to which you agree or disagree with the following:

	Strongly Disagree	Disagree	Neutral	Agree	Strongly Agree
In our school, teachers are expected to work with specialists and other teachers to resolve problems.					
In our school, teachers formally schedule time to collaborate about teaching and learning practices.					
Specialists (e.g., ESOL teachers, special educators, reading teachers) and classroom teachers plan together for students they teach in common.					
Teachers are on their own to solve classroom problems in this school.					
In this school, it is seen as a sign of weakness if a teacher asks for help.					
Teachers are uncomfortable asking for helpwhen they have a behavior problem in their classroom.					
Teachers in this school work together to design instruction. Teachers in this school coordinate instructional goals across grade levels.					
Teachers in this school consult with each other to improve their own classroom management.					
I am more likely to ask a colleague to work with me on my instruction than to ask them to work with the student.					

APPENDIX B

School Consultation Process Log

Consultant Name:_____

Grade Level of Case:_____

Session Date:_____

1. **Consultation problem-solving stage.**
   a. List what stage of the problem-solving process you are currently engaged in (i.e., Contracting; Problem Identification/Problem Analysis; Intervention Planning; Intervention Implementation, Progress Monitoring, and Performance Feedback; Post-Intervention Planning and Closure).
   b. What components of this stage have you completed thus far?
   c. What components of this stage remain to be completed?
2. **Consultant–consultee working relationship.**
   a. What is the collaborative working dynamic you are experiencing in your case? Embed transcribed excerpts to demonstrate your assessment of collaboration and describe what is demonstrated by the assessment.
3. **Marginalized/oppressed group reflection.★**
   a. How do the identities/experiences of the triad affect the quality of the consultation relationship?
4. **Communication skills.**
   a. Reflect on your use of communication/language within the consultation session, including specific skills such as clarifications, paraphrases, reflecting feelings, and summarizing. Embed transcribed excerpts to demonstrate your points.
      i. What communication strategies were successful?
      ii. What could you have done or said differently?

5. **Request(s) for feedback during supervision.**
   a. What are your next steps in the case, and the problem-solving process?
   b. What would you like to discuss further in supervision? As much as possible, try to answer your own questions in this section of the log. Your initial thoughts should be considered in collaboration with a supervisor.

★This section was added to the Process Log by Dr. Stacy Williams, a faculty member in the University at Albany School Psychology Program, and it is included here with her permission.

APPENDIX C

Basic Listening Skills Rubrics

Paraphrasing

<u>Operational Definition:</u> Paraphrasing is when the consultant checks their own understanding of what the consultee has said by attempting to restate what the consultee has said using the consultant's own words. Paraphrasing is not a point-by-point, exact restatement of what the consultee has said. The consultant checks their own understanding of what the consultee has said by using objective, observable, and/or measurable terms and language. A non-example of paraphrasing is when the consultant infers understanding of what the consultee has said without attempting to check the consultant's own understanding. Paraphrases also attempt to highlight what the consultant views as the most important information shared by the consultee.

- Examples of stems:
    - So, what I think I'm hearing you say is . . .
    - Let me see if this sounds right . . .
    - Let me see if I'm understanding you . . .
    - It sounds like . . .
- Non-examples of stems:
    - What you mean is . . .
    - What you're trying to say is . . .
    - You're saying that . . .

Paraphrasing Component (3 total)	Component Demonstrated 1 point	Component NOT Demonstrated 0 points	Points (0 or 1)
1) Consultant checks understanding of what the consultant has said using the consultant's own words.	Consultant restates what the consultee said using the consultant's own words to check understanding of what the consultee has said.	Consultant does either of the following: (1) restates what has been said by consultee using exact, word-for-word language used by consultee, or (2) does not restate what has been said.	
2) Consultant restates what consultee has said with more observable and/or measurable and/or concise words.	Consultant does the following: (1) attempts to restate what the consultee said using more observable and/or measurable and/or concise words, and (2) addresses the main point(s).	Consultant does any of the following: (1) restates subjective or inferential language used by the consultee, (2) adds subjective or inferential language, (3) does not attempt to describe what has been stated using objective and measurable terms, and/or (4) focuses on information beyond main point.	
3) Consultant uses a paraphrasing stem that checks, rather than infers understanding of what the consultee has stated, or paraphrases without using a stem.	Consultant uses a phrase similar to those mentioned below, or paraphrases without a stem: – So what I think I'm hearing you say is . . . – Let me see if this sounds right . . . – Let me see if I'm understanding you . . .	Consultant uses a phrase that may imply preemptive understanding. An inappropriate phrase may be one mentioned, or one similar these: – What you mean is . . . – What you're trying to say is . . . – You're saying that . . .	

TOTAL PARAPHRASING SCORE
Circle total number of points

Inaccurate (0 points)	Partially Accurate (1 point)	Mostly Accurate (2 points)	Accurate (3 points)

Clarifying

<u>Operational Definition:</u> Clarification is the process by which the consultant follows up with the consultee on information that the consultee has provided to request elaboration of previous statements. Clarifications are directly related to what the consultee has said and are used to make information and target variables observable and measurable. Clarifications can be clarifying questions or clarifying statements. Non-examples of clarification include when the consultant infers understanding of what the consultee has said, makes assumptions without checking in with the consultee, or uses statements/questions that do not pertain to information provided by the consultee and thereby shifts the direction of problem-solving to the consultant's own agenda.

- Examples of clarifying question stems:
    - How does . . . look in your class?
    - Would you tell me a little more about that?
    - What do you mean when you say . . . ?
- Examples of clarifying statement stems:
    - Tell me more about . . .
    - Help me understand more about . . .
    - Please give me an example of . . .
    - Let's talk about what happens when . . .
    - Explain to me what you mean by . . .
- Non-examples of stems:
    - What you mean is . . .
    - What you're saying is . . .
    - You're saying that . . .

Clarifying Component (3 total)	Component Demonstrated 1 point	Component NOT Demonstrated 0 points	Points (0 or 1)
1) Consultant's clarification is directly related to what the consultee has already stated.	Consultant uses a clarification to request elaboration on something that the consultee already stated. *– You said that . . . (followed by statement or question)*	Consultant uses a statement or question that does not relate to what the consultee has said or shifts the direction of the consultation to an alternative focus.	
2) The clarification attempts to make information observable and measurable.	Consultant uses a question/statement to request observable and/or measurable information from the consultee that elaborates on the information provided. Examples include: *– How often does . . . occur?* *– When does . . . occur?* *– Tell me what . . . looks like.*	Consultant does any of the following: (1) adds subjective or inferential language and/or (2) does not attempt to request observable/measurable information.	

Clarifying Component (3 total)	Component Demonstrated 1 point	Component NOT Demonstrated 0 points	Points (0 or 1)
3) Consultant uses a clarification stem that aims to request elaboration, rather than infer understanding of what consultee has stated.	Consultant uses a stem similar to those described below: – *Tell me more about . . .* – *Explain to me what you mean by . . .*	Consultant uses a stem that may imply preemptive understanding. An inappropriate stem may be one mentioned below: – *What you mean is . . .* – *What you're saying is . . .* – *You're saying that . . .*	

TOTAL CLARIFYING SCORE
Circle total number of points

Inaccurate (0 points)	**Partially Accurate** (1 point)	**Mostly Accurate** (2 points)	**Accurate** (3 points)

Reflecting Feelings (Formerly Perception Checking)

Operational Definition: Reflecting Feelings is when the consultant acknowledges the feelings of the consultee that they believe are present in the consultation. Furthermore, the consultant checks their understanding of the consultee's feelings in a non-judgmental manner. The objectives of reflecting feelings are to recognize affect or feelings that are emerging during the consultation and to determine if the consultant's perceptions of the consultee's feelings are accurate. Although the consultant may not correctly identify the feeling, reflecting feelings creates an opportunity for the consultee to correct the consultant's present understanding of the consultee's feelings. A non-example of reflecting feelings is when the consultant implies/infers how the consultee is feeling without attempting to check the consultant's own perceptions, or when a consultant glosses over or ignores affect when it is presented in the consultation.

- Examples of stems:
  - *That seems* [insert feeling] . . .
- Non-examples of stems:
  - *Oh, that does sound very* [insert feeling] . . .

Reflecting Feelings Component (3 total)	Component Demonstrated 1 point	Component NOT Demonstrated 0 points	Points (0 or 1)
1) Consultant checks understanding of what consultee is feeling.	The consultant restates the feelings of the consultee that they believe are present using the consultant's own words.	Consultant does not check emotion when it is present in the consultation.	
2) Consultant checks understanding of what consultee is feeling in a nonjudgmental way.	Consultant attempts to check his/ her perception of what the consultee is feeling in a nonjudgmental manner.	Consultant does any of the following: (1) uses a condescending/harsh tone, or (2) responds to the consultee in a judgmental/biased manner either verbally or non-verbally.	
3) The consultant is able to accurately restate the consultee's feelings if present or allow room for correction if not accurate.	The consultant either: (1) accurately understands consultee's emotions or (2) enables the consultee the opportunity to correct the consultant's understanding.	The consultant does any of the following: (1) implies what consultee is feeling without attempting to check their understanding or (2) inaccurately labels what consultant is feeling without enabling the consultee the opportunity to correct the reflection of feelings.	

TOTAL REFLECTING FEELINGS SCORE
Circle total number of points

Inaccurate (0 points)	Partially Accurate (1 point)	Mostly Accurate (2 points)	Accurate (3 points)

APPENDIX D

Six Big Ideas Informing School Consultation Problem-Solving

Big Ideas
1 Complex problems, such as those found in schools, rarely have simple or linear solutions.
2 The problems school consultants attempt to solve are situated within a school-based context and should be defined accordingly.
3 Everything we do is an intervention, beginning from the earliest consultation interactions and including the establishment of a shared problem conceptualization occurring during *PID/PA*.
4 Problem operationalization stems from listening and seeking clarification, not from asking scripted questions, and communication skills are critical.
5 Accurate problem operationalization precedes well-matched intervention planning.
6 More data aren't necessarily better data when it comes to understanding and solving problems.

APPENDIX E

Adherence to the School Consultation Process

Please indicate which stage(s) of consultation were observed in the video by indicating the components completed within the stages covered.

Consultant Name:_____   Date of Consultation Session:_____

Was a problem-solving stage a continuation from a previous meeting?
(Circle Yes or No)

Which stage(s) was/were continued?_____

Name of Observer:_____   Date of Observation:_____

Contracting Stage	*Was Item Completed?*
Discussed consultee's expectations and prior experiences consulting	Yes No Unsure
Introduced the school consultation assumptions, expectations, and process	Yes No Unsure
Explained the stage-based problem-solving process	Yes No Unsure
Clarified school as the context for problem-solving, including the concept of instructional match	Yes No Unsure
Explained potential application of problem-solving at multiple tiers in addition to individual students	Yes No Unsure
Clarified shared ownership of the problem and the consultation process	Yes No Unsure
Clarified non-evaluative nature of the consultation process	Yes No Unsure
Explained the parameters of confidentiality	Yes No Unsure
Checked for consultee agreement and commitment to participate	Yes No Unsure
Scheduled follow-up meeting/ongoing schedule	Yes No Unsure

Problem Identification and Problem Analysis	Was Item Completed?
Created shared understanding of consultee's concern(s) using collaborative communication skills	Yes No Unsure
Defined concern(s) in observable terms	Yes No Unsure
Defined concern in the context of the school/classroom and considered the role of instructional match/mismatch	Yes No Unsure
Followed up with additional data collection such as record or work sample review, observation, or instructional assessment	Yes No Unsure
Prioritized concerns	Yes No Unsure
Established a plan to measure current performance (i.e., Baseline)	Yes No Unsure
Established baseline measurement of performance	Yes No Unsure
Set performance goals based on baseline data	Yes No Unsure

Intervention Planning	Was Item Completed?
Elicited consultee's ideas/strategies	Yes No Unsure
Discussed all of these: What classroom-based strategy will meet goals? Where will strategy be implemented? When can strategy be implemented? How often will strategy be implemented? Who will be responsible?	Yes No Unsure
Considered conditions to create/maintain instructional match	Yes No Unsure
Considered if multiple students can benefit from the intervention	Yes No Unsure
Documented specifics of what, when, how often, and who	Yes No Unsure

Intervention Implementation, Monitoring, and Performance Feedback	Was Item Completed?
Continued meeting while intervention was being implemented	Yes No Unsure
Clarified what's working and what needs refining	Yes No Unsure
Elicited consultee's perception of progress	Yes No Unsure
Provided performance feedback regarding level of adherence to intervention with consideration given to implementation changes as needed	Yes No Unsure
Collaboratively reviewed and discussed data	Yes No Unsure
Compared progress with goals	Yes No Unsure

Post-Intervention Planning and Closure	Was Item Completed?
Assessed all of these: (a) goals were met, (b) consultee can implement independently if needed. (c) strategies are fading/faded	Yes No Unsure
Elicited consultee's plans to maintain student progress	Yes No Unsure
Determined documentation of efforts	Yes No Unsure
Considered addressing other priority areas not yet addressed	Yes No Unsure
If case is explicitly closed, let consultee know how support can be accessed in the future	Yes No Unsure
Discussed further communication with parents, colleagues, teams	Yes No Unsure

APPENDIX F

Student's Name_____ Grade_____ Date of Birth_____ Date Started_____
Teacher's Name_____ Case Manager_____ School_____

GOAL ATTAINMENT SCALE (GAS)

Step 1: Initial description of concern				
Step 2: Prioritize	Importance 1 2 3 4 (student at instructional level? Y N)	Importance 1 2 3 4 (student at instructional level? Y N)	Importance 1 2 3 4 (student at instructional level? Y N)	Importance 1 2 3 4 (student at instructional level? Y N)
Step 3: Observable/ measurable statement of current performance (following baseline)	Date collected_____	Date collected_____	Date collected_____	Date collected_____
Step 4: Short-term goal: Expected performance in weeks (4–6 weeks)	Date consistently attained_____	Date consistently attained_____	Date consistently attained_____	Date consistently attained_____
Step 5: Interim goal: Expected behavior in weeks	Date consistently attained_____	Date consistently attained_____	Date consistently attained_____	Date consistently attained_____
Step 6: Long-term goal: Expected behavior in weeks	Date consistently attained_____	Date consistently attained_____	Date consistently attained_____	Date consistently attained_____

Operational Definition of Academic/Behavioral Performance:

Priority # ___
on GAS

KEY

What specific academic/behaviors will be recorded?

When will the behavior be recorded?

Where will the behavior be recorded?

Baseline (Step 3)

End Baseline

Describe intervention design and materials	When and how often?	Persons responsible	Motivational strategies?

Date	Summary of Meetings	Follow-up Activities	Next Meeting Date and Time

APPENDIX G

Intervention Script and Adherence Checklist for Responding to Refusal Behavior

Adapted from Smith, J. (2017). *The use of brief functional analysis to reduce refusal behavior in a first-grade student with an autism spectrum disorder.* (Unpublished second year professional practice portfolio). University of Cincinnati, Cincinnati, OH.

Materials

- Token Board with numbers
- X tokens

Intervention Script

1. At the start of a refusal (see operational definition at end of script) provide Jack with two prompts (can include verbal, physical, or gestural prompts) to comply with original instruction.
2. If after two prompts, Jack has not complied with the original instruction, place an X token over the number 1 box and tell Jack, "You earned an X for not listening. Two more X's, you will have a time out."
3. After giving the first X, instruct Jack to complete the original instruction. If he begins to refuse again, follow steps 1–3.
4. Once Jack has received three X's, tell him, "It's time for a time out, sit in the hallway."
5. Prompt Jack to sit outside the work room (close the door behind you).
6. Show Jack a visual timer of one minute. If he is calm after one minute, tell him it is time to work and go back to the original task.
7. If Jack's behavior escalates and he attempts to run or becomes aggressive, go to the safe room and follow time out procedures in there.
8. If in the safe room, show Jack a visual timer through the window for one minute. If he is calm, go back to the workroom and have him complete the original task.

9. Add one-minute intervals to his timer as necessary until he is calm. Time outs should be in a room or area with no or very few items such as the safe room or the room next to the safe room when possible. For instance, the sensory room cannot be considered a time out location because Jack likes to go in there to play and it has preferred items in it.

10. Jack may not have access to any preferred items at this time, which includes Mickey Mouse Doll, Chewy, Kindle, Blanket, Pillow, Lights off, Adult Attention or any other preferred items. All items should be taken away at this time including papers or objects that he attempts to take out of the work-room with him.

11. Once Jack has calmed down (stopped crying, yelling, kicking, hitting, etc.) tell Jack, "Thank you for calming down. It's time to finish your work, let's go back."

12. Instruct Jack to complete the original task that caused his refusal behavior. Once he completes the task, place the correct number on his choice token board.

13. If Jack begins to refuse again, complete steps 1–12 until he has complied with the task.

Refusal Behaviors

Operational Definition: Any instance of student crying for longer than ten seconds, pushing adult or objects with hands or feet, kicking adult or objects with feet, hitting adult or object with an open hand or a closed fist, grabbing items he is not supposed to have, throwing items, yelling for longer than ten seconds, screaming for longer than ten seconds, running/walking away from task or assigned area, or falling to the floor when given a directive or a demand has been placed on him.

Examples of Refusal Behavior

- Teacher instructs student to begin work time. Student pushes items off the table and crawls under the table.
- Teacher and student are walking in the hallway. Student sees an instrument in the hallway. Student grabs instrument. Teacher tells student, "No," and takes the instrument from student. Student pushes teacher and hits teacher to get the instrument back.
- Teacher tells student it is time to go to gym. Student points to sensory room. Teacher tells student, "Gym first, then sensory room." Student runs toward the door. Teacher blocks door. Student hits, kicks, and pushes in an attempt to get out of the door.

Data Collection Plan to Monitor Progress

University of Cincinnati school psychology practicum students will observe the 2:00 PM to 2:30 work time 2x per week. During ten-second intervals, compliance will be recorded using momentary time sampling and refusals will be recorded using partial interval recording.

Adherence checks will consist of the two practicum students completing a checklist on the steps followed in the intervention script 1x per week.

Adherence Check for Jack's Intervention

Name of Teacher:
Date:

1. _____ Before beginning the session, Mickey Mouse Doll is placed out of reach
2. _____ Student is asked to choose reinforcement from his choice board
3. _____ Student places reinforcement token on his token board
4. _____ Teacher prompts student to complete activity 1 and places the number 1 on the token board
5. _____ Teacher prompts student to complete activity 2 and places the number 2 on the token board
6. _____ Teacher prompts student to complete activity 3 and places the number 3 on the token board
7. _____ Teacher prompts student to complete activity 4 and places the number 4 on the token board (this activity can be student's choice or the teacher's choice)
8. _____ Teacher provides praise throughout the session
9. _____ Teacher provides redirection as needed to stay on task
10. _____ Teacher provides student with chosen reinforcement as soon as the fourth token is earned

Total Checked_____
Total Available _____
Adherence % (Total Checked/Total Available)_____

Adherence Check for Jack's Timeouts

Name of Teacher:
Date:
1. When a refusal occurs:
_____ Provides student two prompts to comply with original instruction
_____ Places X token over number box if student does not comply with original instructions and explains why the X was placed
_____ Instructs student to complete original instructions

2. When the student receives three X's:
_____ Tells him that it is time for a time out and to sit in the hallway
_____ Prompts him to sit outside the work room
_____ Sets and shows him a visual timer of one minute
If student is calm after one minute:
_____ Goes back into workroom and instructs him to complete the original task
If student is <u>not</u> calm after one minute:
_____ Takes him to safe room

3. When student is in safe room:
_____ Does not let him have access to any preferred items
_____ Shows him a visual timer of one minute through the window
If student is calm after one minute:
_____ Takes him back to the workroom and instructs him to complete the original task
If student is <u>not</u> calm after one minute:
_____ Adds one minute intervals to timer until he is calm
Once calm:
_____ Thanks him for calming down and tells him that is time to finish his work
_____ Takes him back to the workroom and instructs him to complete the original task

Total Checked_____
Total Available _____
Adherence % (Total Checked/Total Available)_____

APPENDIX H

Self-Assessment of Consultation Competence

From Burkhouse, K. S. (2012). Educating a reflective school consultant: Multi-faceted techniques. In S. Rosenfield (Ed.), *Becoming a school consultant: Lessons learned*. Routledge.

Name:	Date:	Circle one: PRE MID POST RETRO-PRE

NA = No prior knowledge or skill in this area

AW = Awareness: able to generally articulate concept

CU = Conceptual Understanding: able to clearly articulate concept and describe appropriate actions

SA = Skill Acquisition: able to demonstrate skill or knowledge in structured or simulated settings

AP = Application of Skills: able to use skill or knowledge flexibly in actual setting

Consultation Skill Area	NA AW CU SA AP
Collaboration and Consultative Skills	
Form working relationships with diverse consultees	
Understand consultee's strengths and needs	
Flexibly adhere to problem-solving process	
Successfully address difficulties that arise in consultation	
Use Student Documentation Form (SDF) to facilitate consultation process	
Share problem-solving process with consultee and make joint decisions through the process	

(Continued)

(*Continued*)

Consultation Skill Area	NA	AW	CU	SA	AP

Interpersonal Communication Skills

Clarify consultee's concerns through use of paraphrasing, summarizing, and asking questions

Reflect feelings of consultee

Adapt communication to meet needs of consultee

Respond to non-verbal cues of consultee

Reflect on thoughts and ideas of consultee

Use clarifying questions appropriately

Acknowledge differences of opinions and resolve conflicts

Problem-Solving Process

Address all areas of contracting

Create a shared understanding of consultee's concerns

Conceptualize consultee's concerns in observable and measurable terms

Gather data based on curriculum expectations to aid in problem-solving process

Assess student's instructional match

Conduct Curriculum Based Assessment (CBA) and/or Instructional Assessment (IA) appropriately in cases

Conduct systematic observations across multiple settings

Prioritize concerns of consultee

Problem-Solving Process Continued

Set measurable goals with consultee

Elicit teacher's ideas for strategies in coordination with goals

Discuss intervention plans related to EBI

Use instructional match in intervention design and selection

Incorporate student's or group's prior knowledge into intervention plan

Select materials to build on student's skills

Anticipate potential barriers to implementation

Evaluate student progress using data

Follow-up and monitor implementation of intervention plan

Rework conceptualization of problem and intervention based on data

Professional Interaction Skills

Work through obstacles and difficult issues with supervisor

Focus on best interest of consultee and client

Respect the culture and practices of the school

Interact effectively with school personnel

Consider cultural differences in consultation triad

Recognize, respect, and respond appropriately to the effects of personal values and belief systems of self and others in the consultation process

Exhibit caring, respectful, empathic, congruent and open consultation interactions

Consultation Skill Area	NA	AW	CU	SA	AP

Be willing to admit that you do not know an answer and be willing to explore possible solutions with others

Demonstrate willingness to learn from others throughout consultation experience

Give and solicit feedback to maintain, revise, or terminate consultation activities

Relate to peers in professional manner

Engage in self-evaluation of strengths and weaknesses to modify personal behaviors that may influence consultation process

Demonstrate investment in becoming a skilled consultant

Systems Change

View self as change agent and continue development the role of change agent

Conduct system-wide needs assessments

Identify benefits and consequences from proposed change efforts

Evaluate programs that seek systemic change

APPENDIX I

Consultant Self-Efficacy Scale (Guiney et al., 2014)

Name:_____

Please read each of the following statements carefully and indicate the extent to which you feel confident about what is described. Rate each statement on a scale from 1 (Not At All Confident) to 9 (Extremely Confident).

How confident are you that you. . .	1 = Not at all 9 = Extremely
1. Can remain aware of the potential impact of your personal experiences while consulting	1 2 3 4 5 6 7 8 9
2. Can reflect on your performance after a consultation session has finished	1 2 3 4 5 6 7 8 9
3. Can identify areas for improvement in future consultation sessions after a session has concluded	1 2 3 4 5 6 7 8 9
4. Can critically evaluate the success of a consultation case after it has been terminated	1 2 3 4 5 6 7 8 9
5. Can identify areas for improvement in future consultation cases after a case has been terminated	1 2 3 4 5 6 7 8 9
6. Can establish a strong working relationship with most consultees	1 2 3 4 5 6 7 8 9
7. Can demonstrate nonverbal behaviors that indicate you are attending to your consultee	1 2 3 4 5 6 7 8 9
8. Can establish a working relationship with a consultee who demonstrates resistance to consultation	1 2 3 4 5 6 7 8 9

How confident are you that you. . .	1 = Not at all					9 = Extremely			
9. Can establish a working relationship with a consultee who is consulting with you only because it is a prereferral requirement	1	2	3	4	5	6	7	8	9
10. Can establish a collaborative relationship that respects your consultee's expertise and knowledge	1	2	3	4	5	6	7	8	9
11. Can ask open-ended questions to encourage a consultee to further explore his or her concerns	1	2	3	4	5	6	7	8	9
12. Can frame a consultee's concerns in terms of observable, measurable behaviors	1	2	3	4	5	6	7	8	9
13. Can elicit responses from a consultee that will lead to problem identification	1	2	3	4	5	6	7	8	9
14. Can redirect the focus back to the student when the discussion strays to other topics (such as non-work-related problems)	1	2	3	4	5	6	7	8	9
15. Can successfully use reframing (helping your consultee see the problem from a different perspective)	1	2	3	4	5	6	7	8	9
16. Can restore a consultee's objectivity when necessary or appropriate	1	2	3	4	5	6	7	8	9
17. Can address a lack of confidence when detected in your consultee	1	2	3	4	5	6	7	8	9
18. Can recognize and deal with theme interference or transference from your consultee	1	2	3	4	5	6	7	8	9
19. Can collaborate with a consultee to list potential interventions to address the identified problem	1	2	3	4	5	6	7	8	9
20. Can assist the consultee to select an intervention that will be effective in addressing the client's problem(s)	1	2	3	4	5	6	7	8	9
21. Can plan for the collection of data to monitor the effectiveness of an intervention that is implemented	1	2	3	4	5	6	7	8	9
22. Can help consultees develop data-collection skills so that they will have the ability to make data-driven decisions in the future	1	2	3	4	5	6	7	8	9
23. Can plan for the collection of behavioral data to monitor an intervention	1	2	3	4	5	6	7	8	9
24. Can evaluate the effectiveness of an intervention that is implemented	1	2	3	4	5	6	7	8	9
25. Can work with a consultee to plan ways of generalizing the effects of an intervention beyond the setting in which it is used	1	2	3	4	5	6	7	8	9
26. Can develop means of fading an intervention once it has been successful	1	2	3	4	5	6	7	8	9
27. Have knowledge of evidence-based interventions to address academic difficulties	1	2	3	4	5	6	7	8	9

(Continued)

(*Continued*)

How confident are you that you. . .	1 = Not at all					9 = Extremely			
28. Can find information regarding evidence-based interventions for addressing new or unfamiliar referral problems	1	2	3	4	5	6	7	8	9
29. Can guide the consultation process through stages from contracting through termination	1	2	3	4	5	6	7	8	9
30. Can explain the process of consultation to a new consultee	1	2	3	4	5	6	7	8	9
31. Can evaluate the consultation experience with a consultee upon termination of a case	1	2	3	4	5	6	7	8	9
32. Can utilize the process of consultation to address academic difficulties	1	2	3	4	5	6	7	8	9
33. Can utilize the process of consultation to address social-emotional difficulties	1	2	3	4	5	6	7	8	9
34. Can implement a behavioral consultation (BC) or problem-solving consultation model when necessary or appropriate	1	2	3	4	5	6	7	8	9
35. Can implement a mental health consultation model when necessary or appropriate	1	2	3	4	5	6	7	8	9
36. Can implement a systems-level or organizational consultation model when necessary or appropriate	1	2	3	4	5	6	7	8	9
37. Can consult with a teacher around a client (student) with ADHD	1	2	3	4	5	6	7	8	9
38. Can consult with a teacher around a client (student) with a pervasive developmental disorder (PDD)	1	2	3	4	5	6	7	8	9
39. Can consult with a teacher around a client (student) who is an English language learner (ELL)	1	2	3	4	5	6	7	8	9
40. Can consult effectively with someone of a cultural background that is different from yours	1	2	3	4	5	6	7	8	9
41. Can consult effectively with a teacher when the client (student) is from a different cultural background than your own	1	2	3	4	5	6	7	8	9
42. Can recognize your inherent biases or assumptions about clients and/or consultees based on cultural background	1	2	3	4	5	6	7	8	9
43. Can remain aware of how your cultural background may affect the assumptions you make about consultees, clients or consultation cases	1	2	3	4	5	6	7	8	9
44. Can recognize how your consultee's cultural background may affect the way in which he or she approaches a consultation experience	1	2	3	4	5	6	7	8	9
45. Can recognize when your personal beliefs are affecting your approach to a consultee or case	1	2	3	4	5	6	7	8	9

APPENDIX J

Deliberate Practice of Communication Skills Activity Sequence

The following can be completed using a variety of free online tools (e.g., a combination of Flip and Qualtrics) or online learning systems. The same activity can be completed for each of the four videos provided in Chapter 4, Activity 4.10.

Step 1: CITs establish awareness and conceptual understanding

- Instructors teach and model communication skills via assigned readings, lectures, modeling, and micro skills practice opportunities (e.g., activities throughout this book).
- CITs complete micro skills practice opportunities.
- Instructors/supervisors collect assignments, review them, and provide feedback.

Step 2: CITs view and respond to a consultee's simulated request for assistance

- CITs view a video of a consultee request for assistance (see Chapter 4, Activity 4.10 for four unique practice videos) and record a video response to the consultee. CITs may view and record as many times as needed before submitting their best response.

Step 3: CITs reflect on their response and learning

- After submitting their response, CITs self-reflect regarding their application of paraphrases, clarifications, and reflection of feelings using an online survey with these items. They also consider other skills used and any questions they have for the course instructor. The survey is provided at the end of this Appendix.

Step 4: Instructor review and feedback

- The instructor reviews the CIT's video submission while simultaneously reviewing the CIT's self-reflection responses.
- The instructor records their video feedback for the CIT's about skill application and understanding, and responds to any questions from the CIT.
- Feedback often includes one or more of the following:
  - Praise for accurate skill application;
  - Tips for enhancing skill application (e.g., making a question open-ended, making a paraphrase more concise);
  - Corrections of misunderstandings (e.g., CIT misidentifies the application of a skill);
  - Corrections of skill omission, commission, or misapplication (e.g., CIT does not reflect feelings though consultee emotion was evident);
  - Answering questions (e.g., CITs ask about things like if their clarification focused on an appropriate target); and
  - Words of encouragement (e.g., "You've made some excellent strides so far this semester. I am looking forward to seeing your response next week!").

CIT Self-Reflection Survey

Name: _____

1. Circle "Yes" if you applied a clarification (clarifying question or statement) in your response, or "No" if you did not. Clarifications: (1) are directly related to what the consultee has already stated, (2) attempt to make information observable/measurable, and (3) use a stem to request elaboration, rather than infer understanding of what consultee has stated.

   ○ Yes   ○ No

2. If you used a clarification, please specify why you thought that would be a helpful skill to use. In other words, with what purpose did you clarify? If you did not clarify, why did you choose not to do so?

3. Circle "Yes" if you applied a paraphrase in your response or "No" if you did not. Paraphrases: (1) check understanding using consultant's own words, (2) restate what the consultee said using observable/measurable words, and (3) use a stem that checks understanding of what consultee has stated.

   ○ Yes   ○ No

4. If you used a paraphrase, please specify why you thought that would be a helpful skill to use. In other words, with what purpose did you paraphrase? If you did not, why did you choose not to do so?

5. Circle "Yes" if you applied a reflection of feelings (formerly perception check) in your response or "No" if you did not. Reflections of feelings: (1) check understanding of what the consultee is feeling, IF emotion is present in the consultee's statement, (2) check understanding of what consultee is feeling in a nonjudgmental way, and (3) accurately restate the consultee's feelings.

   ○ Yes   ○ No

6. If you used a reflection of feelings, please specify why you thought that would be a helpful skill to use. In other words, with what purpose did you reflect feelings? If you did not, why did you choose not to do so?

7. If you used any other communication skills, please specify which skills and with what purpose.

8. What other questions or comments, if any, do you have for your course instructor at this time?

REFERENCES

Aguilar, E. (2016). *The art of coaching teams: Building resilient communities that transform schools.* Jossey-Bass.

Aguilar, E. (2018). *Onward: Cultivating emotional resilience in educators.* Jossey-bass.

Aguilar, E., & Cohen, L. (2022). *The PD book: 7 habits that transform professional development.* Jossey-Bass.

Alpert, J. L., & Meyers, J. (Eds.). (1983). *Training in consultation: Perspectives from mental health, behavioral, and organizational consultation.* C. C. Thomas.

American Psychological Association. (2006). Evidence-based practice in psychology. *American Psychologist, 61*(4), 271–285. https://doi.org/10.1037/0003-066X.61.4.271

American Psychological Association. (2013). Guidelines for the practice of telepsychology. *American Psychologist, 68*(9), 791–800. https://doi.org/10.1037/a0035001

American Psychological Association. (2015). Guidelines for clinical supervision in health service psychology. *American Psychologist, 70*(1), 33–46. https://doi.org/10.1037/a0038112

American Psychological Association. (2017a). *Ethical principles of psychologists and code of conduct* (2002, amended effective June 1, 2010, and January 1, 2017). https://www.apa.org/ethics/code/

American Psychological Association. (2017b). *Guidelines for education and training at the doctoral and postdoctoral level in consulting psychology (CP)/organizational consulting psychology.* https://www.apa.org/about/policy/education-training.pdf

American Psychological Association. (2017c). *Multicultural guidelines: An ecological approach to context, identity, and intersectionality.* http://www.apa.org/about/policy/multicultural-guidelines.pdf

American Psychological Association/Carnegie Conference. (1997, June 26–28). *Bringing to scale educational innovation and school reform: Partnerships in urban education.* Conference Proceedings. American Psychological Association & Carnegie Corporation of New York.

Anderson, H., & Goolishian, H. A. (1988). Human systems as linguistic systems: Preliminary and evolving ideas about the implications for clinical theory. *Family Process, 27*(4), 371–393. https://doi.org/10.1111/j.1545-5300.1988.00371.x

Anton-LaHart, J., & Rosenfield, S. (2004). A survey of preservice consultation training in school psychology programs. *Journal of Educational and Psychological Consultation, 15*(1), 41–62. https://doi.org/10.1207/s1532768xjepc1501_2

Archer, A. L., & Hughes, C. A. (2011). *Explicit instruction: Effective and efficient teaching.* Guilford Press.

Argyris, C., Putnam, R., & Smith, D. M. (1985). *Action science: Concepts, methods, and skills for research and intervention.* Jossey-Bass.

Augusterfer, E. F., O'Neal, C. R., Martin, S. W., Sheikh, T. L., & Mollica, R. F. (2020). The role of telemental health, tele-consultation, and tele-supervision in post-disaster and low-resource settings. *Current Psychiatry Reports, 22*(85), 1–10. https://doi.org/10.1007/s11920-020-01209-5

Bahr, M. W., Leduc, J. D., Hild, M. A., Davis, S. E., Summers, J. K., & McNeal, B. (2017). Evidence for the expanding role of consultation in the practice of school psychologists. *Psychology in the Schools, 54*(6), 581–595. https://doi.org/10.1002/pits.22020

Bailenson, J. N. (2021). Nonverbal overload: A theoretical argument for the causes of Zoom fatigue. *Technology, Mind, and Behavior, 2*(1). https://doi.org/10.1037/tmb0000030

Baker, C. N., Peele, H. Daniels, M., Saybe, M., Whalen, K., Overstreet, S., & The New Orleans Trauma-Informed Schools Learning Collaborative. (2021). The experience of covid-19 and its impact on teachers' mental health, coping, and teaching. *School Psychology Review, 50*(4), 491–594. https://doi.org/10.1080/2372966X.2020.1855473

Bailey, J. S., & Burch, M. R. (2017). *Research methods in applied behavior analysis.* Routledge.

Barnett, J. E. (2020). Ethical, legal, and professional issues in consultation for psychologists. In C. A. Falender & E. P. Shafranske (Eds.), *Consultation in psychology: A competency-based approach* (pp. 53–70). American Psychological Association.

Barrett, C. (2012). Making the instructional match salient for the teacher. In S. A. Rosenfield (Ed.), *Becoming a school consultant: Lessons learned* (pp. 127–138). Routledge.

Barrett, C., Gadke, D. L., & VanDerHeyden, A. M. (2020). At what cost? Introduction to the special issue "return on investment for academic and behavioral assessment and intervention." *School Psychology Review, 49*(4), 347–358. https://doi.org/10.1080/2372966X.2020.1817718

Barrett, C. A., Newman, D. S., & Hazel, C. E. (2018, February). *Systems-level consultation: Expanding your role for the benefit of all.* Mini-skills workshop presented at the annual convention of the National Association of School Psychologists.

Batsche, G., Elliott, J., Graden, J., Grimes, J., Kovaleski, J., Prasse, D., . . . Tilly, D. (2005). *Response to intervention: Policy considerations and implementation.* National Association of State Directors of Special Education.

Belar, C. D. (2009). Advancing the culture of competence. *Training and Education in Professional Psychology, 3*(Suppl. 4), S63–S65. https://doi.org/10.1037/a0017541

Benishek, L. E., Gregory, M. E., Hodges, K., Newell, M., Hughes, A. M., Marlow, S. Lacerenza, C., Rosenfield, S., & Salas, E. (2016) Bringing the science of team training to school-based teams. *Theory Into Practice, 55*(2), 112-119, https://doi.org/10.1080/00405841.2016.1148987

Benn, A. L. (2004). *Communities of practice: Study of one school's first year of implementation of a new problem-solving model* (Unpublished doctoral dissertation). University of Maryland.

Bergan, J. R. (1977). *Behavioral consultation.* Charles E. Merrill.

Bergan, J. R., & Kratochwill, T. R. (1990). *Applied clinical psychology: Behavioral consultation and therapy.* Plenum Press.

Berger, J. (2012). Who owns the classroom homework problem? In S. A. Rosenfield (Ed.), *Becoming a school consultant: Lessons learned* (pp. 163–176). Routledge.

Berger, W. (2014). *A more beautiful question: The power of inquiry to spark breakthrough ideas.* Bloomsbury.

Bernal, G., Jiménez-Chafey, M. I., & Domenech Rodríguez, M. M. (2009). Cultural adaptation of treatments: A resource for considering culture in evidence-based practice. *Professional Psychology: Research and Practice, 40*(4), 361–368. https://doi.org/10.1037/a0016401

Bersoff, D. N., & Grieger, R. I. (1971). An interview model for the psychosituational assessment of children's behavior. *American Journal of Orthopsychiatry, 41*(3), 483–493. https://doi.org/10.1111/j.1939-0025.1971.tb01134.x

Bice-Urbach, B. J., & Kratochwill, T. R. (2016). Teleconsultation: The use of technology to improve evidence-based practices in rural communities. *Journal of School Psychology, 56,* 27–43. https://doi.org/10.1016/j.jsp.2016.02.001

Bice-Urbach, B. J., Kratochwill, T. R., & Fischer, A. J. (2018). Teleconsultation: Application of provision of consultation for school consultants. *Journal of Educational and Psychological Consultation, 28*(3), 255–278. https://doi.org/10.1080/10474412.2017.1389651

Blanton, L. P., Pugach, M. C., & Boveda, M. (2018). Interrogating the intersections between general and special education in the history of teacher reform. *Journal of Teacher Education, 69*(4), 354–366. https://doi.org/10.1177/0022487118778539

Bloom, B. S. (1976). *Human characteristics and school learning.* McGraw-Hill.

Boland, J. E., Fonseca, P., Mermelstein, I., & Williamson, M. (2022). Zoom disrupts the rhythm of conversation. *Journal of Experimental Psychology: General, 151*(6), 1272–1282. https://doi.org/10.1037/xge0001150

Borgelt, C., & Conoley, J. C. (1999). Psychology in the schools: Systems intervention case examples. In C. R. Reynolds & T. B. Gutkin (Eds.), *The handbook of school psychology* (3rd ed., pp. 1056–1076). Wiley.

Bradshaw, C. P., Mitchell, M. M., O'Brennan, L. M., & Leaf, P. J. (2010). Multilevel exploration of factors contributing to the overrepresentation of black students in office disciplinary referrals. *Journal of Educational Psychology, 102*(2), 508–520. https://doi.org/10.1037/a0018450

Brown, E. (2019). African American teachers' experiences with racial micro-aggressions. *Educational Studies, 55*(2), 180–196. https://doi.org/10.1080/00131946.2018.1500914

Brown, J. M., Naser, S. C., Griffin, C. B., Grapin, S. L., & Proctor, S. L. (2022). A multicultural, gender, and sexually diverse affirming school-based consultation framework. *Psychology in the Schools, 59*(1), 14–33. https://doi.org/10.1002/pits.22593

Bryk, A. S. (2015). 2014 AERA distinguished lecture: Accelerating how we learn to improve. *Educational Researcher, 44*(9), 467–477. https://doi.org/10.3102/0013189X15621543

Burkhouse, K. S. (2012). Educating a reflective school consultant: Multi-faceted techniques. In S. A. Rosenfield (Ed.), *Becoming a school consultant: Lessons learned* (pp. 25–47). Routledge.

Burns, M. K., Jimerson, S. R., VanDerHeyden, A. M., & Deno, S. L. (2016). Toward a unified response-to-intervention model: Multi-tiered systems of support. In S. R. Jimerson, M. K. Burns, & A. M. VanDer Heyden (Eds.), *Handbook of response to intervention* (pp. 719–732). Springer.

Burns, M. K., & Parker, D. C. (2014). *Curriculum-based assessment for instructional design: Using data to individual instruction.* Guilford.

Caplan, G. (1970). *The theory and practice of mental health consultation.* Basic Books.

Carner, L. A. (1982). Developing a consultative contract. In J. L. Alpert (Ed.), *Psychological consultation in educational settings* (pp. 8–32). Jossey-Bass

Castillo, J. M., Curtis, M. J., & Gelley, C. (2012). School psychology - part 2: School psychologists' professional practices and implications for the field. *Communiqué, 40*(8), 4-6..

Clare, M. M. (2022). Qualitative research methods render and advance consultation practice: Here's why that matters. *Journal of Educational and Psychological Consultation, 32*(1), 9–21. https://doi.org/10.1080/10474412.2020.1768859

Clinkscales, A., Barrett, C. A., & Spear, S. E. (2022). The role of racial match between students and teachers in school-based consultation. *School Psychology Review.* Advanced online publication. https://doi.org/10.1080/2372966X.2022.2087477

Collier-Meek, M. A., Sanetti, L. M. H., Levin, J. R., Kratochwill, T. R., & Boyle, A. M. (2019). Evaluating implementation supports delivered within problem-solving consultation. *Journal of School Psychology, 72,* 91–111. https://doi.org/10.1016/j.jsp.2018.12.002

Conoley, J. C., & Conoley, C. W. (2010). Why does collaboration work? Linking positive psychology and collaboration. *Journal of Educational and Psychological Consultation, 20*(1), 75–82. https://doi.org/10.1080/10474410903554902

Conoley, J. C., Powers, K., & Gutkin, T. B. (2020). How is school psychology doing: Why hasn't school psychology realized its promise? *School Psychology, 35*(6), 367–374. https://doi.org/10.1037/spq0000404

Cramer, K., & Rosenfield, S. (2004). Clinical supervision of consultation. *The Clinical Supervisor, 22*(1), 111–124. https://doi.org/10.1300/J001v22n01_08

Curtis, M. J., Castillo, J. M., & Cohen, R. M. (2008). Best practices in system-level change. In A. Thomas & J. Grimes (Eds.), *Best practices in school psychology V* (pp. 887–902). National Association of School Psychologists.

Daly, E. J. III, Doll, B., Schulte, A. C., & Fenning, P. (2011). The competencies initiative in American professional psychology: Implications for school psychology preparation. *Psychology in the Schools, 48*(9), 872–886. https://doi.org/10.1002/pits.20603

Darling-Hammond, L., Schachner, A., Edgerton, A. K., Badrinarayan, A., Cardichon, J., Cookson, P. W., Jr., Griffith, M., Klevan, S., Maier, A., Martinez, M., Melnick, H., Truong, N., & Wojcikiewicz, S. (2020). *Restarting and reinventing school: Learning in the time of COVID and beyond.* Learning Policy Institute.

Dart, E. H., Cook, C. R., Collins, T. A., Gresham, F. M., & Chenier, J. S. (2012). Test driving interventions to increase treatment integrity and student outcomes. *School Psychology Review, 41*(4), 467–481. https://doi.org/10.1080/02796015.2012.12087500

de Brey, C., Musu, L., McFarland, J., Wilkinson-Flicker, S., Diliberti, M., Zhang, A., Branstetter, C., & Wang, X. (2019). *Status and trends in the education of racial and ethnic groups 2018* (NCES 2019–038). U.S. Department of Education. National Center for Education Statistics. https://nces.ed.gov/pubsearch/.

Delise, L. A., Gorman, C. A., Brooks, A. M., Rentsch, J. R., & Steele-Johnson, D. (2010). The effects of team training on team outcomes: A meta-analysis. *Performance Improvement Quarterly, 22*(4), 53–80. https://doi.org/10.1002/piq.20068

Desimone, L. M., & Garet, M. S. (2015). Best practices in teachers' professional development in the United States. *Psychology, Society and Education, 7*(3), 252–263. https://doi.org/10.25115/psye.v7i3.515

Dillon, J. T. (1979). Defects of questioning as an interview technique. *Psychology in the Schools, 16*(4), 575–580. https://doi.org/10.1002/1520-6807(197910)16:4<575::AID-PITS 2310160422>3.0.CO;2-B

Di Stefano, G., Gino, F., Pisano, G. P., Staats, B. (2014). *Learning by thinking: How reflection aids performance.* Harvard Business School.

Doll, B., Haack, K., Kosse, S., Osterloh, M., Siemers, E., & Pray, B. (2005). The dilemma of pragmatics: Why schools don't use quality team consultation practices. *Journal of Educational and Psychological Consultation, 16*(3), 127–155. https://doi.org/10.1207/s1532768xjepc1603_1

Donohoo, J. (2017). *Collective efficacy: How educators' beliefs impact student learning.* Corwin/ Sage.

Dougherty, A. M. (2013). *Psychological consultation and collaboration in school and community settings* (6th ed.). Brooks/Cole.

Dougherty, A. M., Tack, F. E., Fullam, C. B., & Hammer, L. A. (1996). Disengagement: A neglected aspect of the consultation process. *Journal of Educational and Psychological Consultation, 7*(3), 259–274. https://doi.org/10.1207/s1532768xjepc0703_5

Doyle, A. C. (1894). *Round the red lamp: Being facts and fancies of medical life.* D. Appleton.

Dunning, D. (2011). The Dunning-Kruger effect: On being ignorant of one's own ignorance. In J. M. Olson & M. P. Zanna (Eds.), *Advances in experimental social psychology* (Vol. 44, pp. 247–296). Academic Press.

D'zurilla, T. J., & Goldfried, M. R. (1971). Problem solving and behavior modification. *Journal of Abnormal Psychology, 78*(1), 107–126. https://doi.org/10.1037/h0031360

Eddy, C. L., Huang, F. L., Cohen, D. R., Baker, K. M., Edwards, K. D., Herman, K. C., & Reinke, W. M. (2020). Does teacher emotional exhaustion and efficacy predict student discipline sanctions? *School Psychology Review, 49*(3), 239–255. https://doi.org/10.1080/2372966X.2020.1733340

Embry, D. D., & Biglan, A. (2008). Evidence-based kernels: Fundamental units of behavioral influence. *Clinical Child Family Psychology Review, 11*(3), 75–113. https://doi.org/10.1007/s10567-008-0036-x

Erchul, W. P. (2011). School consultation and response to intervention: A tale of two literatures. *Journal of Educational and Psychological Consultation, 21*(3), 191–208. https://doi.org/10.1080/10474412.2011.595198

Erchul, W. P., Grissom, P. F., Getty, K. C., & Bennett, M. S. (2014). Researching interpersonal influence within school consultation: Social power base and relational communication perspectives. In W. P. Erchul & S. Sheridan (Eds.), *Handbook of research in school consultation* (2nd ed., pp. 349–385). Routledge.

Erchul, W. P., Raven, B. H., & Whichard, S. M. (2001). School psychologist and teacher perceptions of social power in consultation. *Journal of School Psychology, 39*(6), 483–497. https://doi.org/10.1016/S0022-4405(01)00085-1

Erchul, W. P., Schulte, A. C., Johnson, A. H., & Geraghty, C. A. (2019). Adults as change agents: Applications of behavioral consultation. In S. G. Little & A. Akin-Little (Eds.), *Behavioral interventions in schools: Evidence-based positive strategies* (pp. 171–188). American Psychological Association.

Erchul, W. P., & Sheridan, S. (Eds.). (2014). *Handbook of research in school consultation* (2nd ed.). Routledge.

Ericsson, K. A. (Ed.). (2009). *Development of professional expertise: Toward measurement of expert performance and design of optimal learning environments.* Cambridge University Press.

Ericsson, K. A., & Pool, R. (2016). *Peak: Secrets from the new science of expertise.* Houghton Mifflin Harcourt.

Evans, A. C., Jr. (2021). Can psychology really help address racism? We must challenge long-held biases in psychology if we want to have an impact. *APA Monitor, 52*(3), 10. https://www.apa.org/monitor/2021/04/ceo

Fallon, L. M., Collier-Meek, M. A., Famolare, G. M., DeFouw, E. R., & Gould, K. M. (2022). Electronically delivered support to promote intervention implementation fidelity: A research synthesis. *School Psychology Review, 51*(2), 221–236. https://doi.org/10.1080/2372966X.2020.1853485

Fallon, L. M., Collier-Meek, M. A., Maggin, D. M., Sanetti, L. M., & Johnson, A. H. (2015). Is performance feedback for educators an evidence-based practice? A systematic review and evaluation based on single-case research. *Exceptional Children, 81*(2), 227–246. https://doi.org/10.1177/0014402914551738

Farbman, D. A. (2015). *The case for improving and expanding time in school: A review of key research and practice*. National Center on Time and Learning.

Farmer, R. L., Goforth, A. N., Kim, S. Y., Naser, S. C., Lockwood, A. B., & Affrunti, N. W. (2021). Status of school psychology in 2020, part 2: Professional practices in the NASP membership survey. *NASP Research Reports, 5*(3), 1–17.

Fenning, P., Diaz, Y., Valley-Gray, S., Cash, R. G., Spearman, C., Hazel, C. E., Grunewald, S., Riccio, C., & Harris, A. (2015). Perceptions of competencies among school psychology trainers and practitioners: What matters? *Psychology in the Schools, 52*(10), 1032–1041. https://doi.org/10.1002/pits.21877

Fischer, A. J., Dart, E. H., LeBlanc, H., Hartman, K. L., Steeves, R. O., & Gresham, F. M. (2017). An investigation of the acceptability of videoconferencing within a school-based behavioral consultation framework. *Psychology in the Schools, 53*(3), 240–252. https://doi.org/10.1002/pits.21900

Fischer, A. J., Erchul, W. P., & Schultz, B. K. (2018). Teleconsultation as the new frontier of educational and psychological consultation: Introduction to the special issue. *Journal of Educational and Psychological Consultation, 28*(3), 249–254. https://doi.org/10.1080/104 74412.2018.1425880

Fisher, E., & Huchting, K. (2019). Consultation to increase educational access and improve conditions for LGBTQ youth [Special issue]. *Journal of Educational and Psychological Consultation, 29*(1).

Florell, D. (2022). Telesupervision. In D. J. Simon & M. E. Swerdlik (Eds.), *Supervision in school psychology: The developmental, ecological, problem-solving model* (2nd ed., pp. 395–410). Routledge.

Fouad, N. A., Grus, C. L., Hatcher, R. L., Kaslow, N. J., Hutchings, P. S., Madson, M. B., Collins, F. L., Jr., & Crossman, R. E. (2009). Competency benchmarks: A model for understanding and measuring competence in professional psychology across training levels. *Training and Education in Professional Psychology, 3*(Suppl. 4), S5–S26. https://doi.org/10.1037/a0015832

French, J. R. P., Jr., & Raven, B. (1959). The bases of social power. In D. Cartwright (Ed.), *Studies in social power* (pp. 150–167). University of Michigan, Institute for Social Research.

Frieder, J. E., Peterson, S. M., Woodward, J., Crane, J., & Garner, M. (2009). Teleconsultation in school settings: Linking classroom teachers and behavior analysts through web-based technology. *Behavior Analysis in Practice, 2*(2), 32–39. https://doi.org/10.1007/BF03391746

Fuchs, L. S., & Fuchs, D. (2011). *Using CBM for progress monitoring in written expression and spelling*. National Center on Student Progress Monitoring. https://files.eric.ed.gov/fulltext/ED519251.pdf

Gallessich, J. (1982). *The profession and practice of consultation: A handbook for consultants, trainers of consultants, and consumers of consultation services*. Jossey-Bass.

Garmston, R. J., & Wellman, B. M. (2016). *The adaptive school: A sourcebook for developing collaborative groups* (3rd ed.). Rowman & Littlefield.

Gawande, A. (2013, July 29). Slow ideas: Some innovations spread fast. How do you speed the ones that don't? *The New Yorker*. https://www.newyorker.com/magazine/2013/07/29/slow-ideas

Geller, A. (2021, September 17). *Should you cancel teacher data team meetings? You might be surprised*. https://corp.smartbrief.com/original/2021/09/should-you-cancel-teacher-data-team-meetings-you-might-be-surprised

Gickling, E. E., Gravois, T. A., & Angell, V. (2016). *Instructional assessment: An essential path for guiding reading instruction.* ICAT Publishing.

Gifford, K. (2012). What do you do when there are multiple concerns? Using problem identification to clarify and prioritize a teacher's concerns. In S. A. Rosenfield (Ed.), *Becoming a school consultant: Lessons learned* (pp. 85–98). Routledge.

Glaser, J. E. (2014). *Conversational intelligence: How great leaders build trust and get extraordinary results.* Bibliomotion, Inc.

Gonsalvez, C. J., Brockman, R., & Hill, H. R. M. (2016). Video feedback in CBT supervision: Review and illustration of two specific techniques. *The Cognitive Behavior Therapist, 9*(e24), 1–15. https://doi.org/10.1017/S1754470X1500029X

Goodyear, R. K., Borders, L. D., Chang, C.Y., Guiffrida, D.A., Hutman, H., Kemer, G., Watkins, C. E., Jr., & White, E. (2016). Prioritizing questions and methods for an international and interdisciplinary supervision research agenda: Suggestions by eight scholars. *The Clinical Supervisor, 35*(1), 117–154. https://doi.org/10.1080/07325223.2016.1153991

Grant, A. (2021). *Think again: The power of knowing what you don't know.* Viking.

Gravois, T. A. (2013). Aligned service delivery: Ending the era of triage education. In L. C. Burrello, W. Sailor, & J. Kleinhammer-Tramill (Eds.), *Unifying educational systems: Leadership and policy perspectives* (pp. 109–134). Routledge.

Gravois, T. A., Gickling, E. E., & Rosenfield, S. (2011). *Training in instructional consultation, assessment, and teaming.* ICAT Publishing.

Guiney, M. C., Harris, A., Zusho, A., & Cancelli, A. (2014). School psychologists' sense of self-efficacy for consultation. *Journal of Educational and Psychological Consultation, 24*(1), 28–54. https://doi.org/10.1080/10474412.2014.870486

Guiney, M. C., & Zibulsky, J. (2017). Competent consultation: Developing self-efficacy for process and problem aspects of consultation. *Journal of Educational and Psychological Consultation, 27*(1), 52–71. https://doi.org/10.1080/10474412.2016.1171718

Guiney, M. G., & Proctor, S. L. (2022). Infusing intersectionality theory into multicultural supervision practices: A case narrative centering Latinx, LGBT-QIA+, and undocumented structural identities. In S. L. Proctor & D. Rivera (Eds.), *Critical theories for school psychology and counselling: A foundation for equity and inclusion in school-based practice* (pp. 161–178). Routledge.

Gustafson, E. (2012). The importance of collaborative communication. In S. A. Rosenfield (Ed.), *Becoming a school consultant: Lessons learned* (pp. 73–84). Routledge.

Gutkin, T. B. (1999). Collaborative versus directive/prescriptive/expert school-based consultation: Reviewing and resolving a false dichotomy. *Journal of School Psychology, 37*(2), 161–190. https://doi.org/10.1016/S0022-4405(99)00003-5

Gutkin, T. B., & Conoley, J. C. (1990). Reconceptualizing school psychology from a service delivery perspective: Implications for practice, training, and research. *Journal of School Psychology, 28*(3), 203–223. https://doi.org/10.1016/0022-4405(90)90012-V

Gutkin, T. B., & Curtis, M. J. (2009). School-based consultation: The science and practice of indirect service delivery. In T. B. Gutkin & C. R. Reynolds (Eds.), *Handbook of school psychology* (4th ed., pp. 591–635). Wiley.

Guva, G. (2004). How to respond to teachers, who ask for help but not for consultation. In N. M. Lambert, I. Hylander, & J. H. Sandoval (Eds.), *Consultee-centered consultation: Improving the quality of professional services in schools and community organizations* (pp. 255–264). Lawrence Erlbaum Associates.

Hackman, J. R., & Wageman, R. (2007). Asking the right questions about leadership: Discussion and conclusions. *American Psychologist, 62*(1), 43–47. https://doi.org/10.1037/0003-066X.62.1.43

Hari, J. (2022). *Stolen focus: Why you can't pay attention – and how to think deeply again.* Crown.

Hall, E. T. (1976). *Beyond culture.* Random House.

Hall, G., & Hord, S. (2020). *Implementing change: Patterns, principles, and potholes* (5th ed.). Pearson.

Hargreaves, A. (2019). Teacher collaboration: 30 years of research on its nature, forms, limitations and effects. *Teachers and Teaching: Theory and Practice, 25*(5), 603–621. https://doi.org/10.1080/13540602.2019.1639499

Hargreaves, A., & Fullan, M. (2012). *Professional capital: Transforming teaching in every school.* Teachers College Press.

Hatzichristou, C., Lampropoulou, A., Georgouleas, G., & Mihou, S. (2017). A multilevel approach to system-level consultation: Critical components and transnational considerations. In C. Hatzichristou & S. Rosenfield (Eds.), *The international handbook of consultation in educational settings* (pp. 70–93). Routledge.

Hatzichristou, C., & Rosenfield, S. (Eds.). (2017). *The international handbook of consultation in educational settings.* Routledge.

Hazel, C. E., Laviolette, G. T., & Lineman, J. M. (2010). Training professional psychologists in school-based consultation: What the syllabi suggest. *Training and Education in Professional Psychology, 4*(4), 235–243. https://doi.org/10.1037/a0020072

Hazel, C. E., Newman, D. S., & Barrett, C. A. (2016). Conducting rigorous survey research in the study of school-based consultation. *Journal of Educational and Psychological Consultation, 26*(2), 111–138. https://doi.org/10.1080/10474412.2015.1137762

Heckman-Stone, C. (2004). Trainee preferences for feedback and evaluation in clinical supervision. *The Clinical Supervisor, 22*(1), 21–23. https://doi.org/10.1300/J001v22n01_03

Higgins, E. T. (1999). "Saying is believing" effects: When sharing reality about something biases knowledge and evaluations. In L. L. Thompson, J. M. Levine, & D. M. Messick (Eds.), *Shared cognition in organizations: The management of knowledge* (pp. 33–49). Lawrence Erlbaum.

Huberman, M. (1993). The model of the independent artisan in teachers' professional relations. In J. W. Little & M. W. McLaughlin (Eds.), *Teachers' work: Individuals, colleagues and contexts.* (pp. 11–50). Teachers' College Press.

Hylander, I. (2004). Analysis of conceptual change in consultee-centered consultation. In N. M. Lambert, I. Hylander, & J. H. Sandoval (Eds.), *Consultee-centered consultation: Improving the quality of professional services in schools and community organizations* (pp. 45–61). Lawrence Erlbaum Associates.

Hylander, I. (2012). Conceptual change through consultee-centered consultation: A theoretical model. *Consulting Psychology Journal: Practice and Research, 64*(1), 29–45. https://doi.org/10.1037/a0027986

Hylander, I. (2017). Establishing psychological consultation services to promote student well-being in schools and preschools. In C. Hatzichristou & S. Rosenfield (Eds.), *The international handbook of consultation in educational settings* (pp. 15–34). Routledge.

Illback, R. J. (2014). Organization development and change facilitation in school settings: Theoretical and empirical foundations. In W. P. Erchul & S. Sheridan (Eds.), *Handbook of research in school consultation* (2nd ed., pp. 276–303). Routledge.

Ingraham, C. L. (2000). Consultation through a multicultural lens: Multicultural and crosscultural consultation in schools. *School Psychology Review, 29*(3), 320–343. https://doi.org/10.1080/02796015.2000.12086018

Ingraham, C. L. (2014). Studying multicultural aspects of consultation. In W. P. Erchul & S. Sheridan (Eds.), *Handbook of research in school consultation* (2nd ed., pp. 323–348). Routledge.

Ingraham, C. L. (2017). Training and education of consultants. In C. Hatzichristou & S. Rosenfield (Eds.), *The international handbook of consultation in educational settings* (pp. 291–311). Routledge.

Ingraham, C. L., Johnson, E. M., & Lopez, K. (2022). What kinds of support do novice consultants request and receive? A constructivist grounded theory investigation. *Journal of Educational and Psychological Consultation, 32*(1), 69–105. https://doi.org/10.1080/10474412.2020.1816473

Ivey, A. E., Packard, N. G., & Ivey, M. B. (2018). *Basic attending skills: Foundations of Empathic relationships and problem solving* (6th ed.). Microtraining Associates.

Joyce, B., & Showers, B. (2002). *Student achievement through staff development* (3rd ed.). ASCD.

Kaiser, L. T., & Newman, D. S. (2023). Best practices in instructional consultation. In P. L. Harrison, A. Thomas, & S. L. Proctor (Eds.), *Best practices in school psychology: Data-based and collaborative decision making* (7th ed., pp. 309–322). National Association of School Psychologists.

Kaiser, L. T., Rosenfield, S., & Gravois, T. A. (2009). Teachers' perception of satisfaction, skill development, and skill application after instructional consultation services. *Journal of Learning Disabilities, 42*(5), 444–457. https://doi.org/10.1177/0022219409339062

Kaslow, N. J. (2004). Competencies in professional psychology. *American Psychologist, 59*(8), 774–781. https://doi.org/10.1037/0003-066X.59.8.774

Kaslow, N. J., Grus, C. L., Campbell, L. F., Fouad, N. A., Hatcher, R. L., & Rodolfa, E. R. (2009). Competency assessment toolkit for professional psychology. *Training and Education in Professional Psychology, 3*(Suppl. 4), S27–S45. https://doi.org/10.1037/a0015833

Kazdin, A. E. (2020). *Single case research designs: Methods for clinical and applied settings* (3rd ed.). Oxford University Press.

Kegan, R., & Lahey, L. L. (2001). *How the way we talk can change the way we work*. Jossey-Bass.

Kendall, P. C., & Beidas, R. S. (2007). Smoothing the trail for dissemination of evidence-based practices for youth: Flexibility within fidelity. *Professional Psychology: Research and Practice, 38*(1), 13–20. https://doi.org/10.1037/0735-7028.38.1.13

King, H. C., Bloomfield, B. S., Wu, S., & Fischer, A. J. (2022). A systematic review of school teleconsultation: Implications for research and practice. *School Psychology Review, 51*(2), 237–256. https://doi.org/10.1080/2372966X.2021.1894478

Knotek, S. (2003). Bias in problem solving and the social process of student study teams: A qualitative investigation. *The Journal of Special Education, 37*(1), 2–14. https://doi.org/10.1177/00224669030370010101

Kohli, R. (2021). *Teachers of Color: Resisting racism and reclaiming education*. Harvard Education Press.

Kratochwill, T. R., Altschaefl, M. R., & Bice-Urbach, B. (2014). Best practices in school-based problem-solving consultation: Applications in prevention and intervention systems. In P. L. Harrison & A. Thomas (Eds.), *Best practices in school psychology: Data-based and collaborative decision making* (pp. 461–482). National Association of School Psychologists.

Kratochwill, T. R., & Bergan, J. R. (1990). *Behavioral consultation in applied settings: An individual guide*. Plenum Press.

Kratochwill, T. R., & Stoiber, K. C. (2002). Evidence-based interventions in school psychology: Conceptual foundations of the procedural and coding manual of division 16 and the society for the study of school psychology task force. *School Psychology Quarterly, 17*(4), 341–389. https://doi.org/10.1521/scpq.17.4.341.20872

Kruger, J., & Dunning, D. (1999). Unskilled and unaware of it: How difficulties in recognizing one's own incompetence lead to inflated self-assessments. *Journal of Personality and Social Psychology, 77*(6), 1121–1134. https://doi.org/10.1037/0022-3514.77.6.1121

Kruse, S., Louis, K. S., & Bryk, A. (1994). Building professional community in schools. *Issues in Restructuring Schools, 6*(3), 67–71.

Kuhfeld, M., Soland, J., Tarasawa, B., Johnson, A., Ruzek, E., & Liu, J. (2020). Projecting the potential impact of COVID-19 school closures on academic achievement. *Educational Researcher, 49*(8), 549–565. https://doi.org/10.3102/0013189X20965918

Laidley, D., Bambino, D., McIntyre, D., Quate, S., & Quinn, J. (2001). The paseo of circles of identity. In *The national school reform faculty resource book*. National School Reform Faculty.

Lambert, N. M., Hylander, I., & Sandoval, J. H. (Eds.). (2004). *Consultee-centered consultation: Improving the quality of professional services in schools and community organizations*. Lawrence Erlbaum Associates.

La Salle, T. P., Wang, C., Wu, C., & Neves, J. R. (2020). Racial mismatch among minoritized students and white teachers: Implications and recommendations for moving forward. *Journal of Educational and Psychological Consultation, 30*(3), 314–343. https://doi.org/10.1080/10474412.2019.1673759

Leech, N., Gullet, S., Cummings, M. H., & Haug, C. (2022). The challenges of remote K-12 education during the COVID-19 pandemic: Differences by grade level. *Online Learning, 26*(1), 245–267. https://doi.org/10.24059/olj.v26i1.2609

Leverson, M., Smith, K., McIntosh, K., Rose, J., & Pinkelman, S. (2021). PBIS cultural responsiveness field guide: Resources for trainers and coaches. *Center on Positive Behavioral Interventions and Supports*. https://www.pbis.org/resource/pbis-cultural-responsiveness-field-guide-resources-fortrainers-and-coaches

Lin, T., Stone, S. J., Heckman, T. G., & Anderson, T. (2021). Zoom-in to zone out: Therapists report less therapeutic skill in telepsychology versus face-to-face therapy during the COVID-19 pandemic. *Psychotherapy, 58*(4), 449–459. https://doi.org/10.1037/pst0000398

Little, J. W. (2007). Professional communication and collaboration. In W. D. Hawley & D. L. Rollie (Eds.), *The keys to effective schools: Education reform as a continuous improvement* (pp. 51–65). Corwin Press.

London, M., & Diamante, T. (2018). *Learning interventions for consultants: Building the talent that drives business*. American Psychological Association.

Lowman, R. L. (2015). Series editor forward. In J. Glover & H. L. Friedman (Eds.), *Transcultural competence: Navigating cultural differences in the global community* (pp. vii–x). American Psychological Association.

Lowman, R. L., & Cooper, S. E. (2017). *The ethical practice of consulting psychology*. American Psychological Association.

Luevano, C., & Collins, T. A. (2020). Culturally appropriate math problem-solving instruction with English language learners. *School Psychology Review, 49*(2), 144–160. https://doi.org/10.1080/2372966X.2020.1717243

Maital, S. L. (2017). Thinking in the box: A tool for promoting innovative problem-solving in Israeli school psychology services. In C. Hatzichristou & S. Rosenfield (Eds.), *The international handbook of consultation in educational settings* (pp. 232–249). Routledge.

Malone, C. M., Briggs, C., Ricks, E., Middleton, K., Fisher, S., & Connell, J. (2016). Development and initial examination of the school psychology multicultural competence scale. *Contemporary School Psychology, 20*(3), 230–239. https://doi.org/10.1007/s40688-015-0079-1

Martens, B. K., DiGennaro Reed, F. D., & Magnuson, J. D. (2014). Behavioral consultation: Contemporary research and emerging challenges. In W. P. Erchul & S. Sheridan (Eds.), *Handbook of research in school consultation* (2nd ed., pp. 180–209). Routledge.

Meckler, L., & Rabinowitz, K. (2019, December 27). America's schools are more diverse than ever. But the teachers are still mostly white. *The Washington Post.* https://www.washingtonpost.com/graphics/2019/local/education/teacher-diversity/

Meyers, J., Meyers, A. B., & Grogg, K. (2004). Prevention through consultation: A model to guide future developments in the field of school psychology. *Journal of Educational and Psychological Consultation, 15*(3–4), 257–276. https://doi.org/10.1207/s1532768xjepc153&4_4

Meyers, J., & Nastasi, B. (1999). Primary prevention in school settings. In C. Reynolds & T. Gutkin (Eds.), *Handbook of school psychology* (3rd ed., pp. 764–799). Wiley.

Michelsen, E. (2004). Anger and gender in consultation. In N. M. Lambert, I. Hylander, & J. H. Sandoval (Eds.), *Consultee-centered consultation: Improving the quality of professional services in schools and community organizations* (pp. 291–299). Lawrence Erlbaum Associates Publishers.

Miller, G. A. (1969). Psychology as a means of promoting human welfare. *American Psychologist, 24*(12), 1063–1075. https://doi.org/10.1037/h0028988

Miller, S. D., Hubble, M. A., & Chow, D. (2020). *Better results: Using deliberate practice to improve therapeutic effectiveness.* American Psychological Association.

Miranda, A. H. (Ed.). (2016). *Consultation across cultural contexts: Consultee-centered case studies.* Routledge.

Morrison-Smith, S., & Ruiz, J. (2020). Challenges and barriers in virtual teams: A literature review. *Springer Nature Applied Sciences, 2*(6), 1–33. https://doi.org/10.1007/s42452-020-2801-5

National Association of School Psychologists. (2017). *Understanding intersectionality* (Handout). Author.

National Association of School Psychologists. (2020a). *Framework for effective school discipline.* Author. http://www.nasponline.org/discipline-framework

National Association of School Psychologists. (2020b). *The professional standards of the national association of school psychologists.* Author. https://www.nasponline.org/x55315.xml

National Association of School Psychologists. (2021). *Shortages in school psychology: Challenges to meeting the growing needs of U.S. students and schools.* Research Summary. https://www.nasponline.org/x43315.xml

National Association of School Psychologists. (2022a). *Advocacy toolkit promoting equity, diversity, and social–emotional learning.* Handout. https://www.nasponline.org/Documents/Research%20and%20Policy/Advocacy%20Resources/EDI%20and%20SEL%20Advocacy%20Toolkit/Advocacy_toolkit_promoting_EDI_and_SEL.pdf

National Association of School Psychologists. (2022b). *Grade retention and social promotion.* Position Statement.

National Education Association. (2022, October). *Elevating the education professions: Solving educator shortages by making public education an attractive and competitive career path.* https://www.nea.org/sites/default/files/2022-10/29302-solving-educator-shortage-report-final-oct-11-2022.pdf

Newell, M. L. (2012). Transforming knowledge to skill: Evaluating the consultation competence of novice school-based consultants. *Consulting Psychology Journal: Practice and Research, 64*(1), 8–28. https://doi.org/10.1037/a0027741

Newell, M. L., & Coffee, G. (2015). School psychologists as systems-level consultants: Interdisciplinary perspectives. *Journal of Educational & Psychological Consultation, 25*(2–3), 67–71. https://doi.org/10.1080/10474412.2015.1016227

Newell, M. L., Newell, T. S., & Looser, J. A. (2013). Examining how novice consultants address cultural factors during consultation: Illustration of a computer-simulated case-study method. *Consulting Psychology Journal: Practice and Research, 65*(1), 74–86. https://doi.org/10.1037/a0032598

Newell, M. L., Tindall, C., Reed, K., & Zwolski, S. (2020). School-based consultation. In C. A. Falender & E. P. Shafranske (Eds.), *Consultation in psychology: A competency-based approach* (pp. 201–219). American Psychological Association.

Newman, D. (2012). Supervision of school-based consultation training: Addressing the concerns of novice consultants. In S. Rosenfield (Ed.), *Becoming a school consultant: Lessons learned* (pp. 49–70). New York, NY: Routledge.

Newman, D. S. (2020). *The school psychology internship: A guide for interns and supervisors* (2nd ed.). Routledge.

Newman, D. S. (2021). Journal of educational and psychological consultation editor's vision: Ecological perspectives on consultation scholarship during a time of need. *Journal of Educational and Psychological Consultation, 31*(1), 1–7. https://doi.org/10.1080/104744 12.2020.1857108

Newman, D. S., Barrett, C. A., & Hazel, C. E. (2015). School consultation practices in the early career: Does training matter? *Consulting Psychology Journal: Practice and Research, 67*(4), 326–347. https://doi.org/10.1037/cpb0000048

Newman, D. S., Gerrard, M. K., Villarreal, J. N., & Kaiser, L. T. (2022). Deliberate practice of consultation microskills: An exploratory study of training. *Training and Education in Professional Psychology, 16*(3), 263–271. https://doi.org/10.1037/tep0000368

Newman, D. S., Hazel, C., Barrett, C., Chaudhari, S. D., & Fetterman, H. (2018). Early career school psychologists' perceptions of consultative service delivery: The more things change, the more they stay the same. *Journal of Educational and Psychological Consultation, 28*(2), 105–136. https://doi.org/10.1080/10474412.2017.1378106

Newman, D. S., & Ingraham, C. L. (2017). Consultee-centered consultation: Contemporary perspectives and a framework for the future. *Journal of Educational and Psychological Consultation, 27*(1), 1–12. https://doi.org/10.1080/10474412.2016.1175307

Newman, D. S., & Ingraham, C. L. (2020). Cross-university dialogues to support multicultural school consultation training. *Journal of School Psychology, 81,* 11–27. https://doi.org/10.1016/j.jsp.2020.06.001

Newman, D. S., McKenney, E., Silva, A. E., Clare, M., Salmon, D., & Jackson, S. (2017). A qualitative metasynthesis of school consultation process research: What we know and where to go. *Journal of Educational and Psychological Consultation, 27*(1), 13–51. https://doi.org/10.1080/10474412.2015.1127164

Newman, D. S., Salmon, D., Cavanaugh, K., & Schneider, M. F. (2014). The consulting role in a response-to-intervention context: An exploratory study of instructional consultation. *Journal of Applied School Psychology, 30*(3), 278–304. https://doi.org/10.10 80/15377903.2014.924456

Newman, D. S., Villarreal, J. N., Gerrard, M. K., McIntire, H., Barrett, C. A., & Kaiser, L. T. (2022). Deliberate practice of consultation communication skills: A randomized controlled trial. *School Psychology, 37*(3), 225–235. https://doi.org/10.1037/spq000 0494

Noell, G. H., Volz, J. R., Henderson, M. Y., & Williams, K. L. (2017). Evaluating an integrated support model for increasing treatment plan implementation following consultation in schools. *School Psychology Quarterly, 32*(4), 525–538. https://doi.org/10.1037/spq0000195

O'Bryon, E. C., & Rogers, M. R. (2016). Using consultation to support English learners: The experiences of bilingual school psychologists. *Psychology in the Schools, 53*(3), 225–239. https://doi.org/10.1002/pits.21904

Organization for Economic Cooperation and Development (OECD). (2019). *TALIS 2018 results (Volume I): Teachers and school leaders as lifelong learners.* OECD Publishing. https://doi.org/10.1787/1d0bc92a-en

O'Roark, A. M. (2002). Assessment and intervention issues in international organizational consulting. In R. L. Lowman (Ed.), *Handbook of organizational consulting psychology: Theory, skills, and techniques* (pp. 516–544). Jossey-Bass.

Ortiz, S. O., & Melo, K. E. (2017). Foundations for consultation in educational settings with second language learners. In C. Hatzichristou & S. Rosenfield (Eds.), *The international handbook of consultation in educational settings* (pp. 137–159). Routledge.

Owens, J. S., Schwartz, M. E., Erchul, W. P., Himawan, L. K., Evans, S. W., Coles, E. K., & Schulte, A. C. (2017). Teacher perceptions of school consultant social influence strategies: Replication and expansion. *Journal of Educational and Psychological Consultation, 27*(4), 411–436. https://doi.org/10.1080/10474412.2016.1275649

Parker, J. S., Castillo, J. M., Sabnis, S., Daye, J., & Hanson, P. (2020). Culturally responsive consultation among practicing school psychologists. *Journal of Educational and Psychological Consultation, 30*(2), 119–155. https://doi.org/10.1080/10474412.2019.1680293

Pas, E. T. (2012). Case metamorphosis through consultation. In S. A. Rosenfield (Ed.), *Becoming a school consultant: Lessons learned* (pp. 195–209). Routledge.

Pearson. (2013). *Pearson BOSS™ user's guide.* https://images.pearsonclinical.com/images/Assets/BOSS/BOSS_UsersGuide.pdf

Pickering, C. (2012). Relationship building and objectivity loss: The importance of the process in consultation. In S. A. Rosenfield (Ed.), *Becoming a school consultant: Lessons learned* (pp. 111–124). Routledge.

Pluymert, K. (2014). Problem-solving foundations for psychological services. In P. L. Harrison, & A. Thomas (Eds.), *Best practices in school psychology data-based and collaborative decision making* (pp. 25–39). National Association of School Psychologists.

Pressley, T. (2021). Factors contribution to teacher burnout during covid-19. *Educational Researcher, 50*(5), 325–327. https://doi.org/10.3102/0013189X211004138

Pugach, M. C., Blanton, L. P., & Correa, V. I. (2011). A historical perspective on the role of collaboration in teacher education reform: Making good on the promise of teaching all students. *Teacher Education and Special Education, 34*(3), 183–200. https://doi.org/10.1177/0888406411406141

Quintero, E. (2017, Summer). Elevating relationships: How collaboration shapes teaching and learning. *American Educator, 41*(3), 18–21.

Reinke, W. M., Lewis-Palmer, T., & Merrell, K. (2008). The classroom check-up: A classwide teacher consultation model for increasing praise and decreasing disruptive behavior. *School Psychology Review, 37*(3), 315–332. https://doi.org/10.1080/02796015.2008.12087879

Reschly, A. L., & Reschly, D. J. (2014). School consultation and response to intervention: Convergence, divergence, and future directions for research and practice. In W. P. Erchul & S. Sheridan (Eds.), *Handbook of research in school consultation* (2nd ed., pp. 495–512). Routledge.

Ridgard, T. J., Laracy, S. D., Dupaul, G. J., Shapiro, E. S., & Power, T. J. (2015). Trauma-informed care in schools: A social justice imperative. *Communiqué, 44*(2), 12–15.

Rock, D., & Grant, H. (2016, November 4). Why diverse teams are smarter? *Harvard Business Review.* https://hbr.org/2016/11/why-diverse-teams-are-smarter

Rodriguez, R. R., & Walls, N. E. (2000). Culturally educated questioning: Toward a skills-based approach in multicultural counselor training. *Applied & Preventive Psychology, 9*(2), 89–99. https://doi.org/10.1016/S0962-1849(00)80008-6

Roediger III, H. L., Watson, J. M., McDermott, K. B., & Gallo, D. A. (2001). Factors that determine false recall: A multiple regression analysis. *Psychonomic Bulletin & Review, 8*, 385–407. https://doi.org/10.3758/BF03196177

Rosenfield, S. (1987). *Instructional consultation.* Erlbaum Associates.

Rosenfield, S. (1991). The relationship variable in behavioral consultation. *Journal of Behavioral Education, 1*(3), 329–336.

Rosenfield, S. A. (Ed.). (2012). *Becoming a school consultant: Lessons Learned.* Routledge.

Rosenfield, S. A. (2013). Consultation in the schools – are we there yet? *Consulting Psychology Journal: Practice and Research, 65*(4), 303–308. https://doi.org/10.1037/a0035652

Rosenfield, S. A. (2014). Best practices in instructional consultation and instructional consultation teams. In P. L. Harrison & A. Thomas (Eds.), *Best practices in school psychology: Data-based and collaborative decision making* (pp. 509–524). National Association of School Psychologists.

Rosenfield, S. A. (2022). Strengthening the school in school psychology training and practice. *School Psychology Review, 51*(6), 785–794. https://doi.org/10.1080/23729 66X.2021.1993032

Rosenfield, S. A., & Gravois, T. A. (1996). *Instructional consultation teams: Collaborating for change.* Guilford.

Rosenfield, S. A., Gravois, T. A., & Silva, A. E. (2014). Bringing instructional consultation to scale: Research and development of IC and IC teams. In W. P. Erchul & S. Sheridan (Eds.), *Handbook of research in school consultation* (2nd ed., pp. 248–275). Routledge.

Rosenfield, S., Kaiser, L., & Cramer, K. (in press). Instructional consultation. In L. Theodore, M. Bray, & B. Bracken (Eds.), *Desk reference in school psychology.* Oxford University Press.

Rosenfield, S. A., Levinsohn-Klyap, M., & Cramer, K. (2010). Educating consultants for practice in the schools. In E. Vasquez, T. Crespi, & C. Riccio (Eds.), *Handbook of education, training, and supervision of school psychologists in school and community* (Vol. 1, pp. 259–278). Routledge.

Rosenfield, S. A., Newell, M., Zwolski, S., Jr., & Benishek, L. E. (2018). Evaluating problem-solving teams in K–12 schools: Do they work? *American Psychologist, 73*(4), 407–419. https://doi.org/10.1037/amp0000254

Rosenfield, S. A., & Rubinson, F. (1985). Incorporating curriculum-based assessment through consultation, *Exceptional Children, 52*(3), 282–287. https://doi.org/10.1177/ 001440298505200309

Rousmaniere, T., Goodyear, R. K., Miller, S. D., & Wampold, B. E. (Eds.). (2017). *The cycle of excellence: Using deliberate practice to improve supervision and training.* John Wiley & Sons.

Sabnis, S., Castillo, J. M., & Wolgemuth, J. R. (2020). RTI, equity, and the return to the status quo: Implications for consultants. *Journal of Educational and Psychological Consultation, 30*(3), 285–313. https://doi.org/10.1080/10474412.2019.1674152

Sander, J. B., Hernández Finch, M. E., & Newell, M. (2016). Introduction to special issue on multicultural competence in consultation. *Journal of Educational and Psychological Consultation, 26*(3), 213–219. https://doi.org/10.1080/10474412.2015.1089777

Sandoval, J. H. (2014). *An introduction to consultee-centered consultation in schools: A step-by-step guide in the process and skills.* Routledge.

Sanetti, L. M. H., & Collier-Meek, M. A. (2015). Data-driven delivery of implementation supports in a multi-tiered framework: A pilot study. *Psychology in the Schools, 52*(8), 815–828. https://doi.org/10.1002/pits.21861

Sanetti, L. M. H., & Collier-Meek, M. A. (2019). Increasing implementation science literacy to address the research-to-practice gap in school psychology. *Journal of School Psychology, 76*, 33–47. https://doi.org/10.1016/j.jsp.2019.07.008

Sanetti, L. M. H., Fallon, L. M., & Collier-Meek, M. A. (2013). Increasing teacher treatment integrity through performance feedback provided by school personnel. *Psychology in the Schools, 50*(2), 134–150. https://doi.org/10.1002/pits.21664

Sarason, S. B. (1971). *The culture of the school and the problem of change*. Allyn & Bacon.

Sarason, S. B. (1982). *The culture of the school and the problem of change* (2nd ed.). Allyn & Bacon.

Sarason, S. B. (1995). *School change: The personal development of a point of view*. Teachers College Press.

Sarason, S. B. (1996). *Revisiting "The culture of the school and the problem of change."* Teachers College Press.

Sarason, S. B. (2003). Teaching as a lonely profession. In R. L. Fried (Ed.), *The skeptical visionary* (pp. 41–45). Temple University Press. (Original work published in 1966).

Sarason, S. B., Levine, M., Goldenberg, I., Cherlin, D., & Bennett, E. (1966). *Psychology in community settings: Clinical, educational, vocational, social aspects*. Wiley.

Schein, E. H. (1999). *Process consultation revisited: Building the helping relationship*. Addison-Wesley.

Schein, E. H. (2009). *Helping: How to offer, give, and receive help*. Berrett-Koehler.

Schein, E. H. (2013). *Humble inquiry: The gentle art of asking instead of telling*. Berrett-Koehler.

Schein, E. H. (2016). *Humble consulting: How to provide real help faster*. Berrett-Koehler.

Schein, E. H., Turner, R. A., Schein, P. A., & Hayes, T. L. (2021). A long and beautiful conversation with Edgar Schein: His journey through seven decades of social psychology, anthropology, and organizational life. *Consulting Psychology Journal: Practice and Research, 73*(4), 289–301. https://doi.org/10.1037/cpb0000213

Schon, D. A. (1983). *The reflective practitioner: How professionals think in action*. Basic Books.

Schumacher-Martinez, R., & Proctor, S. L. (Eds.). (2020). Untangling the grip of white privilege in education through consultation and systems change [Special issue]. *Journal of Educational and Psychological Consultation, 30*(3).

Schussler, L. (2012). Improving an English language learner client's comprehension through consultee-centered consultation. In S. A. Rosenfield (Ed.), *Becoming a school consultant: Lessons learned* (pp. 139–159). Routledge.

Senge, P. M., Cambron-McCabe, N., Lucas, T., Smith, B., Dutton, J., & Kleiner, A. (2012). *Schools that learn: A fifth discipline field book for educators, parents, and everyone who cares about education*. Doubleday.

Senge, P. M., Kleiner, A., Roberts, C., Ross, R. B., & Smith, B. J. (1994). *The fifth discipline field book: Strategies and tools for building a learning organization*. Doubleday.

Shapiro, E. S. (2011). *Academic skills problems: Direct assessment and intervention* (4th ed.). Guilford.

Shaw, S. R. (2021). Implementing evidence-based practices in school psychology: Excavation by de-implementing the disproved. *Canadian Journal of School Psychology, 36*(2), 91–97. https://doi.org/10.1177/08295735211000513

Sheridan, S. M., Clarke, B. L., & Ransom, K. A. (2014). The past, present, and future of conjoint behavioral consultation research. In W. P. Erchul & S. M. Sheridan (Eds.), *Handbook of research in school consultation* (2nd ed., pp. 210–247). Erlbaum.

Sheridan, S. M., & Garbacz, S. A. (2021). Centering families: Advancing a new vision for school psychology. *School Psychology Review*. Advanced online publication. https://doi.org/10.1080/2372966X.2021.1954860

Sheridan, S. M., & Kratochwill, T. R. (2008). *Conjoint behavioral consultation: Promoting family-school connections and interventions* (2nd ed.). Springer.

Sherry, E. (2012). Making the case for consultee-centered consultation: A novice consultant's perception of culture and relationships. In S. A. Rosenfield (Ed.), *Becoming a school consultant: Lessons learned* (pp. 99–109). Routledge.

Shriberg, D., & Fenning, P. A. (Eds.). (2009). School consultants as agents of social justice: Implications for practice [Special issue]. *Journal of Educational and Psychological Consultation, 19*(1).

Silva, A. E., Newman, D. S., Guiney, M. C., Valley-Gray, S., & Barrett, C. A. (2016). Supervision and mentoring for early career school psychologists: Availability, access, structure, and implications. *Psychology in the Schools, 53*(5), 502–516. https://doi.org/10.1002/pits.21921

Silverstein, S. (1974). *Where the sidewalk ends: The poems & drawings of Shel Silverstein.* Harper Collins.

Skiba, R., Reynolds, C. R., Graham, S., Sheras, P., Conoley, J. C., & Garcia-Vasquez, E. (2006). Are zero tolerance policies effective in the schools? An evidentiary review and recommendations. In *A Report by the American Psychological Association zero tolerance task force.* American Psychological Association. https://www.apa.org/pubs/reports/zero-tolerance-report.pdf

Slavin, R. E. (2020). How evidence-based reform will transform research and practice in education. *Educational Psychologist, 55*(1), 21–31. https://doi.org/10.1080/00461520.2019.1611432

Simon, D. J. (2016). *School-centered interventions: Evidence-based strategies for social, emotional, and academic success.* American Psychological Association.

Smith, J. (2017). *The use of brief functional analysis to reduce refusal behavior in a first-grade student with an autism spectrum disorder* (Unpublished second year professional practice portfolio). University of Cincinnati.

Staats, C. (2016). Understanding implicit bias: What educators should know. *American Educator, Winter 2015–2016,* 29–43. https://www.aft.org/ae/winter2015-2016/staats

Stoltenberg, C. D. (1993). Supervising consultants in training: An application of a model of supervision. *Journal of Counseling & Development, 72*(2), 131–138. https://doi.org/10.1002/j.1556-6676.1993.tb00911.x

Stone, D., Patton, B., & Heen, S. (1999). *Difficult conversations: How to discuss what matters most.* Penguin Books.

Stoner, G., & Green, S. (1992). Reconsidering the scientist-practitioner model for school psychology practice. *School Psychology Review, 21*(1), 155–167. https://doi.org/10.1080/02796015.1992.12085602

Sullivan, A. L., Harris, B., Miller, F. G., Fallon, L. M., Weeks, M. R., Malone, C. M., Kulkarni, T., Proctor, S. L., Johnson, A. H., Rossen, E., Nguyen, T., & Shaver, E. (2021). A call to action for school psychology to address covid-19 health disparities and advance social justice. *School Psychology, 36*(5), 410–421. https://doi.org/10.1037/spq0000463

Sussman, K., Burns, M. K., & Lembke, E. S. (2022). Effects of ECHO MTSS teleconsultation model on self-efficacy of data-based individualization of academic interventions. *Journal of Educational and Psychological Consultation, 32*(4), 395–415. https://doi.org/10.1080/10474412.2021.1996243

Szarko, J. E. (2022). Letter to a first-year school psychologist. *Communiqué, 51*(4), 26–27.

Tannen, D. (2007). *You just don't understand.* William Morrow Paperbacks.

Tannen, D. (2017). *You're the only one I can tell: Inside the language of women's friendships.* Ballantine Books.

Tarquin, K. A., & Truscott, S. D. (2006). Survey of school psychology students' perceptions of their practicum experiences. *Psychology in the Schools, 43*(6), 727–736. https://doi.org/10.1002/pits.20182

Teachers and Parents as Partners. (2022). http://cyfs.unl.edu/TAPP/

Thomas, J. T. (2010). *The ethics of supervision and consultation: Practical guidance for mental health professionals.* American Psychological Association.

Truscott, S. D., Cohen, C. E., Sams, D. P., Sanborn, K. J., & Frank, A. J. (2005). The current state (s) of prereferral intervention teams: A report from two national surveys. *Remedial and Special Education, 26*(3), 130–140. https://psycnet.apa.org/doi/10.1177/07419325 050260030101

Truscott, S. D., Kearney, M. A., Matthews, Y. T., & Daniel, K. (2017). Conducting school-based consultation as publishable research. In C. Hatzichristou & S. Rosenfield (Eds.), *The international handbook of consultation in educational settings* (pp. 357–377). Routledge.

Truscott, S. D., Truscott, D. M., Washington, M. L., & McLendon, K. E. (2022). Understanding school-based consultation as engineering using a mix of methods. *Journal of Educational and Psychological Consultation, 32*(1), 106–123. https://doi.org/10.1080/10474412.202 1.1954528

Tsakiris, E. (2012). Leaving no teacher behind: Widening the view and changing the perspective. In S. A. Rosenfield (Ed.), *Becoming a school consultant: Lessons learned* (pp. 211–231). Routledge.

U.S. Commission on Civil Rights. (2018). *Public education funding inequity in an era of increasing concentration of poverty and resegregation* [Briefing report]. https://www.usccr.gov/pubs/2018/2018-01-10-Education-Inequity.pdf

Vaganek, M. (2012). A teacher's concerns for one student reveals a classroom-wide bullying concern. In S. A. Rosenfield (Ed.), *Becoming a school consultant: Lessons learned* (pp. 177–192). Routledge.

Van Den Bergh, L., Denessen, E., Hornstra, L., Voeten, M., & Holland, R. W. (2010). The implicit prejudiced attitudes of teachers: Relations to teacher expectations and the ethnic achievement gap. *American Educational Research Journal, 47*(2), 497–527. https://doi.org/10.3102/0002831209353594

VanDerHeyden, A. M. (2014). Commentary: Evidence-based practice in school-based consultation research. In W. P. Erchul & S. Sheridan (Eds.), *Handbook of research in school consultation* (2nd ed., pp. 138–149). Routledge.

Visone, J. D., Mongillo, M. B., & Liu, Y. (2022). Teachers' perceptions of collaboration within an evolving teacher evaluation context. *Journal of Educational Change, 23*(4), 421–450. https://doi.org/10.1007/s10833-021-09424-4

Viswanathan, M., Golin, C. E., Jones, C. D., Ashok, M., Blalock, S. J., Wines, R. C., ... Lohr, K. N. (2012). Interventions to improve adherence to self-administered medications for chronic diseases in the United States: A systematic review. *Annals of internal medicine, 157*(11), 785–795. https://doi.org/10.7326/0003-4819-157-11-201212040-00538

Vu, P., Bruckman Shanahan, K., Rosenfield, S., Gravois, T., Koehler, J., Kaiser, L., Berger, J., Vaganek, M., & Gottfredson, G. D. (2013). Experimental evaluation of the effects of Instructional Consultation Teams on teacher efficacy, instructional practices, collaboration, and job satisfaction. *International Journal of School and Educational Psychology, 1*(2), 67–81. https://psycnet.apa.org/doi/10.1080/21683603.2013.790774

Watzlawick, P. (1978). *The language of change: Elements of therapeutic communication.* W. W. Norton & Co.

Wilcox, G., Chatlos, S. B., McClure, E., Flowers, J., & Makarenko, E. (2021). De-Implementation: A missing piece in bridging the research to practice gap in school psychology. *Contemporary School Psychology*, Advance online publication. https://doi.org/10.1007/s40688-021-00399-w

Witte, A. L., Schumacher, R. E., & Sheridan, S. M. (2022). The effectiveness of technology-delivered conjoint behavioral consultation: Addressing rural student and family needs. *Journal of Educational and Psychological Consultation*. Advance online publication. https://doi.org/10.1080/10474412.2022.2083624

Wolf, M. M. (1978). Social validity: The case for subjective measurement or how applied behavior analysis is finding its heart. *Journal of Applied Behavior Analysis, 11*(2), 203–214. https://psycnet.apa.org/doi/10.1901/jaba.1978.11-203

Worrell, F. C., Naecker, J. E., Gerchow, C. E., Green, C., Kunesh, C. E., & Casey, A. (2017). Complicating the thinking of trainee consultants in consultee-centered consultation. In C. Hatzichristou & S. Rosenfield (Eds.), *The international handbook of consultation in educational settings* (pp. 332–354). Routledge.

Wyner, N. B. (1991). Unlocking cultures of teaching: Working with diversity. In N. B. Wyner (Ed.), *Current perspectives on the culture of schools*. Brookline Books.

Yoshida, R. K. (1983). Are multidisciplinary teams worth the investment? *School Psychology Review, 12*(2), 137–143.

Young, A. N. (2022). Guide to providing culturally competent behavioral health services via telehealth. *Practice Innovations, 7*(3), 170–177. https://doi.org/10.1037/pri0000173

Ysseldyke, J. E., & Christenson, S. (2002). *Functional assessment of academic behavior: Creating successful learning environments*. Sopris West.

Ysseldyke, J. E., Burns, M. K., Dawson, M., Kelly, B., Morrison, D., Ortiz, S., Rosenfield, S., & Telzrow, C. (2006). *School psychology: A blueprint for training and practice III*. National Association of School Psychologists.

Zins, J. E., & Erchul, W. P. (2002). Best practices in school consultation. In A. Thomas & J. Grimes (Eds.), *Best practices in school psychology IV* (pp. 625–643). National Association of School Psychologists.

INDEX

Milton Keynes UK
Ingram Content Group UK Ltd.
UKHW020327030124
435379UK00009B/60